THE SEARCH FOR A THEOLOGY OF CHILDHOOD

Also by Brendan Hyde

First Steps in Religious Education
(together with Richard Rymarz)

THE SEARCH FOR A THEOLOGY OF CHILDHOOD

Essays by Jerome W. Berryman from 1978-2009
Edited by Brendan Hyde

Modotti Press
(An Imprint of Connor Court Publishing)

Published in 2013 by Connor Court Publishing Pty Ltd.

Copyright © Brendan Hyde 2013

ALL RIGHTS RESERVED. This book contains material protected under International and Federal Copyright Laws and Treaties. Any unauthorised reprint or use of this material is prohibited. No part of this book may be reproduced or transmitted in any form or by any means, electronic or mechanical, including photocopying, recording, or by any information storage and retrieval system without express written permission from the publisher.

Modotti Press (An Imprint of Connor Court Publishing Pty Ltd)
PO Box 224W
Ballarat VIC 3350
sales@connorcourt.com
www.connorcourt.com

ISBN: 9781921421887 (pbk)

Cover design by M. Giordano. Photo of Jerome Berryman at his office at Christ Church Cathedral, Texas, where he was the Canon Educator from 1984-1994. (Used with permission, courtesy of Jerome Berryman).

Printed in Australia

TABLE OF CONTENTS

Acknowledgements

Preface

A note about referencing

Introduction: Teaching the Christian's strange language:
   Berryman, religious education and spirituality
   (Brendan Hyde)   1

PART 1: Maria Montessori and religious education

   Preface to Part 1   21
1. Montessori and religious education   23
2. Montessori religious education: E.M. Standing (1887-1967)   39
3. Preface to the English edition of *The religious potential of the child*   51

PART 2: Children and religious language

   Preface to Part 2   73
4. The chaplain's strange language: A unique contribution to the health care team   75
5. The illusive use of religious language in childhood   103
6. Silence is stranger than it used to be: Teaching silence and the future of humankind   121

PART 3: Children, spirituality and religious education

    Preface to Part 3   143

7. Spirituality, religious education and the dormouse   145

8. The nonverbal nature of spirituality and religious language   169

PART 4: Play, imagination and the creative process

    Preface to Part 4   189

9. Imagination   191

10. Caring for sick children: The parish, the hospital and theological play   195

11. Laughter, power and motivation in religious education   207

12. Playful orthodoxy: Reconnecting religion and creativity by education   231

PART 5: Ethical considerations when working with children

    Preface to Part 5   257

13. Discussing the ethics of research on children   259

14. Children in worship: An ethic of respect   279

15. Theologizing with children: A parable approach   291

    Endnotes   315

Acknowledgements

The research for this compilation was undertaken during my sabbatical at the Centre for the Theology of Childhood, in Denver, Colorado, USA, in December and January of 2009/2010. I would like to acknowledge the support, generosity, patience and good humor of Reverend Dr Jerome W. Berryman, Senior Fellow of the Centre for the Theology of Childhood. Access to the vast number of archived books, texts and journals of the Centre was invaluable. Without it, this book would not have been completed.

I would also like to acknowledge the support of my own institution, the Australian Catholic University, for enabling me to visit the Centre for the Theology of Childhood, and for funding this important venture. The learning which has resulted from this undertaking has been invaluable and I am extremely grateful for the University's backing and encouragement.

Special acknowledgement needs to be made of Tim Alderson, who, at the time, was the Director of the Godly Play Foundation in California. Tim's tremendous encouragement and support for this project was greatly appreciated.

The staff of Connor Court publishing also need to be acknowledged for their enthusiasm and support in publishing this work, in particular Anthony Cappello and Michael Gilchrist.

As well, I would like to acknowledge the help of my son, Thomas, as my "research assistant". He proved a competent and enthusiastic aide to both myself and to Reverend Dr Berryman in organizing the archival library space at the Centre – and he was introduced to *Lord of the Rings* – one of the magnificent books he stumbled across and read while at the Centre.

Preface

Whether or not one agrees or disagrees with his approach and thesis, few would dispute the significant and unique contribution of Jerome W. Berryman to the field of religious education. Influenced initially by the work of Maria Montessori, as well as those who came after her, in particular Sofia Cavalletti, Berryman developed an approach to religious education and the pastoral care of children which is today being drawn upon in the United States of America, Mexico, Canada, England, Scotland, Wales, Spain, Germany, Finland, Tanzania, Kenya, Korea, and more recently, in Australia. While many readers may be familiar with his more recent publications, *The Complete Guide to Godly Play* (2002) and *Teaching Godly Play* (2009), Berryman's work in fact spans a period of more than thirty years, dating back to the mid 1970s. His work is attested to by numerous academic and professional articles and chapters in books which outline the development of his thinking and thought process which eventually resulted in Godly Play and its theory. However, many of these writings are either no longer in print, or have been "lost" among archival material, and are therefore inaccessible to most readers and scholars of religious education.

This publication represents an attempt to collate and assemble for the first time, and in one volume, some of these major writings of Jerome W. Berryman. Collectively, they detail his search for a theology of childhood. Many of the writings which have been selected here include those which are now largely inaccessible for many readers. I have chosen not to include selections from the published books that Berryman has authored, as these stand as entire works in and of themselves and are, for the most part, still available in print. They are also well known to most readers.

The writings in this book have been organized around five themes: (1) Maria Montessori and religious education; (2) children and religious language; (3) children, spirituality and religious education; (4) play, imagination and the creative process; and (5) ethical considerations when working with children. The contributions in each of these themes have not necessarily been arranged in chronological order. They have instead been placed together in such a way so as to illustrate the development of thought in relation to the particular themes of Berryman's writing. Due to the vast number of publications, it has not been possible to include them all in one volume. Instead, the editor has taken the liberty of selecting from Berryman's bibliography those contributions which are particularly indicative of his thinking in relation to each of the themes.

Every attempt has also been made to present these works intact as Berryman had originally composed them. For instance, where Berryman used numerals in his original text rather than numbers written as words, the numerals have been retained in this compilation. It is also important to note that American spelling has been used throughout, in keeping with the North American context out of which Berryman has written. For consistency, each of my short prefaces to each of the five sections in this compilation has also utilized American spelling.

In presenting this collection of writings, it is my hope that they will stimulate further discussion and the ongoing development of Berryman's work. It is also hoped that they might lead to a greater appreciation and understanding of a theology of childhood, as well as the concepts and theory which underpin the practice of Godly Play as an approach to religious education for both children and adults, as these have often been misunderstood and misrepresented. Finally, it is hoped that this collection might provide a valuable point of reference for both scholars and practitioners of religious education.

Brendan Hyde
August 2012

A note about Referencing

Since the works of Berryman collected in this volume span not only three decades, but also a variety of journals and book chapter publications – each containing its own particular referencing style – some editorial decisions needed to be made in terms of the style guide to be used in this publication. Such judgments have been made according to the following two principles:

1. Where Berryman employed endnotes in the original published work, the original endnotes have been maintained and preserved, gathered together at the end of this volume;
2. Where in-text citations and a reference list at the end of the contribution were used in the original, these have been maintained in this present volume, as they appeared in the original publication.

The editor wishes to make this important note about the referencing here, at the beginning of this collection of writings, lest the reader may be led to believe that the referencing is both disorganised and chaotic. Rather, an attempt has been made to steer a careful path between faithfulness to Berryman's original work, and consistency in terms of an edited collection of such works.

Every effort has been made to contact all copyright holders. The publishers will be happy to make good in future editions any errors or omissions brought to their attention.

Introduction

Teaching the Christians' Strange Language: Berryman, Religious Education and Spirituality

By Brendan Hyde

Among the many who have made substantiative contributions to the theory, practice and development of religious education, Jerome W. Berryman's work exemplifies a creative synthesis of praxis, foundational theory and methodology, which makes it unique. His writing spans a period of well over thirty years, beginning in the early 1970s and continuing through to the present day. By way of an introduction, this chapter presents a short background to Jerome Berryman, and briefly surveys some of the major themes of this writing.

Background

Jerome Woods Berryman was born in 1937 in Ashland, Kansas, a small farming and ranching community. He graduated with a Bachelor of Arts from the University of Kansas in 1959, and shortly afterwards, from the Princeton Theological Seminary in 1962 with a Master of Divinity. He later returned to the Princeton Theological Seminary to graduate with a Doctor of Ministry in 1996. He also graduated with the degree of Juris Doctor from the University of Tulsa Law School in 1969 and read theology at Oxford University's Mansfield College during the summer of 1966.

However, it was during his time at Princeton Seminary (his middle year in 1960, to be precise) when his exploration into children and religious education originated. He realised that children were seldom mentioned in theological discussion. When he took the Christian education class, which was required for all students at the Seminary, he quickly understood that adult education and educational theory seemed to dominate the process. Children were viewed largely as empty vessels that needed to be filled, and the emphasis seemed to be on getting the doctrine right – and to convince children to believe it! According to Berryman (2009a) no one seriously considered that children might already know God, and that what they may in fact need is to learn how to construct their own personal meaning about this reality.

Berryman's own personal experience of growing up on the prairies of western Kansas suggested to him that children's knowledge of God was largely nonverbal and undifferentiated. Interestingly, most of the Christian mystics over the centuries had conveyed similar ideas when they tried to explain their own experiences of God. If this is the case, Berryman believed that perhaps what children needed was not to have their heads filled with information and propositional truths, but rather to learn the art of how to use an appropriate language to identify and reflect on their experience of God. Herein lay the first difficulty. Although children learn to use a variety of different languages associated with the various subject areas of the school curriculum, such as the language of mathematics and the language of science, religious language is not emphasized in schools. As well, when for example children learn the language of mathematics, they have already experienced the *practical functions* of adding and subtracting as they pile up blocks or take them away in their play. However, the Christian language system is concerned with the functions of identity (sacred story), stimulating exploration of Christian meaning (parable), making accessible the actions of the Christian community (liturgical action), and opening the way to experiencing the presence of the mystery of God directly (contemplative silence). How then does one teach such a strange language?

It would take Berryman another ten years, from his middle year at the Princeton Seminary in 1960 until the early 1970s working in churches and schools (as a Presbyterian minister) before a method for teaching Christian language to children would be discovered – the Montessori Method. Berryman decided upon this method because he believed that it could connect the child's intuition of God with the language of the Church by the playful interaction in a Montessori-like setting.

And so in 1971-1972, Jerome, his wife Thea and their two young children, Alyda and Coleen, moved to Italy for twelve months so that he could study Maria Montessori's educational approach at the Centre for Advanced Montessori Studies in Bergamo. There, as well as developing an appreciation for the Italian culture and cuisine (a liking for which he still enjoys very much to this day), Berryman met Sofia Cavalletti, who had already developed an approach to religious education grounded in the Montessori Method. The friendship and collegiality between he and Cavalletti would prove to be a long-lasting one for many years to come. Berryman studied the approach to religious education that Cavalletti had developed with great enthusiasm. Although it was firmly rooted in the Montessori Method, it would take Berryman more than another ten years to adapt, develop and refine his own approach to religious education. It would take longer still to devise a name for this process and to describe what he and Thea discovered from the children they worked with on a weekly basis.

Upon returning to the United States of America in 1973, Berryman began to teach in Montessori and other schools. He also served various positions over the course of the coming decade in the Texas Medical Centre in Houston and as a Fellow at the Institute of Religion. These included teaching the pastoral care of children, medical ethics, the relation of science and religion, and faith development courses in a range of pastoral care programs in the Texas Medical Centre's hospitals, as well as at the Institute of Religion. During this time, he continued to adapt and develop his approach to religious education, influenced greatly and primarily by the Montessori Method, secondly by Cavalletti's approach, and thirdly by his experience with sick children. He authored and presented several papers during this period documenting his work with children (largely in a pastoral care context) in which he referred to his developing approach to religious education as *theological play*. Notable among these are those titled *The Parish, the Hospital, and Theological Play* (1982) and *The Chaplain's Strange Language* (1985b), both of which have been included in this book. Experimental classrooms were set up at Pines Presbyterian church and then at the Institute of Religion where he and Thea met children on Saturdays for theological play.

In 1984 he was ordained as an Episcopal priest, and served at the Christ Church Cathedral in downtown Houston until 1994, briefly as a consultant, and then as Canon Educator. During this period he and Thea continued working with and observing children from the ages of about 3 to 5, and about ages 6 to 12. The classroom was moved to the Cathedral from the Institute of Religion, and was set up for further research and for refining Berryman's process of theological play. The sessions for which the children came lasted around 2 hours. During these sessions, a lesson consisting of sacred story, parable, or a liturgical action (which included an opportunity for group wondering) was presented by a storyteller using two and three dimensional materials. This was followed by a lengthy time in which the children responded through choosing their own work. The sessions concluded with prayers and a feast (consisting usually of fruit juice and biscuits), since the sessions themselves mirrored closely the pattern of Christian worship. Soon eight beautiful classrooms were built for children's theological play at the Cathedral.

Towards the end of his period in the Texas Medical Centre, and after much research, adaptation and refinement, Berryman devised the name "Godly Play" for his process and way of religious education. His seminal work *Godly Play: A Way of Religious Education* was published in 1991 (reprinted in 1995) and documented from a theoretical and practical stance, the essence of the process of theological play with children. In it Berryman detailed the necessity and centrality of play for learning the language of God and of God's people. He detailed the necessity of the imagination in Godly Play, and the steps involved in the creative process, of which play was at the heart. The final chapter presented his early understanding of the theology of childhood, drawing an important connection between two gateways of knowing – play (nonverbal communication) and language.

In the years which followed, Berryman was invited to present workshops, teach courses, give lectures and present academic papers about his approach to religious education, not just in the United States of America, but all over the world. The workshops were designed to train others in the method he had developed so that they could use Godly Play with children in their own religious contexts. Today the Godly Play approach to religious education is widely known, and is drawn upon in countries such as England, Wales, Scotland, Spain, Finland, Germany, Mexico, Canada, Tanzania, Kenya, Korea, and Australia, as well as the United States.

From 1998 until 2007, Berryman was the Executive Director of the Centre for the Theology of Childhood, currently located in Denver, Colorado. The Centre is now the research and development arm of the Godly Play Foundation, which was established in late 2007. Although originally situated in Houston, Texas, the Foundation is now situated at the Church of Our Saviour in San Gabriel, California. In 2007, Berryman retired as the Executive Director, and was appointed Senior Fellow of the Centre for the Theology of Childhood.

As both a recognised scholar and practitioner, Berryman was awarded an honorary Doctor of Divinity by the General Theological Seminary in New York City (2009) and an honorary doctorate from the Virginia Theological Seminary in Alexandria, Virginia (2010). He is also a member of the International Seminar for Religious Education and Values, and served on the board of the Association of Professors and Researchers in Religious Education in the United States. As well, Berryman is also a former member of the American Bar Association and belonged to the Family Law section.

There is one other pertinent factor to note in relation to Berryman's background. It concerns his collegial relationship with James Fowler and Sam Keen. In the mid-1970s, Berryman read some of Fowler's work and was so excited by what he read that he booked a flight to visit him at the Harvard Divinity School. A short time later, Berryman brought both Fowler and Keen together for a dialogue in which each outlined their different perspectives on faith. This took place at the Institute of Religion in the Texas Medical Centre on 10 May 1975. Berryman subsequently came to edit the book *Life Maps* (1978c), which captured the essence of the dialogue between Fowler and Keen. This book would prove to be so significant that there would be four re-printings of it. The influence of Fowler in particular on Berryman's thinking would prove to be great, as the next section of this introductory chapter illustrates.

A survey of the major themes of Berryman's writing

Berryman often describes himself as merely trying to be good a teacher of children. While this is undoubtedly the case, his numerous contributions to both academic and professional journals, as well as his own authored books and book chapters certainly render him a scholar – and he is recognized as such by the academic community. His writings have drawn on philosophy, theology, psychology, anthropology and contemporary research to explore, describe and detail his thinking in relation to both the theory and practice in the field. There are definite themes which can be identified in his writing which, although occasionally overlapping, can be delineated and seen to affirm each other. These are the themes around which this book has been organized. They are briefly discussed here in order to orient the reader to the work which follows.

Maria Montessori and religious education

The primary influence of the Montessori Method upon Berryman's own approach to religious education cannot be overstated. Berryman (1980) notes that both religious educators and Montessorians have overlooked her contribution to religious education. Yet, according to Berryman, it was at the very core of her life and work. Montessori found the child to be not only the focus of her work, but also the metaphor for her method. Through close observation of the child and the child's capabilities, Montessori's spiral curriculum for religious education moved through the creative use of symbols, images, concepts, rules and structures (Berryman 1992). Berryman notes that although her theory might be dated generally, her practice of religious education is not. She made creative contributions to religious education through her attention to the learning environment and the use of sensorial materials within that environment for children to manipulate (Berryman 1990).

In particular, it was the work of Sofia Cavalletti (1979), a third generation interpreter of Montessori religious education that influenced Berryman's development of a method for religious education for children initially. Cavalletti and her colleagues had expanded Montessori's innovating method for catechetical instruction with young children. The method, known as *The Catechesis of the Good Shepherd* used sensorial materials in a specially prepared environment (the atrium) to enable children to "make meaning and find direction" (Berryman 1983a, 11) in their lives in relation to the Christian story. Berryman (1978a, 1983a) writes extensively on Cavalletti, the relationship of her work to Montessori, and of the influence of her work on the development of his own method of religious education, which became known as Godly Play. He was among the first to provide what was at the time a complete and comprehensive bibliography of Cavalletti's writing (Berryman 1978a).

It was Berryman who was a leader in bringing Sofia Cavalletti to the United States in the early 1980s to present workshops on her method of religious education, and it was Berryman who provided the impetus for having her seminal work *The Religious Potential of the Child* (1979), originally published in Italian, translated into English, in which he wrote the preface (Berryman, 1983a, published by Paulist Press). In this preface to the English edition, Berryman discusses Cavalletti's method of undertaking research, the assumptions which underpin her research and her theory of Christian Education. Although a great admirer of Cavalletti and her work with children, Berryman is not blinded by his high regard, and his preface to this work is both enthusiastic and balanced. For instance, he questions whether many of the case studies presented in her work serve to demonstrate the religious potential of the child. He also notes the lack of conformity of reporting the cases. Some of the cases are third hand reports about children, or "reports of adults about their own childhood ... and parents talking about their own children" (9).

Nonetheless, the influence of the Montessori tradition on Berryman, and in particular the influence of Cavelletti's utilization of the Montessori Method in religious education, cannot be overstated. This influence continues to surface in almost all of his writings, both implicitly and explicitly, and his gratitude for her work remains warm and friendly.

Children and religious language
Since the central thesis of Berryman's thinking involves children learning to master the art of using religious language so as to confront and creatively cope with the existential issues of their lives, it is of little surprise to find that much of his writing focuses on this theme. Berryman argues that children's rapid growth means that they are living primarily at the edges of their being and knowing, and that playing in language at these edges requires a special kind of art which

many children seem to have naturally. It requires only the support of adults in order for them to draw upon their experience and to provide the Christian language system in a beneficial way.

If one were to critique Berryman's work in relation to this particular theme, it would be to note his growing reliance upon developmental psychology, and in particular, structuralist approaches to advance his argument. Berryman relies initially upon the work of Piaget, and to a lesser extent, Erikson and their notion of stages of cognitive development. He also proceeds to draw upon others who modelled their theories upon Piagetian stages, notably James Fowler and Lawrence Kohlberg (see for example, Berryman 1983b, 1985a). Theories of cognitive development are problematic because they tend to view development as a linear trajectory. Development begins at a particular stage, and proceeds along a straight path until the highest stage is attained. By implication one cannot attain a particular stage of development until one has "passed through" each of the stages which precede it. Taking Fowler's (1981) stages of faith development as an example, one cannot attain the stage of Synthetic – Conventional faith (occurring in early adolescence in which the emergent capacity is the forming of a personal myth) until one has passed through the stage of Mythic – Literal faith (occurring in middle childhood, in which the new capacity consists of the rise of narrative and the emergence of story, drama and myth as ways of giving coherence to experience). Much of the academic literature suggests that development is much more complex. It does not occur along an even path, and there are regressions as well as progressions along the trajectory (see for example Cupit 2007).

It is pertinent to note here in relation to Fowler (1981) that each of the stages of faith development he proposes are quite broad. For example, his third stage – Synthetic-Conventional faith – is summarized by a number of features, including experiences of the world extending beyond the family, a synthesis of values and information, as well as the emergent capacity of forming personal myth. This itself represents a deviation from the trajectory of Piaget's work. Strict Piagetian developmentalists would consider the proposed stages of Fowler's model "defective" since the structures through which the individual passes to attain the following stage of development are too expansive.

Nonetheless, the way in which Berryman utilizes these theories within his writing clearly indicates that he regards developmental psychology not as providing definitive answers in relation to cognitive development, but rather as providing signposts which point towards phenomena rather than capturing them precisely (see for example Berryman 1992). It is also important to note that much of Berryman's writing in relation to this theme initially occurs shortly after the theories of James Fowler and Lawrence Kohlberg were published. One would expect then that Berryman would draw upon theories which were current at the time of writing. It is also relevant to note that Berryman has continued, where appropriate, to draw upon these theories in instances where they offer plausible insights and explanations, which advance the thesis of his writing.

Children, spirituality and religious education

For Berryman, the notions of play, religious education and spirituality are intrinsically connected. Berryman's main contribution to this particular theme is his articulation of the nonverbal dimension of spirituality, particularly in relation to young children, who have not yet *mastered* the ability to communicate verbally. Spirituality is primarily nonverbal and, in young children, it is signalled by play. The task of the religious educator is to guide the child from nonverbal spirituality into religious language, and to keep that language rooted in the creative spirituality of the child (Berryman 2002).

For Berryman, the optimal way for this to be achieved is within a community of shared values, beliefs, and a shared language system – a Christian community. Again, critics may take issue with this proposition. The scholarly literature suggests that all people are inherently spiritual, irrespective of whether or not they belong to or practise a religious tradition (see for example O'Murchu 1997; Hyde 2008; Tacey 2000). Some would maintain that Berryman is arguing that, unless the innate spirituality of children is guided to be expressed in traditional religious language, the spirituality of the child somehow remains incomplete or immature. For many, this would render the erroneous notion that religion is the larger sphere into which spirituality needs necessarily to be situated. Such thinking echoes Ranson's (2002) proposition that the spiritual experience of an individual must proceed to reflection and be placed within a shared context of particular beliefs and values – a believing, worshipping community, in which religious language gives the individual a theology with which to articulate spirituality. The difficulty here, as Meehan (2002) notes, is that many people today rightly consider themselves to be spiritual, yet for various reasons, do not belong to or practise any religious tradition. One cannot dismiss their spirituality on the grounds that they do have a theology to articulate it. Berryman would, however, question whether such people have a mature language system, such as those offered by the world's major religions, to enable them to articulate and share their spirituality in a supportive community.

A close examination of Berryman's writing in relation to this theme suggests his acute awareness of the tensions which exist. And, Berryman clearly acknowledges the context out of which he writes and operates. Whether or not one agrees with his proposition, Berryman's writings in relation to children, spirituality and religious education are scholarly and offer both academics and practitioners valuable insights into the spirituality of children and its expression both nonverbally and in language.

Play, imagination and the creative process

The concepts of play, imagination and the creative process are central to Berryman's approach to religious education with both children and adults. For Berryman, play is at the heart of creativity, and creativity is at the heart of all creatures created in the image of the Creator. Play is connected to smiles and laughter – nonverbal communication – which are the key signals of play for human beings. Yet play is a serious business. Play with God in a community of children guided by adult mentors is the way children and adults enter the creative process to confront their existential issues and limits by playing at the edges of their knowing and being. The role of the imagination in play and the creative process cannot be overstated. Rather than enabling one to retreat from reality, the creative process takes one deeper into reality. Therefore religious education for both children and adults must be grounded in play and imagination, and must enable the participants to engage freely in the creative process.

In his writing, Berryman in particular utilizes Garvey's (1977) description of play as being pleasurable and spontaneous, as having no extrinsic goals, as involving deep engagement on the part of the players, and as having systematic relations to what is not play: creativity, language learning, problem solving, the development of social roles, and other cognitive and social phenomena. Critics may question whether all play for children is in fact always pleasurable. For instance, some play can involve pain and discomfort, such as when one plays football and gets injured, or when one is practising for a particular sport and one experiences muscle soreness and the like. That type of pain is certainly not pleasurable! However, Berryman would argue that, in the long run, such pain is in the service of the satisfaction derived from the overall achievement. When one plays a game in which one wins, the pain that may have been experienced quickly fades as the elation of having won the game takes over. If one loses, one looks forward to the next game, and the continued improvement that practice can bring.

In discussing creativity, Berryman draws again upon the insights from developmental psychology, in particular the work of Csikszentmihalyi (1975, 1996) and Gardner (1983, 1993, 1999). The notion of multiple intelligences as proposed by Howard Gardner, and upon which Berryman draws, has been the subject of much critique. Many would argue that each of the separate intelligences identified by Gardner are not, in fact, separate intelligences, but are instead a reframing of intelligence as different cognitive abilities (see for example Elliott 1998; Zohar and Marshall 2000). In other words, verbal-linguistic, musical-rhythmic and so forth are all indicative of cognitive abilities, not separate intelligences. That Berryman (1991, 2005) draws upon Gardner's thesis to suggest different creativity styles, for many, could then be problematic.

Yet, again, Berryman does not draw upon developmental psychology in his discussion of creativity as a definitive explanation. Rather, he crafts the insights from the work of Gardner (and others) so that they act as signposts which provide possible perspectives in shedding light upon the concept of creativity for guiding the teacher's way of communication with children.

Berryman's discussion of the creative process is helpful. He draws upon the work of Loder (1981) to outline five steps indicating how, in playing at the edges of knowing and being, an individual might develop a new and creative insight to cope with existential issues. The first stage consists of a disruption of one's circle of meaning, wherein an established idea or meaning is broken in some way, for instance, by being challenged. The second step in the creative process involves the scanning for a new frame of meaning to cope with the disruption, and to restore cohesion. The third step is insight. A new and more adequate pattern is formed and becomes a new frame of meaning, using the symbols of the given domain to develop the idea. Until this point the process has been largely nonverbal. The fourth step, which is the point at which closure begins, involves the new insight being articulated, verbalized and evaluated by the rules and structures of the particular domain in which it was discovered until there is closure, which comprises the fifth step.

Ethical considerations when working with children

Some may not immediately recognize this as a theme of Berryman's writing, but it is not surprising since, from 1974 until 1984, he taught and consulted on medical ethics at the Institute of Religion in the Texas Medical Centre in Houston. This theme is one which surfaces in much of his work, at least implicitly, often woven into the fabric of the text itself. Examples of this include his outlining of the power relation between children and adults (Berryman 1989) and the "double bind" (Berryman, 2009b). As well, there are some articles in which he explicitly writes about ethical considerations, particularly in conducting research with children (for example Berryman 1978b).

Although structuralist theories again influence Berryman's writing here, in particular Piaget and Kohlberg in his earlier writings, the issue Berryman addresses is in relation to the child's right to be heard and consulted in research and worship contexts. While children do not think and feel as adults so, "the conclusion that they should not be included in the ethical discussion is a cruel distortion of what I consider to be the main purpose of having an ethical discussion with another human being, especially a child" (Berryman 1978b, 85).

In many ways Berryman was ahead of his time in this respect. He advocates for the rights of the child, based on scriptural accounts of Jesus and his respect for children, in relation to ethics, theology and religious education in ways that later writers, for example Bunge (2001) and Grajczonek (2007), would eventually come to do. His writing in this area focuses on the practical – putting ethics into action when engaging with children.

Conclusion

The five themes outlined above form the parts into which this book has been organized. The writings of Berryman which have been selected and placed within each theme speak clearly and unambiguously for themselves. Some of the writings included may be unfamiliar to some readers. The editor was able to access these from among the archival material at the Centre for the Theology of Childhood, in Denver, Colorado and the editor's sincere thanks is expressed to Jerome W. Berryman for allowing him to include these in this volume. For many, these writings would remain otherwise inaccessible.

So, while at times the Christian's strange language is still perplexing today, especially to those not fluent in its creative art, it remains both curious and intriguing, and Berryman's writing reflects a remarkable journey of scholarship and research to keep this language deeply rooted in children, yet open and creative to meet the future. This marks the spirit of Godly Play which Berryman has termed "playful orthodoxy". It is the hope of the editor that the contributions included here will serve to provoke thought, stimulate discussion, and inspire further investigation by a new generation of scholars and religious educators.

References

Berryman, J.W. 1978a. "Sofia Cavalletti: A brief introduction and bibliography." *The Constructive Triangle* 5(1): 32-45.

_____. 1978b. "Talking ethics with the child." In *Research on Children: Medical Imperatives, Ethical Quandaries and Legal Constraints*, edited by J. van Eys Baltimore: University Park Press.

_____. (Ed.). 1978c. *Life Maps: Conversations on the Journey of Faith*. Waco, Texas: Word Books.

_____. 1980. "Montessori and religious education." *Religious Education* 75(3): 294-307.

_____. 1982. "The parish, the hospital, and theological play." *Liturgy* 2(2): 47-53.

_____. 1983a. "Preface to the English edition." Pp. 3-20 in *The Religious Potential of the Child: The Description of an Axperience with Children From Ages Three to Six*. New Jersey: Paulist Press.

_____. 1983b. "The rite of anointing and the pastoral care of sick children." Pp. 63-77 in *The Sacred Play of Children*, edited by D. Apostolos-Cappadonna. New York: The Seabury Press.

_____. 1985a. "Children's spirituality and religious language." *British Journal of Religious Education,* 7 (3):120-127.

_____. 1985b. "The chaplain's strange language: A unique contribution to the health care team." Pp. 16-39 in *Life, Faith, Hope and Magic: The Chaplaincy in Pediatric Cancer Care*, edited by J. van Eys & E.J. Mahnke. Austin, Texas: The University of Texas Press.

_____. 1988. "Maria Montessori." P. 424 in *Harper's Encyclopaedia of Religious Education*, edited by I.V. Cully & K.B. Cully. San Francisco: HarperSanFrancisco.

_____. 1989. "Children in worship: An ethic of respect". *Liturgy: Ethics and Justice* 4(7): 53-59.

_____. 1991. *Godly Play: A Way of Religious Education*. San Francisco: HarperCollins.

_____. 1992. "Faith development and the language of faith." Pp. 21-55 in *Handbook of Children's Religious Education*, edited by D. Ratcliff. Birmingham, Alabama: Religious Education Press.

_____. 2001. "The nonverbal nature of spirituality and religious language." Pp 9-21 in *Spiritual Education: Cultural, Religious and Social Differences. New Perspectives for the 21st Century*, edited by J. Erricker, C.Ota, & C. Erricker. Brighton, UK: Sussex Academic Press.

_____. 2005. "Playful orthodoxy: Reconnecting religion and creativity by education." *Sewanee Theological Review* 48(4): 437-455.

_____. 2009a. *Teaching Godly Play: How to Mentor the Spiritual Development of Children*. Denver, CO: Morehouse Educational Resources.

_____. 2009b. "Theologizing with children: A parable approach."

Pp. 197-213 in *Hovering Over the Face of the Deep: Philosophy, Theology and Children*, edited by G. Iversen, G. Mitchell & G. Pollard. Munster: Waxmann.

Bunge, M. 2001. *The Child in Christian Thought*. Grand Rapids, Michigan: Wm. B. Eerdmans.

Cupid, G. 2007. "The marriage of science and spirit: Dynamic systems theory and the development of spirituality." *International Journal of Children's Spirituality* 12(2):105-116.

Elliott, M. 1998. "Multiple intelligences and other delusions: Gifted children in the Catholic religion classroom." *Word in Life* 48(3): 22-28.

Fowler, J. W. 1981. *Stages of Faith: The Psychology of Human Development and the Quest for Meaning*. San Francisco: Harper & Row.

Garvey, C. 1977. *Play*. Cambridge, MA: Harvard University Press.

Grajczonek, J. 2007. "From the Vatican to the classroom. Part 2: Examining intertextuality and alignment among church, local diocesan and school religious education documents." *Journal of Religious Education* 56(4): 2-9.

Hyde, B. 2008. *Children and Spirituality: Searching for Meaning and Connectedness*. London: Jessica Kingsley.

Loder, J.E. 1981. *The Transforming Moment: Understanding Convictional Experiences*. San Francisco: Harper & Row.

Meehan, C. 2002. "Confusion and competing claims in the spiritual development debate." *International Journal of Children's Spirituality* 7(3): 291-308.

O'Murchu, D. 1997. *Reclaiming Spirituality: A New Spiritual Framework for Today's World*. Dublin: Gateway.

Ranson, D. 2002. *Across the Great Divide: Bridging Spirituality and Religion Today*. Strathfield, NSW: St. Paul's Publications.

Tacey, D. 2000. *ReEnchantment: The New Australian Spirituality*. Sydney: HarperCollins.

Zohar, D., & Marshall, I. 2000. *SQ: Spiritual Intelligence: The Ultimate Intelligence*. London: Bloomsbury.

Part One

Maria Montessori and Religious Education

Preface to Part One

The work of Maria Montessori is, to a great extent, a prerequisite for understanding the context of the writings of Jerome W. Berryman. This is because the theoretical and conceptual underpinnings for Berryman's approach to religious education with children (and adults) stem initially from the work of Montessori and her approach to education generally, as well as from the influences of those who initially applied Montessori's concepts to religious education. The writings of Berryman presented in this section reflect and convey his understanding and engagement with Montessori and the Montessori Method, and his place among the generational interpreters of Montessori religious education.

Berryman describes himself as a fourth generation interpreter of Montessori religious education. While Maria Montessori herself represents the first generation, E.M Standing, Montessori's first biographer, is the second generation interpreter. Sofia Cavalletti is the leader of the third generation.

Accordingly, the first of the writings presented in this section explores in depth Montessori's contribution to religious education. In it, Berryman notes that although Montessori's contribution to religious education is significant, it has often been overlooked by religious educators and Montessorians alike. Yet, and as Berryman argues convincingly, it was at the core of her life and work.

Berryman's second contribution in this section briefly articulates the work of E.M Standing (1887-1967) of the second generation of interpreters of Montessori religious education. In this contribution we are introduced to Standing, and in particular to his seminal work, *The Child in the Church*.

The third contribution comes from Berryman's preface to the English edition (1983) of Cavalletti's seminal work *The Religious*

Potential of the Child, which was first published in 1979 in Italian. Berryman's contribution to this work cannot be overstated and is of great significance. It was the influence of Berryman in particular, which resulted in the first English translation of Cavalletti's work. Although a great admirer of Cavalletti and her work with children, Berryman is not blinded by his high regard, and his preface to this work is both enthusiastic and balanced. In this preface he discusses Cavalletti's method of undertaking research, the assumptions which underpin her research and her theory of Christian Education.

1
Montessori and Religious Education[1]

Maria Montessori (1870-1952) is much more interesting and important as a person than as an educational saint. Her contribution to religious education has been ironically overlooked by many religious educators and Montessorians. It was at the core of her life and work.

Montessori and religion

The last public statement Montessori worked on before her death in 1952 was for the Catholic Montessori Guild which had just been formed in England. Two years earlier she had expressed to Standing, her trusted follower and biographer, that she longed to form a religious order devoted to serving children and their families through the use of her method.

In 1922 when Montessori was fifty-two years old she said that with the opportunity to begin a school and center in Barcelona "... the Montessori Method was furnished with a long-sought opportunity of penetrating deeper into the life of the child's soul, and of thus fulfilling its true educational mission".[2] This school fit Montessori's personal agenda because it centered around a children's chapel and learning center.

When Montessori was about forty years of age she and her close colleagues swore an oath "before the Blessed Sacrament" to serve the Catholic Church in the reform of humanity. This was the same period when she resigned from her academic post at the University of Rome and had her name removed from the list of practicing physicians there.

From about 1910 on, Montessori turned from the academic community, from formal research and from the writing of technical papers toward the business of the Movement and keeping her growing entourage and family afloat. She supported herself by giving courses, by book royalties, by the sale of didactic materials and by finding patrons. From that point on she was also caught in the tension of longing to be a scientist and longing to be a child advocate. To a very great extent she accomplished all of these things, although, as we shall see, the articulation of her theory did suffer from a lack of systematic treatment.

On Christmas Eve in 1916 she could be heard sobbing as she sat among the government officials who helped her build her school in Barcelona. They were at Mass in the Church of Our Lady of Pompei. After Mass she told her close co-worker, Anna Maccheroni:

> Many who haven't understood me think that I'm a sentimental romantic who dreams only of seeing children, of kissing them, of telling them fairy tales, that I want to visit schools to watch them, to cuddle them and give them caramels. They weary me! I am a rigorous scientific investigator, not a literary idealist like Rousseau. I seek to discover the man in the child, to see in him the true human spirit, the design of the Creator: the scientific and religious truth. It is to this end that I apply my method of study, which respects human nature. I don't need to teach anything to children: it is they who, placed in a favorable environment, teach me, reveal to me spiritual secrets as long as their souls have not been deformed.[3]

Montessori's method of theory building and research to discover "the scientific and religious truth" used neither the paradigm articulated in her scientific training nor that of the church to guide her. She did not seem to fit anywhere, but her instinct told her she was on the right path.

Montessori's way of doing research

Montessori began her research by assuming a particular nature of the child. This "elevated nature" revealed a child who was self-directed, loved order, had an ability for deep concentration, worked best through his or her senses, respected other people and their work and seriously played at learning. This "elevated nature" was something only a few others had seen. It was observed by Tolstoy, Tagore, Froebel, Itard, Seguin and Pestalozzi. Most adults, however, did not believe such a child existed. Montessori noted:

> They cannot admit that the child was concealing, as behind a mask, his elevated nature, his formidable energies and initiative; nor can they admit the statement that it was a psychological ignorance on the part of the educator which was to be blamed for this state of affairs. They prefer to attribute to the adult's competence successes in the children.[4]

Montessori described her method for discovering the child behind the mask in her first book, *The Montessori Methods*[5]. It sold out the whole first edition of five thousand copies in four days when it appeared in America in April of 1912. Published in Italy in 1909, this book appeared about a century after Pestalozzi's own reports on his first experiments.

The environment Montessori set up to prevent adult misconceptions from distorting the behavior and growth of the children seems commonplace today. It was almost unthinkable at the turn-of-the-century. The scaled-down furniture, sensorial learning materials, and the freedom of movement in the classroom opposed the assumptions of Montessori's day. She allowed constructive, spontaneous movement for physical and psychological development as well as to see what materials the children profitably used and spontaneously selected from the open shelves. She removed materials children did not "prove" important to their development. They were given real tasks such as cleaning and preparing meals with the indirect help of the adults. The afternoon was spent outside gardening, building, potting, playing, etc.

The child that appeared from behind his or her mask in this "prepared environment" Montessori called "normal." The process of de-programming the adult mask was called "normalization." The natural law of the child had been uncovered.

Children who did not normalize, however, were excluded from the school. Parents who did not "show the greatest respect and deference toward the Directress" had their families excluded. The experiment was controlled to succeed.

When Montessori used the word, "experiment," she did not mean a formal experiment as we think of it today. She meant something more like clinical observation. Her record keeping included physical measurements, family interviews, scoring concentration cycles, counting the usage of each material, noting where "spontaneous" movements took the children in the environment, etc. She was not a dispassionate observer, however, as she sometimes implied.

Montessori intervened in the environment to halt any behavior which "... offends or annoys others, or whatever tends toward rough or ill-bred acts." To shape behavior in a positive way she noted, "The child needs to be charmed in every way, by the glance as well as by the pose."[6]

Most of the verbal and non-verbal intervention was indirect. Montessori aimed to reinforce positive tendencies or re-direct negative tendencies just before the child might act. She did not want to scold or over-praise. She valued the fragile but developing individual character of each child's self-direction. She also knew that some acts would right themselves. This would strengthen moral judgment and will by such self-overcoming. The art of discipline was for her "... to discern which are the acts to hinder and which are those to observe."

Montessori was not just interested in classroom discipline. By intuition she knew that she also had to observe herself interacting with the children. In this total ecology the "reciprocal influence" was as important as her influence on the child.

The clarification of her reciprocal influence principle of mutual child-adult relations had been made by 1922. It had far ranging implications. She wrote in *The Child in the Church:*

> There are some of those who think that the child's only value for humanity lies in the fact that he will some day be an adult. In this way they detract from the true value of childhood by shifting it only into the future. This cannot be justified. The child is a human entity having importance in himself; he is not just a transition on the way to adulthood. We ought not to consider the child and the adult merely as successive phases in the individual's life. We ought rather to look upon them as two different forms of human life, going on at the same time and exerting upon one another a reciprocal influence.[7]

The adult can be as developmentally damaged when this principle is ignored.

We can infer Montessori's ideal for herself as a clinical observer from her ideal for the teachers she trained. In contrast to the view of William James she felt that the teacher ought to be a "teacher-scientist." James thought that "an intermediary inventive mind" was needed to make the application of a science such as psychology to an art like teaching "by using its originality?"[8]

Despite her training Montessori intuited that observation (at least in the case of human beings) involved one in an irreducible web of empirical method, scientific theory and human aspiration. She stood with one foot in the data-to-theory camp and the other foot in the theory-to-data camp. While she talked natural law and Baconian strategy she also postulated an ideal child and sought that phenomenon in her classroom laboratory. She did what Michael Polanyi later described as personal or tacit knowing. He argued that this is the way science is actually practiced. The false ideal of objective science not only is a self-deception but is dangerous since no one takes responsibility for what he or she sees and acts on.[9]

Montessori's classroom had a built-in Pygmalion effect,[10] but she felt that *all* the children in *"her"* classroom would experience "growth spurts." She also reinforced the experience of making-it-on-your-own which contrasted to the dark side of what Rosenthal and Jacobsen found at Oak-Hall. The children who tried to grow on-their-own without the teacher's self-fulfilling prophecy were found by teachers in that study to be less well-adjusted, less interesting or less affectionate than the ones the teachers thought would grow rapidly. A study of the children Montessori expelled as "incorrigible" might have been interesting.[11]

Teacher self-respect is as important as his or her respect for the children. Montessori did not lack in self-respect, but she also examined herself to see if she were centered enough to allow the children to be themselves and grow on their own.

A final and extremely important aspect of Montessori's participation in the ecology of the classroom is that she loved and valued creativity in herself and in the children. The children and Montessori mutually reinforced each other's creativity in word and "by the glance as well as by the pose."

One often wonders what Montessori, Pestalozzi, Froebel or other creative teachers of the past would think of what *is* done in their names today. Would they even recognize it? There is an attitude of respect for children and a creativity-respecting-creativity between master teacher and child which cannot be packaged or put into books. Montessori *was* her method.

This concludes our discussion of Montessori's approach to clinical observation. In many ways we will be left with what Bruner said of Freud when we turn now to her theory:

> There is no scientific proof for Freudian theory inasmuch as it

is based on Freud's clinical observation of specific individuals ... and it is not even a theory in the conventional sense; it is a metaphor, a way of conceiving man, a drama.[12]

Montessori and religious reality

The reality which Montessori identified, named, and valued in her theory is important for us to discuss, because it is to this reality that she keyed her practice of religious education. It is not entirely clear what her theory of religious reality is, but working back and forth between what she did and what she said concerning religious education we can come to a tentative conclusion about how she organized in theory, what she learned clinically from the children.

To talk about religion Montessori had to distinguish both imagination and fantasy from that phenomenon. Religion could be neither based on sense impressions of the natural world nor illusion. It is another kind of reality.

Montessori first began to break out of her turn-of-the century objectivism box in her book, *Spontaneous Activity in Education*,[13] in 1916. About 57 percent of this book is devoted to a chapter on "Imagination." It moves from a description of a mental faculty to the creative process. It started with a heavy reliance on William James' *Principles of Psychology* and, as James himself did, it moves away from matters of mechanical physiology into matters of religion.

Montessori said, "What we call *creation* is in reality a composition, a construction raised upon a *primitive material* of the mind, which must be collected from the environment by means of the senses."[14] She concluded: "We are unable to 'imagine' things which do not actually present themselves to our senses."

With the authority of James on one side she had the authority of her Church on the other. The Catholic Church's doctrine of *creatio ex nihilo* was interpreted by Montessori to mean that humankind could only create with sense matter. "Thus positive science represents to us the 'redemption' of thought; its purification from original sin, a return to the natural *laws* of psychical energy."[15]

Reality lay straight ahead in the world "out there" known by the senses and ordered by natural law imbedded in its structure. Given this orientation toward creativity one can see why Montessori was concerned about children disengaging from the sensory world and why fantasy was considered non-sense or unreal.

For Montessori art was aimed in the same direction. It recorded incoming data from "out there" and by a mathematical averaging of proportion the artist's mind was able to represent the ideal form. Raphael's *Madonna della Seggiola* was recommended for every Montessori school. Not only was he Italy's "greatest artist," but the painting provided an "elevation of the idea of motherhood to the progress of women and to the protection of her offspring." Though the children did not comprehend the symbolic significance of this painting they did have awakened in them what she called "a religious impression".[16]

Montessori did not explore the "deviated" aspect of fantasy until 1936 in her book, *The Secret of Childhood.*[17] In this book which addressed the discoveries of Freud concerning the unconscious mind she also talked about troubled children: flights from reality ("fugues"), "barriers," "cures," "attachment," "possessiveness," "desire for power," "inferiority complexes," "fear," and "lies." In this book she comes as close as she ever did to a theory of the emotional life of the child. It also clearly shows that fantasy is distinguished from religion. Fantasy is a disordered projection. Religion is a reality.

In her first book in 1909 Montessori had said that we cannot deny *a priori* that there is a "religious sentiment." If we were to do this we would rob humankind of its development.[18] She still maintains her assumption that the essential child is religious but has she left room theoretically?

Montessori was forced to set up a new category for religious reality. She said:

> There are persons who have had non-sensorial impressions and they are persons whose spiritual life was of very great intensity. They have *internal impressions* which cannot be accounted fruits of the imagination, but must be accepted as realities simply perceived. That they are realities *as* affirmed not only by the introspection of normal subjects, but by the effect upon their internal personality.[19]

Religious reality is not perceived through the senses. It is neither perceived in the internal world in the same way that "the hallucinations of the insane are":

> In the madman, an excitement of the cerebral cortex reproduces old images deposited by the external world whence they were taken, with external sensorial characteristics; so that the sufferer really believes that he sees his phantasms with his actual eyes, and that he hears voices which persecute him.[20]

To distinguish between the sense impressions and internal impressions which are non-sensorial without getting confused by the old images experienced internally but which have external sensorial characteristics is difficult. She relied on the introspection of normal subjects to prove this, but she does not cite cases or literature to substantiate her observation. Presumably she is referring to the introspection tradition of Wilhelm Wundt, who in the 1870s set up what was probably the first psychological laboratory in an old auditorium in Leipzig. Wundt and his associates relied greatly on systematic self-observation to find the basic elements of psychology, especially in the area of perception and consciousness.

In practice she relied on outward behavior to signal the child's non-sensorial impression of God. Hallucination was distinguished by observing bad behavior which is defined as disordered. Montessori discussed conversion in this context, because conversion brings order from disorder.

Montessori conceived of aesthetics and morality order as being received from the exterior world which is structured by natural law. Uncovering this external order clarifies moral and aesthetic reality, but it is still not clear how she conceived of religious reality or the experience of God.

By instinct she turns to children for the answer. At the end of *Spontaneous Activity* she cites a case presented in Brussels at a medical meeting in 1911. It discussed the development of the moral and religious feeling in a child. No age is given for the child in her description of the case. She says that it is "the solitary study of this kind which has been brought forward in public congresses on psychology." She does not state the extent or method of her literature search. What is obvious is that her real interest is not in the connection between moral conversion and the religious "internal impression."

Her main interest focused on in the link between the 1911 case and the four cases she had personally observed. They each involved children who had had no previous religious training.

Montessori concluded from this small sample at the end of *Spontaneous Activity* that the "religious sentiment" is "spontaneous" rather than acquired.

Montessori did not discuss how the spontaneous religious sentiment and the "opening of the mind" she referred to as an aspect of the intelligence were connected. General cognition seems to be related to the creative process when discussed in *Spontaneous Activity*.

> When we talk of "opening the mind," we mean a creative phenomenon, which is not the weak result of an impression violently made from without. The opening of the mind is the *active comprehension* which accompanies great emotions, and which is therefore felt as a spiritual event.[21]

Does this "opening" work in the realm of religious reality as well as natural reality? Is it internally felt as being spontaneous religious understanding? Montessori concludes that the ordering of one's *life* not only in moral and aesthetic ways, but totally is a function of the creative process.

At the end of *Spontaneous Activity* Montessori concludes as she did in *The Montessori Method* with poetic and vague references to religion. In 1916, however, she calls the reader's attention to experiments occuring in Barcelona which clarify moral and religious education.

The Barcelona experiment did not add much to Montessori's theory of religious reality, but it added a tremendous amount to her practice of religious education. By this time she had begun to speak of "the supernatural order" to solve the problem *Spontaneous Activity* had raised:

> Not only in the natural but also in the supernatural order there exists an ideal to be realized. Just as the education of physical and psychic life is nothing else than co-operation with the natural forces of growth, so the supernatural education is nothing else than co-operation with God's grace, which provides the real urge to true process of growth in the divine life.[22]

This experiment gave the children the Christian symbol system in sensori-motor and creative ways as the means for such growth.

The Barcelona school had shaded walks, a meadow, pools for fish, cages for pets, and lots of lovely space indoors. The most important room was the children's chapel. Artists were hired to make this room the most beautiful in the school. Integrated into its child-scaled furnishings were materials about the liturgy and sacred history. It was a learning center as well as a place for celebrating the liturgy with a priest specially assigned to the school for this work.

The materials developed in religion during this period produced a spiral curriculum. It was keyed to the needs and capacities of each developmental stage.[23] This curriculum has been in continual development since that time at various places in the world. One outstanding center of experimentation is in Rome.

In 1954, two years after Montessori died, Sofia Cavalletti and Gianna Gobbi began to extend and deepen what Montessori started. By "experimentation" is meant that what the children do not use in their playful work with the materials is thrown away. This child-tested curriculum has been developing now for over sixty-four years in an unbroken line.

Montessori fled from Spain when the Civil War broke out in 1936, she went to the Netherlands. In 1939 she was invited to come to India to give a course by the Theosophical Society. She was interned there by the British during the war because she was an Italian citizen. The British allowed her to travel freely. During this period she personally trained over one thousand Indian teachers. It was during this time that she also continued to reflect on the young child. Beginning with her book, *The Secret of Childhood,* she began to use the model of a "psychic embryo."

In 1946 Montessori returned to Europe. She went back to India in 1947. Talk of starting a Montessori University brought her back. She gave a course in 1947 at Ahmedabad which provided the basis for her book, *The Absorbent Mind.*[24] The bloody partition of India and Pakistan caused her to return to her European home in Amsterdam where schools bearing her name were now flourishing.

Many of the publications from Montessori's India Period (1939-1946) were more "authorized" than written by her. Students listened to the translations of her Italian lectures and made notes which were later published under her name. The *Absorbent Mind* was published in such a volume in English in 1949 in India. Montessori re-worked that version for her Italian publisher. The Italian publication of 1952 was the basis for a second improved English translation by Claude Claremont in 1958 in the United States.

Montessori's summing up in *The Absorbent Mind* continues her refusal to deny *a priori* the existence of a "religious sentiment" in the human species. To do that would be "... to commit a pedagogical error similar to that of denying, *a priori,* to the child, the love of learning for learning's sake."[25] Even to explore the possibility of God's presence, the reality of God had to be assumed and the related religious symbol system used in the exploration.

By the time of *The Absorbent Mind,* forty years after her first book, Montessori had found many names for the mysterious force which moves in the adult, the infant and the whole cosmic ecology. Drawing on her wide interests and broad travels she tried to explain it by re-naming it. Her books were littered with the husks and jargons of the many models she had used to find a theory to match what her practice and clinical observation had shown her.

Montessori called the core of growth process many things. She called it Love. Following Bergson she called it the Life Force. Following Sir Percy Nunn she used his concept of the Home. She called it energy. From her association with the Italian physicist, Luigi Fantappie, she talked of it in terms of syntrophy and entrophy.[26] When she returned to the Christian symbol system she called it God. She did this, however, with an awareness the many religions which call on God, she also had a deep feeling for the inability to speak about what she wished to describe.

Toward the end of *The Absorbent Mind,* Montessori tried to bring together the evolution of the species, the creative process, all her jargon from the many models the had used, the cosmic ecology and God. Now in her late 70s she tried to say it all in one phrase:

> I would like to say a word about this reality, and also about the sayings of the poets and the prophets. This force that we call love is the greatest energy of the universe. But I am using an inadequate expression, for it is more than an energy: it is creation itself. I should put it better if I were to say: "God is love."[27]

She did not mean the pantheisem of created reality but the reality of the creative process. God is known in the process known to humankind as the vast biological and emotional creative dynamic called love. They cannot be separated. The search for God cannot be separated from the search for love. Love draws us into the creative process of the personal or cosmic other. It is especially in the infant, who absorbs and is so absorbing, that humankind has its most profound metaphor for this relationship. Montessori's intuition brought her back again to the infant.

It may be that the experience which Montessori used as the basis for her clinical research and for the theoretical discussion she tried to make, is literally beyond words. The totality cannot be abstracted into bits and pieces by symbols. If this is true, then, the only way that we can find out what Montessori knew is by watching her in the classroom with children or by being in a personal relationship with her. We have only historical glimpses of what that was like, since she was a complex, public figure.

One glimpse which to this author has an authentic ring comes from Sheila Radice. In the fall and winter of 1919 she wrote several *Times Educational Supplement* articles about Montessori. In one of these articles she looked into a classroom:

> ... a group of seven- to eleven-year-olds are at work with the advanced material. In what looks like disorder each child is making his own order, one little boy at geometrical drawings, another at word cards, others with bead frames, another reading. In the middle of the room, the children oblivious to them, are Montessori and Maccheroni, standing and talking in rapid Italian, then bursting into laughter. Later, Montessori repeats the conversation to a visitor, adding a few refinements that have occured to her since and that start them laughing all over again.[28]

The ecology of a classroom with Montessori present was not a ritualistic or repressive experience. Her enjoyment of the creative process promoted the process in the children. They in turn reinforced her own delight and all together they made a place of laughter and playful work.

Montessori and religious education

In 1919 Sheila Radice heard Montessori sigh. "Words, words, words!", she put down another of the innumerable commentaries on the implications of her method. "Let us leave aside these questions of historical comparison and philosophical abstraction and get back to the living child."

Montessori found the child to be not only the focus of her work but also the metaphor for her method. The "God in the Child" referred to in *The Child in the Church*[29] absorbed her as the infant absorbed the God she had in the child of her adult personality. As she learned from the child about adult religion the child learned about his or her species from the adult. The "reciprocal influence" was mutually beneficial, and opened the way to know secrets about children and adults unknown to a science influenced by the assumptions of Descartes and Comte. She overcame her turn-of-the-century Italian scientific training to know children through this relationship, but she did not work out a new paradigm. As a clinician and as a child advocate she had other tasks to do.

Montessori's spiral curriculum for religious education moved through the creative use of images, symbols, concepts, rules and, perhaps, beyond these structures. Because her own intuitive method attached the Christian symbol system to the creative process through all these stages it was never extinguished. Its usefulness did not die out or become dormant. From the child to the levels of adult experiencing no ceiling was placed on the way God was known.

Today we use a hierarchy of systems. Reality is known by a relative continuum of systems ranging from atomic ones, such as rhythmically related energy particles, to cosmic ones, such as finite, curved, expanding space. Each system has its own appropriate set of symbols for probing and describing that part of reality.

The Christian symbol system (and perhaps other religious symbol systems) has become suspect because it refers to no experiential base. The reality of God seems detached from it. Its place in the hierarchy of systems is being squeezed out because it seems hollow.

Without an experience base there is no need to teach this symbol system to children. It is done, however, for motivations which can only further distort the symbol system. If it is true that we know God most adequately in the creative process, then, the Christian symbol system must be attached to that for it to work. The many implications for the theory and practice of religious education are important although they are beyond the scope of this paper.

Montessori's theory is dated; her practice of religious education is not. When her theory is conceived of as "... a metaphor, a way of conceiving man, a drama," perhaps, it is timeless too. As she said, "Let us leave aside these questions of historical comparison and philosophical abstraction and get back to the living child."

Original source:

Berryman, J.W. 1980. "Montessori and religious education." *Religious Education* **75 (3): 294-307.**

2
Montessori Religious Education
E.M. Standing (1887-1967)

This second chapter takes up the life of E.M. Standing. He is especially important because of his interpretations of Montessori's work to the English-speaking world and his special interest in her approach to religious education.

The vocation of teaching

Edwin Mortimer Standing was born on 18 September 1887, in Tananarive, Madagascar. He was called "Ted" and grew up in a Quaker missionary family. When Ted was about six years old, he went to England for his schooling and never returned to Madagascar except, perhaps, to visit.

Ted was educated in Quaker schools and received his university training at the University of Leeds, from which he graduated about 1909 with a B.Sc. in biology. He earned his Diploma in Education at Cambridge University the next year and then went to Germany for a brief period to study at the University of Freiburg.

Ted Standing, like many others, found his vocation when he met Dr. Maria Montessori. They met in 1921, probably at her London Course. She helped him arrange a year in India (1921-1922) as the teacher of the many children of the Sarabhai family. When he returned to Europe, he took her training course again, probably in London, and made himself useful in the Movement from then on.

Ted wrote that this "spiritual technique" was "something akin to a religious conversion ...". Certainly, it was a new way of seeing children: their "sensitive periods," their natural dignity, the significance of their "spontaneous" activities, the wider and more thorough understanding of their needs and "planes of development," and the appreciation of the child as the creator of the adult. It was also a new way of seeing adults. Montessori suggested that working with children in this way can put us more deeply in touch with the Creator. Some found this to be true, and Ted Standing was one of them.

E.M. Standing as Montessori's interpreter

E.M. Standing is best known for his biography, *Maria Montessori: Her Life and Work* (still in print and used today in many Montessori training courses). Montessori wrote: "I am not making any comments on the substance of it because here is an apostle who is voicing his own enthusiastic impressions. I have, however, made some minor corrections in matters of 'historical' detail. I am impatient to see the whole book ..." (see Standing, *Maria,* "Author's Note"). She died before it was finished.

Montessori's style mixed psychology, philosophy, anthropology, history, ethics, and advocacy for children into a passionate and persuasive statement. Some careful, modem readers have become frustrated by this mixture of what we today see as distinct fields of discourse, each with its own kind of logic and way of validating statements. Standing's publications helped un-mix her style. He also pulled together her main ideas, worked out in a long list of publications over many years. Her bibliography today fills a book of its own, some 87 pages long (see Grazzini).

Little was written by Standing about Montessori's religious education, "striking and original as it is," in his biography *(Maria* 69). The subject was beyond the scope of the book. Nevertheless, Christian assumptions are everywhere, especially as the foundation for the "spiritual" training of the teacher.

Standing's books were translated into French, Spanish, Japanese, and perhaps other languages, and he loved the role of the writer. He also wrote poetry and short stories, as well as articles about education. His shorter writings appeared in the *Atlantic, Sower, Irish Rosary, America, Times* (London), and in educational journals. His articles on religious education ranged from one called "Montessori Practice and Thomistic Principle" to another called "The Narrative Method Versus the Catechism."

E.M. Standing's greatest contribution to religious education was his book, *The Child in the Church.* It was first published by Montessori in 1922 in Naples as a booklet of around 52 pages, called *I bambini viventi nella Chiesa (The Children Living in the Church).* Montessori, then about fifty-two years old and living in Barcelona, was reporting on her first experiments in this field.

Standing expanded Montessori's booklet into a larger version of 191 pages in English in 1929. The latest and most expanded version was published in 1965. By this time it had grown to 224 pages and included chapters by other major figures of the second and third generations of Montessorians working in religious education. Mother Isabel Eugenia, RA, M. and F. Lanternier, and Sofia Cavalletti, as well as Standing were represented.

Mother Isabel Eugenia had been the president of the Catholic Montessori Guild and principal of the Maria Assumpta Training College in London. This guild was founded in 1952, the year Montessori died. E.M. Standing, who then called himself "E. Mortimer Standing" was the chairman.

M. Lantemier had a school in Limoges and then in Rennes, France. He was a former French army officer and had integrated the liturgical year into the school's life. It culminated in the re-living of Holy Week. Among other innovations, some 200 wooden figures were moved about amid the buildings and streets of a model Jerusalem to help tell the story.

Sofia Cavelletti also contributed a chapter. In 1954, she began in Rome to use Montessori's approach to religious education, and today her Catechetical Center is the leading source of both inspiration and learning about this approach in the world. Her work will be discussed in the third and last article in this series.

Standing and Montessori

When Ted Standing first met Montessori in 1921, distressing divisions were beginning to appear among Montessorians in England. The split was between those who felt that Montessori had already said everything that needed to be said about child development and education and those who did not. The Movement was in danger of losing its vital spirit and becoming hardened into a kind of orthodoxy imposed by the authority of the founder, often used in a rigid way by her disciples.

In the early 1920s, the battle between the national and the international Montessori organizations in England was so intense that *Punch* could not restrain comment:

> Sing, Muse, the tragic story of the Montessorian split
> And the lurid possibilities arising out of it,
> Revealing how "paedologists," though normally urbane May develop, on occasion, quite a first-class fighting strain (Kramer 275).

The relationship between Montessori and Standing remained one of trust, for he was not given to much innovation. Still, he not only resisted the bitterness of these conflicts but also avoided the cynicism that can result from a disappointed idealism.

One of the reasons for Standing's fairness and calm may have been that he stayed in contact with children, teaching. Also, Standing had contact directly with Montessori when he needed it. In addition, his travel took him to Rome around 1926, where he lived, working "in collaboration with the Dottoressa." It was probably sometime during 1926 that he was baptized as a Roman Catholic.

Being close to Montessori was much different from encountering the Montessori Method in the hands of a conservative disciple. In the *Times Educational Supplement,* Sheila Radice described Montessori and her trusted co-worker Maccheroni standing in the middle of a classroom at the London County Council elementary school in Hornsey Road. A group of seven-to eleven-year-old children were at work with the advanced materials (Kramer 259-260).

In the middle of the room, the children oblivious to them, Montessori and Maccheroni were described as standing and talking in rapid Italian, then bursting into laughter. Later, Montessori repeated the conversation to a visitor, adding a few refinements that had occurred to her since, and that started them laughing all over again.

To Radice, the atmosphere of a classroom where Montessori was actually present is "a sufficient comment on the ritualistic, semi-religious interpretation of the method that one sometimes sees." If Montessori was becoming something of a sacred object to many of her followers, her relations with those with whom she closely worked, children or adults, remained open and creative.

A new way of learning for religious education

Standing wrote: "The difficulty in realizing the immense significance of Dr. Montessori's work is that it presents so many different facets, each fascinating in itself, that it is not easy to see the movement as a whole ... For this reason it is fatally easy to regard it *spezzato (*as Montessori would say), i.e., broken into separate pieces" (Child 77).

To avoid *spezzato,* we will follow the main lines of Standing's summary in the 1929 edition of *The Child in the Church* (chapter ten). When Montessori principles of education are extended "to the study of the Supernatural Order" religious education's key becomes "Liberty in a Prepared Environment."

The "prepared environment" refers to the setting up of a place where the child can be at home in body, mind, and spirit. The little tables and chairs, low shelves, pictures hung at eye-level for the child, and other such details were designed for the child's body. Why take energy away from the child's development by using it to adjust to an adult environment?

The "Materials for Development" in this environment are for the child's mind in an ordinary Montessori classroom, and in religious education they help direct spiritual development. Think of a little child polishing a brass model of a chalice and paten. At one level, there is the bodily activity of mastering the act of polishing. The next level is polishing the chalice and the paten to contribute to their beauty and the common responsibility for the care of the classroom. Third, there is the level where the child consciously ponders the meaning of the presence of the Mystery of God in Holy Communion as the polishing takes place. This approach promotes both development and the integration of body, mind, and spirit.

In an environment with nothing to climb on, Standing wrote, you would never notice that monkeys are naturally developed for climbing. In the same way, children do not reveal their true nature until they can function in an appropriate environment. It is then that the "New Child" appears, tending toward order, deep concentration, self-direction, and a joy and serenity in learning.

Yet, liberty in such an environment does not mean license to do anything you want or to use the developmental materials in any way you wish. Things are to be used for the purpose they are intended. True liberty is to be able to choose well and then "will" the chosen activity. Choices are among constructive alternatives.

A child's mind is not a "sack" to be filled with facts. It is a "dynamic principle" which needs to be approached indirectly for learning. Learning is by personal discovery, not by the imposition of an adult.

Montessori suggested that young children from about three through six or seven years like to use their senses, and children from about six through twelve years prefer the imagination for learning. A child of four years might love to trace his or her finger over a sandpaper letter, but a child of twelve would think that silly.

To not be aware of what Montessori called the "sensitive periods" or periods of "natural interest" is to risk "dropped stitches." The knitting together of knowledge and the person will still take place, but the depth and breadth of the knitting will not be as great. Montessori's favorite example of this was to note how easily young children learn languages as compared to the difficulty adults have. The sensitive period for learning languages, including religious language, is before six years of age.

Standing was fond of quoting G.K. Chesterton on the imagination: "When we are very young we do not need fairy tales. Mere life is interesting enough" (Child 80). He was always quick to assure his readers that Montessori was not against fairy tales. What she was concerned about was disconnecting the imagination from sensorial reality.

Standing cited a child who was killed by jumping out the window to "fly away" with Peter Pan and Wendy. He was outraged at something he saw in a Theosophical school. A visitor passed around photographs of supposed "fairies" flitting about a garden. Some adults take advantage of the credulity of children rather than respecting their developmental needs.

When children can focus on particular developmental materials and carry through their discoveries to completion, a joyful calm takes over. They become ordered in body, mind, and spirit. They also move from the concrete to the abstract as they grow. If you ask a child why he or she no longer does sums with a sensorial material like a bead frame, he or she will say, "I can do it quicker without it."

Teacher preparation for Montessori was not just about knowledge and culture but also "the way in which we regard the child" (Child 52 in 1929 edition). One must be prepared inwardly not to be too much occupied with controlling misbehavior. The primary defect Montessori saw in most teachers was a combination of anger and pride.

Respect is usually reserved for the strong, but children are weak. They cannot defend themselves, so there is nothing to restrain adult anger. This is why teachers need humility before this creation of God. If they do not have such humility, they will never know the power of God that is present there.

The spreading of Montessori religious education

Montessori escaped from Barcelona and the Spanish Civil War on a British warship in 1936. She went to England for the Fifth International Montessori Congress to be held at Lady Margaret Hall, Oxford. Standing by that time was firmly fixed in the orbit that moved about Montessori. At the Congress he was one of three on the Committee for Press Information, although he may rather have been employed as a lecturer or a "Conference Tutor." Two hundred delegates came from nearly every country in Europe as well as from South America and India.

In England interest in Montessori religious education centered around London. Montessori gave a course on religious education at the request of Mother Isabel Eugenis in 1936 at Assumption College.

Pictures in the 1965 edition of *The Child in the Church* show the children at St. Anthony's School working in a well-developed program with materials about the liturgy, sacred history, and with timelines about saints and Church leaders. Sister Stephanie, OSF, the Headmistress, was also involved in the Catholic Montessori Guild as honorary secretary.

In Scotland a major center was in Glasgow. The Sisters of Notre Dame of Namur had a school at Dowanhill. In addition to having some

300 young children in Montessori classes, they had a high school and a training college for teachers. The 1929 edition of *The Child in the Church* includes pictures of their materials on the liturgy, the symbols of the liturgical seasons, and the life of Christ.

Maria Montessori came to Ireland in 1927 to the Ursuline convent, Waterford. The Convent of Mercy held St. Oteran's School, which was a large National School. They had converted their school for young children to the Montessori Method, and in the 1929 edition of *The Child in the Church* there are pictures of their sensorial materials for Montessori religious education as well.

The Dominican convent, Sion Hill, Blackrock, Dublin, Ireland, is of special interest. In 1928 Montessori gave a course in Dublin to representatives of over a dozen Dominican convents. Thirty years later Sofia Cavalletti was invited to give lectures there.

Writing in the 1929 edition of *The Child in the Church,* Cavalletti graciously gave her hosts credit for their contributions to her work: "Some of this has been copied from the Dominican Sisters at the Sion Hill Convent, Blackrock, Dublin – and from other material devised by members of the Catholic Montessori Guild in England" (Child 132).

Cavalletti then went on to suggest what her own contributions had been to that point. First, there were the parables. A child carries out the action with wooden figures, while another reads the parable. "Such figures were presented in a more or less abstract manner in order to differentiate them from the figures used in the Christmas or Easter panorama, since these latter stand for definite historical persons."

Second, she had added several kinds of three-dimensional models. One was the plaster model of Jerusalem for lessons about Holy Week. She also created a model of the Lake of Tiberias and one of the whole of Palestine. A picture in the same edition of the *Child in the Church* also shows her model of the tomb. She has continued to experiment, create many additional materials, and expand the theoretical base for this approach to the present day. This will be discussed in the next essay.

The legacy of E.M. Standing

On February 26, 1962, Sister Margaret Jane of Mount St. Vincent's in Seattle wrote to Standing at McCarthy's Hotel in Fethard, County Tipperary, Ireland. She invited and then "ordered" him to come to Seattle to live. She said, "I want it well understood that you are to be our guest here in this house as long as you wish – absolutely free of charge" (E.M. Standing Archives).

He wrote in his journal on May 28, 1962, that his *"Vita Nuova* begins." E.M. Standing was about 75 years old when he crossed the Atlantic on the Queen Elizabeth to begin his new life. On June 3, he wrote that he saw "snow clad mountains in the distance." The end of his journey by train to Seattle was near.

Standing's last years were very active. (New interest in Montessori education began about 1958 with the opening of Whitby School in Connecticut.) *The Montessori Method: A Revolution in Education* came out in 1962. Standing had been working again on *The Child in the Church* since 1960, and the new version was published in 1965. In addition, Standing and Fr. William Codd, SJ, a professor of education and psychology at Seattle University, set up a Montessori training program at the university.

E.M. Standing died March 4, 1967. Letters of sadness came to Seattle University from all over the world. Mario Montessori wrote from The Netherlands. Friends from India wrote. There were many others.

He left a good portion of his estate, including royalties from the sale of his books, to support the Seattle University Montessori Teacher Education Program.

He also left a legacy of love and respect for children and their religious life, as well as his fair and passionate "impressions" of his Montessori vocation.

References

Grazzini, M. 1965. *Bibliografia Montessori*. Brescia, Italy: La Scuola Editrice.

Kramer, R. 1976. *Maria Montessori*. New York: G.P. Putnam's Sons.

Standing, E.M. 1965. *The Child in the Church*. St. Paul, MN: Catechetical Guild, 1965. (London and Edinburgh: Sands and Co., 1929).

_____. 1957. *Maria Montessori: Her Life and Works*. London: Hollis and Carter Ltd.

_____. 1962. *The Montessori Revolution in Education*. New York: Schocken Books.

Original Source:

Berryman, J.W. 1994. "Montessori religious education: E.M. Standing (1887-1967)." *PACE: Professional Approaches for Christian Educators* **23: 3-7.**

3

Preface to the English Edition of *The Religious Potential of the Child*

This book was published in 1979 in Italian. It describes the experience and tentative conclusions by the author about the religious potential of children based on her work since the spring of 1954. This clinical experience took place in her worship-education center in Rome.

A very important point was made about this book in the Preface to the Italian Edition by Dalmazio Mongillo. He called Cavalletti's approach a "concelebration" *(concelebrazione)*. Propositions stress relationships. In Cavalletti's work the "with-ness" and the quality of that relationship are the most important. This does not minimize knowing the "right" time to present the "right" material in the "right" way, but if we overlook the spirit of Cavalletti's approach we have missed that which we cannot do without.

Your first reading of this book ought to be done with your critical faculties "on hold" so its total spirit can be absorbed. Look at the pictures of the children and their art. Allow the wonder in the book to work. Have patience with the leisurely pace at which the argument of the book is unfolded. When this first reading is finished, however, return to the book and probe it with tough-minded criticism. The author would like that. She does the same.

Before advancing in this Preface any further you need to know something about the relationship between this writer and the author. I first met Sofia Cavalletti in 1971 in Bergamo, Italy. She had come north from Rome to the vicinity of Milan to give some lectures at the

Center for Advanced Montessori Studies in Bergamo where I was a student. We have visited across the Atlantic several times since then and our correspondence has been a lively one.

You need to know that I am both a friend and an admirer of Dr. Cavalletti and her work with children. I would not be a good friend to her or to children if I were blinded by my admiration when I read this book. In any case, it is my opinion that both the questions this book raises and its conclusions are very helpful. It is for both of these reasons that you can have a measure of confidence that this Preface will be a balanced as well as an enthusiastic one.

Before introducing you to the author I would like to make a final introductory point. It is about Cavalletti's intent for this book. In 1978 Cavalletti visited Houston to give a month-long course to an international group of students. We held this through the good offices of the Institute of Religion in the Texas Medical Center where I am professor of theology and ministry and director of the Children's Center. At the conclusion of the course Cavalletti gave each student a small packet of mustard seeds from the Holy Land. I am sure that this book is intended by Dr. Cavalletti to be like those mustard seeds.

Sofia Cavalletti of Rome – and the world

Sofia Cavalletti would be uncomfortable to be introduced personally in this Preface. She would rather have the focus placed totally on the work and the children. This is impossible. The art of religious education is an art in which the artist cannot be separated from the art. As Mongillo suggested, the spirit of this work is indispensable. I must add that Cavalletti personifies that spirit.

The second reason that I must introduce you to the author of this work is more mundane. She is not widely known to the English reading public.

Sofia Cavalletti was born on August 21, 1917, in Rome. The Cavalletti home was and is near the Piazza Navona, the ancient site of

Domitian's Stadium, which we now know in baroque form as a large public square. Her birth took place in the very room where she now has her study.

Two people especially influenced Cavalletti's professional development. Neither was in Rome the year she was born, but both influences would cross paths there. Dr. Maria Montessori, a physician and educator, was one influence and Dr. Eugenio Zolli, the former chief rabbi of Rome, was the other. In 1917 Montessori had moved the center of her work to Barcelona, Spain, and Zolli was vice rabbi in Trieste, the ancient city at the head of the Adriatic Sea.

Maria Montessori's international fame as an educator began in Rome about 1907 when her first "House of Children" was opened on January 7 in the San Lorenzo slum area. Zolli did not arrive in Rome until 1938. At Cavalletti's birth Montessori was about 47 years of age and Zolli was about 36.

As Europe moved toward the Second World War, Montessori accepted an invitation to come to India to give a course for teachers under the auspices of the Theosophical Society. Ironically she was interned there during the war because she carried the passport of the enemy, Italy. The British realized that this educator, child advocate, and worker for peace was not "the enemy" and allowed her to travel. She was able to establish schools as well as to teach teachers. India today still has many flourishing Montessori schools.

After the war Montessori returned to Holland to live. She died there in 1952 and is buried at Noordwijk. She asked to be buried where she fell, a citizen of the world and an advocate for the world's children.

When Zolli came to Rome in 1938 he was 57 years old. On his mother's side of the family there had been rabbis and scholars for over two centuries. His service as chief rabbi was stormy. In 1943 the Germans took over Rome and the persecution of the Jews was at once more severe and systematic. Zolli and his wife, as well as others, went into hiding. In his autobiography, *Before the Dawn*,[30] he said,

"My wife and I suffered much from hunger, cold and anxiety for six months." His daughter, Mirium, he remembered as "ferocious" as she got her parents, paralyzed by the complexity of the situation they were in, to seek shelter.

Zolli suffered from more than hunger, cold, and anxiety. Since about 1917 he had seen visions of Christ. Another Jew, who converted to the way of Christ, Paul of Tarsus, also confronted Zolli by his writings in the New Testament about the spirit overcoming the letter of the Law. On February 13, 1945, Zolli and his wife were baptized into the Roman Catholic Church.

Sofia Cavalletti met the former chief rabbi of Rome in her first Hebrew classes as an undergraduate after the war. Zolli's love of the language and heritage of the Jewish people remained genuine and powerful. Under his influence and training she became a Hebrew scholar. After earning her doctorate Cavalletti became a colleague. It was she who was asked by members of their profession to write Zolli's tributes when he died. She was also given the lonely task of completing his works in progress as well as the works they were collaborating on at his death.

Sofia Cavalletti never met Maria Montessori. In the spring of 1954, two years after Montessori's death, a friend brought her seven-year-old son to Cavalletti for some lessons about religion. The wonder of this event has never ceased to amaze Dr. Cavalletti. The deep joy of the child's response to her opening the Bible and talking with him about God has been the motivation for her unceasing search to know the deeper levels of the child's knowledge of religion and the art of releasing that power and insight.

Cavalletti's ability as a teacher did not go unnoticed by the energetic Miss Costa Gnocchi, who had started a Montessori School at Palazzo Taverna in Rome. She persuaded Cavalletti to teach religion at her school. Gianna Gobbi – a wonderfully competent, creative, and perceptive Montessorian – began to collaborate with Cavalletti. Soon this work attracted so many children that they moved it to its present site in the Cavalletti home at 34 Via Degli Orsini.

In 1957 Cavalletti was asked to give a paper at the International Montessori Congress in Rome.[31] This meeting introduced her to Montessorians around the world and in 1958 she began the international scope of her work with a trip to Dublin to give a course to teachers. One of her latest trips was in the summer of 1980. She returned to Mexico to give a course and to check on the progress of the classes established for children during a previous visit.

In 1963 an international organization, *L'Associazione "Maria Montessori" per la formazione religiosa del bambino,* was founded to develop materials and study the development of the religious potential in children. This group includes people from many countries and professions. It also includes some former students from Dr. Cavalletti's Center, who knew her as children.

Cavalletti's blending of Hebrew studies and religious education is obvious through a review of her bibliography.[32] When this author prepared such a bibliography in 1978 it included 165 citations of book reviews, professional articles, newspaper articles, translations from Hebrew, and books in both areas.

There is also a blending of the practical and the theoretical in Cavalletti's work. She works with children on a weekly basis.

She also reads Hebrew every day. Her work in Jewish and Catholic relations is not widely known but it has been active. Her daily observance and recollection of her own religious life also needs to be mentioned in this regard.

Sofia Cavalletti is the kind of person who puts life and lives together rather than taking them apart. She has put together her interests in serious biblical research and her work with children. She has combined her scholarly and practical interests in both fields. She is an international person who knows not only the ancient languages Greek, Latin, and Hebrew, but also the modern languages Italian, English, French, German, Spanish, and, perhaps, others. One ingredient in her personality more than others seems to allow this to happen. We might call it "objective humility."

There is much in Cavalletti's life and work to take pride in, and she does. On the other hand, she knows that the work she is doing is not really hers but work she holds in trust for God. Her humility is objective because it is not the sentimental kind and because the child's real growth comes from God. This is a fact when she works with a child as clearly as the fact of the sun's rising in the morning and setting in the evening.

Cavalletti's objective humility seems to be at the root of her rich sense of humor and her Roman realism about children and the religious life of all human beings. It also enables her not to be over-controlling in her celebration with children.

Objective humility is also at the root of Cavalletti's openness to continued research and growth. If you were to compare her earlier book on this subject, *Teaching Doctrine and Liturgy*,[33] with the present work, you would be interested in the developments that have taken place between 1961 and 1979. We cannot compare the two books here, but except for their common spirit you would not feel that the same author had written both of them.

There is one final matter of spirit I would like to stress before closing this introduction to Cavalletti and returning to an introduction of this book. Martin Buber's work has also had a great influence on her. During her 1978 visit to Houston it was this section of my library that first attracted her attention. The matter of Jewish wisdom also occupied us one evening, when we had a long and leisurely dinner with Rabbi Hyman Schachtel of Houston, his wife, and Mrs. Berryman.

The rabbi and the professoressa tracked the concepts of Greek wisdom *(sophia)* and Jewish wisdom *(hokmah)* through the centuries of discussion about them. They concluded that *sophia* was a closed realm of knowledge accumulated for its own sake intellectually. Jewish wisdom was by contrast a lived knowledge, a unity of thought and life. Sofia Cavalletti sided with *hokmah* against her name, *sophia*, with ironic pleasure.

In Cavalletti you will find no Greek separation of body and soul nor will you find any Cartesian duality of subject and object in relation to the environment. A "fact" is a lived *datum* relative to one's relationship with "it" as a Thou. Her research cannot be reduced to I-It relationships either in principle or personally. This raises the question of Cavalletti's relation to formal research methods.

To answer the question of how Cavalletti has done her research requires us to rearrange her book a bit. This reorganization will ask questions in a rather linear fashion to probe her more integrated presentation here. We now must turn to questions about assumptions, definitions, methods, and theory.

Cavalletti's way of doing research

To ask questions about Cavalletti's research style we need to ask questions in an order that does not follow the structure of the book. This superficial structure is superimposed on the book to understand the deep structure better by contrast.

Questions about Cavalletti's assumptions for this study seem especially explicit in chapter 4's section, "The Problem of Controls." We must go back to chapter 1 to find her definition of "religious potential." This definition is illustrated by the cases presented in that chapter. This brings us to the heart of the matter.

Chapter 10 presents Cavalletti's central contribution. It is her "Method of Signs." This is the means by which the religious potential is appropriately stimulated toward further growth. It is also the means by which this research is validated.

In chapter 11 Cavalletti arrives at her statement of theory. She brings together the assumptions, definitions, and data derived by the Method of Signs to formulate and organize all of the coherence she has discovered in this procedure. She does this by concepts such as "sensitive periods," "constants," and "objects." We turn first to Cavalletti's assumptions. There seem to be four. The first of these four assumptions to be discussed here is also the most important. She assumes that children experience God. If she did not assume this she would not be able to enter into a relationship with children, the signs, and God to discover if it is true.

Cavalletti has as great a respect for the religious experience of children as she does for that of adults. It is the relationship itself that is important rather than the form. God cannot be fully caught by the logic structures of any age or stage anyway.

Cavalletti's second assumption is that the child's religious potential is a global experience in two ways. It touches the child's total being and is not the function of some isolated psychic or physical mechanism. It is also "natural," she says, so it is essential to what defines being "human" regardless of where the child is born on this globe.

The third assumption Cavalletti makes is that human beings are not fully developing unless their religious potential is stimulated and growing. Religious potential is not a matter of willed commitment, intellectual reasoning, or political force. It is *systemic* to human health.

A fourth assumption is that the religious language Cavalletti works with, the Judeo-Christian tradition, is a language that is very powerful as an agent to describe, evoke, and express the multidimensional aspects of a child's experience of God. It is probably the most powerful tool for knowing this reality. Certainly the language of science is a powerful tool to open up other realities but it functions in a very different framework of knowledge. Other religions such as the Eastern religions do not work as well as the one she uses because they are not as deeply rooted in our Western experience.

With the above assumptions in mind we turn now to Cavalletti's definition of the phenomenon she is investigating. She does this through the use of fifteen cases in chapter 1. There is some question about whether these cases are intended to demonstrate the existence of the child's religious potential or to illustrate its complexity.

The method of reporting in the cases is not uniform. There are third-hand reports about children, reports of adults about their own childhood, unidentified reporters, and parents talking about their own children. The age and the setting for the event described are not always clear. Each description can, however, be interpreted to stand on its own without adding to an accumulative weight of the evidence about the existence of this potential called "religious."

If this presentation of cases in chapter 1 does not demonstrate the presence of the religious potential in young children, it does define the complexity of this phenomenon. The cases also illustrate the grounds Cavalletti has for making this search for the child's religious potential.

The complexity of the phenomenon is suggested by the issues in the cases. Cavalletti has noticed the issues of: religion and guilt in children, the logic of discussing origins and causality, religious interest of children despite a lack of religious training, logic development enabling young children to discuss religious issues in a way that goes beyond what one would predict by their chronological age as normal functioning when talking about other issues, remembered childhood experiences influencing later life, an "attraction" to religious "facts," which means an attraction to religious observances such as the liturgy, and, finally, the issue of children's overcoming "negative environmental conditions," by which is meant an environment where the parents are atheists or are agnostic.

My interpretation of how Cavalletti defines "religious potential" attempts to define it in terms of an experience that the child "has" and that can be observed by the researcher. It reduces the complexity in the case-by-case definition and other Cavalletti statements to four points:

1. The experience of the child is "spontaneous" rather than a response to an adult's prompting.
2. The experience is "complex." It involves feelings, thinking, and moral action although moral consciousness is not expected until about age six.
3. The experience is not limited to cultural conditioning.
4. The experience is "deep" rather than involving only a single function like auditory or visual memory.

This basic experience shows certain shifts when the religious potential is moving toward actualization. This growth can be identified, much like the tests for an appropriate stimulus of the religious potential that will be presented in connection with Cavalletti's theory. Four indicia of growth are:

1. A global and deep joy results.
2. A "mysterious knowledge" results, which no adult told the child.
3. The child is aware of the "invisible" (nonmaterial) meaning in the material environment.
4. A capacity develops for deep and personal prayer that expresses itself in praise and thanksgiving rather than memorized prayers or requests for favors.

The American reader might first associate this discussion by Cavalletti of religious potential with the human potential movement that swept the United States during the 1960s and early 1970s. Esalen, Gestalt, Encounter, and T-Groups were among the banners of this movement. One of the marks of expanding human consciousness was joy, according to this movement. Cavalletti's use of this terminology is linked to her Montessori background rather than to this American phenomenon.

Cavalletti's method to stimulate the religious potential of the child is her "method of signs." The symbol system of the Judeo-Christian tradition is the set of signs she uses. They give children a set of tools by which to make meaning and find direction.

When Cavalletti uses the word "sign," she is indicating a class of words, images, and actions that point into a mystery and participate in the mystery they point out. This mystery is the experience of God.

In English we usually use the word "symbol" to mean the class of words, images, and actions to which Cavalletti gives the name sign. Cavalletti's use of sign is more classical and biblical, more like the Greek word *semeion,* used in the New Testament to indicate the sign quality of the miracles of Jesus. Tillich even translated *semeion* (sign) into English as "sign-event" to give this a better understanding. He observed that such a sign involved one in "numinous astonishment," a knowing of God.[34]

In English the more usual distinction between sign and symbol is one that Tillich used more widely than this particular note on the sign of a miracle. The symbol participates in the reality to which it points. This contrasts to a sign (in English), which is an indicator of a narrow range of meaning and is arbitrarily and neutrally chosen. Examples are the plus sign in math, a stop sign in traffic control, and a *symbol* in symbolic logic. I have added this last example to suggest that the confusion of these terms is not merely a problem in translation from Italian into English. English is inconsistent within its own language.

It is important to note that a symbol points to a mystery both beyond and within a person. The danger in using a symbol is that its meaning is often reduced to either the exterior, transcendent meaning or to the immanent, interior meaning. There is also the added danger of confusing the symbol itself with the meaning it participates in.

Cavalletti has steered clear of the distortions we have just mentioned caused by a misuse of symbols (her "signs"). As we continue this discussion we will return to Cavalletti's use of the word sign to indicate symbolic, multilevel, nonreductionistic communication.

Cavalletti talks of both inner and outer signs. An example of an outer sign is a gesture by the priest during liturgy. This smaller sign participates in a larger meaning, a gesture of God in history such as the Exodus or Easter events.

Inner signs recall actions of the person. These are called forth by liturgical or linguistic events. The remembered experience of fields, seeds, rocks, birds, thorns, and harvest, stored at many levels by the human being, are reframed and given new significance by a sign such as the Parable of the Sower. This re-framing of meaning releases the memories from their literal correspondence to atomic facts in the environment and provides a tool by which one can participate in the experience of God by "entering" the parable and participating in its experience.

To teach how to give children religious language without it being turned into something smaller than a sign is difficult but critical. A sign ought to be as free as the flight of a butterfly and not be pinned to a classification board to be memorized. One needs to model the art of religious language to show children how to ponder the depths of signs like a pebble sinking deeply into a pond. If this art is learned, then wider and wider circles of meaning and application of the signs can be made to life, as the circles on the surface of a pond expand from the point where the pebble entered.

Cavalletti's metaphors of the butterfly and the pebble do not commit her to a position that allows children to make anything out of the Judeo-Christian symbol system they want to or to reduce religion to their private symbol system of fantasy. What she presents to children and how she presents it are both significant. Both the signs and the art of their use have been tested for centuries, so her confidence is not unfounded.

What Cavalletti has rediscovered is a way to present the signs and the art of their use to children in a way that does not distort their use. The translation of religious language into material objects has been a central element in this approach and it is part of the legacy of Maria

Montessori that Cavalletti has extended and refined.

Cavalletti's method of signs is an art. Like any art it is not learned from reading books about the art. One must practice the art and if possible one must practice it with a mentor. It is for this reason that Cavalletti has been hesitant to write more about the method of signs in detail. It must be shown to the potential teacher of children as it must be modeled for the child.

Cavalletti's method of signs is not only her main tool for stimulating the child's religious potential. It is also her main tool for research. The use of the curriculum as a research tool has provided continuous feedback from teachers into the refinement of the art of translating the signs of the Judeo-Christian tradition into materials, the presentation of the materials to the children, and the arrangement of the environment of the worship-education center when Cavalletti's approach is practiced correctly.

Cavalletti's patient search to understand and describe the child's religious potential and by implication to know better the development of religion across the life span reminds me of Madame Curie's search for the nature of radioactivity. The problem with the object of this search is that it is not one that can be reduced and isolated in its pure form as radium was. Cavalletti has not found a substance but a changing field of relationships. Her struggle has been to not allow her theory to close the experience of God into a semantic box and yet to articulate what she knows of these relationships among children, God, adult teachers, and the signs of the tradition. We turn now to her theory to see how this has been done.

Cavalletti's theory of Christian education

Cavalletti's problem in stating her theory or in writing a curriculum that adequately states what she does in her worship-education center is that the quality of the web of relationships must be experienced by the whole person rather than read with our most long-ranged sense, sight. Her theory attempts to balance the variables in this web of relationships despite the difficulties involved in putting them down on paper.

What Cavalletti has discovered in her patient search has been a developmental set of "constants." The constants in her theory are relationships. They are the relationships between the sensitive periods in the child's religious potential for different aspects of objects and different objects from the Judeo-Christian tradition. The objects are not just the linguistic signs but are also the colors, gestures, processions, and other acts of liturgy and the Christian life as well as the acts of God in history. The observable constant implies relationships not observable.

Cavalletti has drawn on her Montessori background for the concept of the "sensitive period." Maria Montessori borrowed this concept from the Dutch botanist Hugo de Vries, whom she met in 1917[35] during a visit to Holland when de Vries was in his seventies. He was famous for his discoveries about plant evolution and at the turn of the century he had confirmed the Mendelian laws of heredity. He noticed parallels between sensitive periods in lower orders of life and what Montessori had described about child development. Montessori applied this concept to human development.

Montessori discussed her concept of sensitive periods from 1917 on until it was fully developed in her late work, *The Absorbent Mind*.[36] In this book she distinguished her concept from the position of the behaviorists such as Watson[37] and the maturationists such as Gesell.[38] Since she was dealing with more than the structures of cognition, she could not be classified as an interactionist, as we would consider Piaget and his theory of adaptation by assimilation and accommodation.

Montessori developed her own jargon. She spoke of the "absorbent mind" as an active force that motivates humankind not only to create the individual self but also to create a unified, creative totality with all of life.[39] It is this drive or force that moves one from the inherited potentials ("nebulae" in Montessori's jargon) to their activation at times of optimum sensitivity (sensitive periods).

Montessori's favorite example was the development of human language. When the sensitive period arrives for language, whatever is at hand in the environment to stimulate that sensitivity will be learned in an optimum way. The "wild child of Aveyron" learned the language of the forest during this period and never successfully learned human language, Montessori suggests. The "dropped stitch" spoiled the sweater.

With regard to specific religious potential, Montessori's help is limited. She did struggle with religious education issues and the part religion had to play in human development, but her conclusions tend to fade away into ambiguity.[40] Cavalletti tries to be more specific, but we must read a bit of Montessori theory back into what she says to extrapolate this interpretation.

The potential is "wired-in" genetically, as a maturationist might hold. It is stimulated in a primary way by God, as a theologian might hold. This experience is given content and shape from the culture, as a behaviorist might hold. The relation with God, however, prevents this cultural determinism to close. The relationship with God keeps it open and, thus, development remains open. It is increasingly conscious and more differentiated across the life span in much the same progression that Fowler has described as a set of faith structures.[41]

It is not especially helpful for Cavalletti to say that the religious potential in the child is "spontaneous." All her theory's relationships involve patterns that are lawful in the sense that they can be roughly predicted. The potential is an innate fact. The stimulus by God is present to open this potential to growth toward actualization. The culture is there in a smaller to wider range of social reference to impact the potential to give it symbolic content and structural form. All these relationships are "natural." What Cavalletti is stressing when she discusses the potential for religion's being spontaneous is that we ought not be over-controlling and that it is not merely a phenomenon of cultural conditioning. God is also at work here.

We can now see what she means by the relationship between the object and the sensitive period's being a "vital act." It is fundamental to the actualization of the religious potential that is necessary for health, as she defines it. It is, therefore, an "exigence," as the translator interpreted Cavalletti's use of the Italian word *esigenza*.

The criteria by which an appropriate relationship between object and sensitive period can be determined have four aspects:

1. The child will feel a deep interest in the object.
2. The child will feel a vital life impulse to do more than notice or name the object. He or she will want to know its meaning and be struck by the wonder the object produces.
3. The child will feel a sense of joy and peace while working with the object and during contemplation of that work.
4. Frustration indicates that either the object is inappropriate to the sensitive period or that it has been formulated or presented in an inappropriate way.

Cavalletti gives examples of an appropriate matching of object and sensitive period. The constants that have been established by her research for the child from about three to six years of age involve such relationships as that between the Good Shepherd and the child or the image of light in the Baptism materials and the child. During the years past six years of age there is more interest in social matters so the communion aspect of Mass and the moral maxims of the New Testament become constants. To fill out this list of constants you need not only to reread the book with this in mind but also to see how they are developed in one of Cavalletti's training courses. One needs to know how the total environment functions in order to make this more clear and that takes us not only beyond the scope of this Preface but also beyond the ability of the medium of print to convey. A clinical experience under supervision is needed, much like the experience needed to learn how to give a child one of Piaget's semiclinical interviews or to do pastoral counseling.

To conclude this sketch of Cavalletti's theory of Christian education it is important to alert the reader to her use of the word "deviation." This also comes from her Montessori background. It does not mean a deviation from the statistical norm but from a norm defined as optimum for the species.

Cavalletti and science

Dr. Cavalletti's investigation of the child's religious potential stands within the framework, the paradigm, of the Christian experience. This research tradition has its own methods and exemplars of method as does the scientific tradition. The angle on reality opened up by this method of Christianity is slightly different from that of science although in medicine and physics there seems to be a great appreciation for nonmaterialistic factors in the creative mix of things today.

Cavalletti's attitude toward science is a paradox. Sometimes she seems uninformed or disinterested, as when she refers to "the psychologists." It does not clarify much to group the humanistic psychologists, the Jungians, the Freudians, the behaviorists, the eclectic, the developmental structuralists, and others into one group to contrast her position against it.

At other times she seems to misunderstand the experimental method. She is not really presenting an experiment here that has both pretesting and posttesting and a control group. She is presenting cases from which a pattern might be said to emerge.

When she speaks of proof it sounds as if she is referring to an absolute proof. Science deals with probabilities. We find absolute proof only in pure logic or when political power is strong enough to enforce a "solution." Cavalletti is too Roman to place undue credence in either logical or political perfection. In practice her attitude is much more one that deals with probabilities and her objective humility is a frame of mind that does not overcontrol the evidence. She has, therefore, a tendency to misrepresent her actual way of allowing the results of her research to stand for themselves.

The paradox shifts again when we look at science's misrepresentation of its tradition. Polanyi[42] has shown from a philosophical and autobiographical perspective that scientific knowledge is not arrived at from pure objectivity. It is really personal knowledge that we create rather than receive or uncover. Kuhn[43] has shown from the sociology of scientific discovery and paradigm change that the larger frameworks within which science works are value laden. This needs to be kept in mind as the formalities of the scientific method are observed to prevent *undue* projection of what one wants to find onto what is "there."

When we take what Cavalletti actually does when she does research with the children and the Christian symbol system and what science is really like when it is also practiced, the two poles of this relationship are closer together than at first realized. Now, the paradox shifts again.

The scientific and religious paradigms for doing research do not investigate the same aspect of reality. They have different assumptions and language based on those assumptions. They cannot, therefore, be considered to be complementary models for reality. When Cavalletti "talks science" and you feel her strained accommodation to that paradigm it is because by intuition she knows that this is not right. She is merely trying to communicate what she knows through a medium she feels will be heard.

The deep structure of Cavalletti's approach to religious education is informed by the secular models but primarily works within the classic creedal formulation of Christ as both human *and* divine. Her theory balances immanence *and* transcendence, nature *and* grace as potent powers, the natural *and* the supernatural realms, and culture *as well as* Christ. Perhaps a diagram will ilustrate:

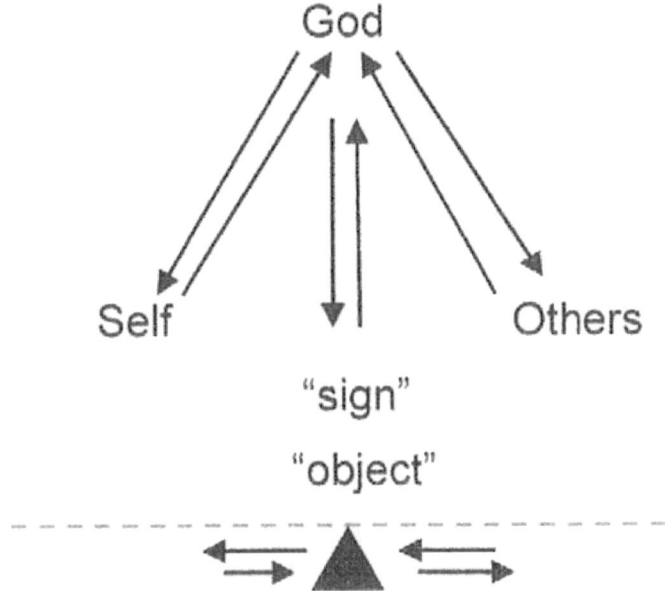

The multiple participations in realities and the signs that participate in those realities are what make religious education impossible to reduce to secular learning theories or theories of human development.

Cavalletti's demonstration that there are constants in the way children interact with signs of the Judeo-Christian tradition and that growth results from the proper use of these signs has implications for both theology and a theological view of human development. Her long absorption in the biblical literature and the worship tradition of the Judeo-Christian tradition has made her discovery a rediscovery of old truths about the Christian research tradition. It is exciting to contemplate the further development of this research that began before science.

This book is valuable in itself and as it stands. My critique is laden with a rather American concern about method, which has been spoken about in terms of the scientific research tradition. Cavalletti has also tried to express herself through that tradition as she perceived it. What I am suggesting as we close this Preface is that different realities have different languages and research traditions. At this time when the warfare between science and religion is more a working partnership, especially in modern physics and medicine, there is a possibility of double paradigm research, respecting both traditions and their research exemplars, such as Christ and Piaget or Moses and Freud, without becoming confused about the contribution or reality investigated by either but to advance both.

Conclusion

The concelebration Cavalletti participates in among children, adults, and God through the Christian signs has a quality of "with-ness" in practice. What this Preface also suggests is that her theoretical approach and method have a with-ness theologically and scientifically. It is a witness that respects all of the points in the web of relationships that make it up. It is also a theory that has within itself a mustard seed quality that leaves room for mystery, wonder, and continued development.

Original Source:

Berryman, J.W. 1983. "Preface to the English edition." In S. Cavalletti. *The Religious Potential of the Child: The Description of an Experience with Children from Ages Three to Six.* **New Jersey: Paulist Press.**

Part Two

Children and Religious Language

Preface to Part Two

The Christian language system and the ability to use this system effectively is one of the key themes in Berryman's writing. It is a theme which appears continually throughout his many articles, papers and book chapters. In fact, Berryman refers to the learning of religious language as an art form, such as learning to paint or to sculpt. The learning of an art form requires far more than acquiring a knowledge of its history and its skills. It entails being able to engage with and use creatively the many elements which comprise that particular art form so as to discern and create meaning. The purpose of mastering the art of using the Christian language system is to enable the individual – both child and adult – to make meaning at the edges of being and knowing, which discloses the presence of the Creator with whom the individual can be in relation in a complex living system of relationships with self, others, nature, and the Creator. Berryman argues that children's rapid growth means that they are living primarily at the edges of being and knowing, and that playing in language at these edges requires a special kind of art which many children seem to have naturally, and which requires only the support of adults in order for them to draw upon and make use of. The role of the adult is to support the development of the art of the Christian language system.

Each of the three contributions in Part Two illustrates Berryman's development of the art of the Christian language system. The first contribution comes from his chapter in *Life, Faith, Hope and Magic: The Chaplaincy in Pediatric Cancer Care* (1985). This highly influential publication (still required reading for students in pediatrics at the University of Texas) brought together a selection of papers which dealt with children who had life-threatening diseases for which there was treatment and hope, but very little certainty for cure. Berryman's chapter focuses on the contribution made by the pediatric chaplain to the health care team by being a master of the art of using religious language, and by enabling children to play at the edges of knowing and being in order to deal creatively with ultimate human limits. In this seminal contribution, many of Berryman's ideas in relation to religious language are outlined. As well, this contribution details his notion of reframing research concerning religious language and young children, in which early conceptions and descriptions of the Godly Play process are presented.

The second contribution explores the function of religious language in child development, and the importance of children being allowed to return again and again to chosen images, of being able to work together in community, and of being able to combine meditation on a chosen image with juxtapositions with other parts of the religious language system to enhance creativity.

In the third contribution, Berryman explores an essential element of the Christian language system – silence. Non-verbal communication is an integral element of this language system, and is one through which young children initially communicate before the development of formal language. It involves a different way of referencing the world than does symbols and the use of verbal language. In this contribution Berryman argues that silence needs to be taught by religious educators because of the connection between silence and the creation of existential meaning. The loss of silence in the postmodern context results in the loss of religious meaning and the impairment of creativity, which, according to Berryman, places the human species at risk.

4

The Chaplain's Strange Language: A Unique Contribution to the Health Care Team

The pediatric chaplain makes a unique contribution to the health care team by being a master of the art of using religious language. This art makes meaning at the limit to life and understanding by using religious language. It is not an end in itself. It is an art to be taught to children and others to deal creatively with ultimate human limits and how to live from that perspective.

Some might say that children do not experience the limit to their knowing and being. It is certainly true they do not experience this limit in the same way that adults do. Children encounter this limit in a more sensorimotor and undifferentiated way than adults do, but like adults they experience this limit in both positive and negative terms.

It is the special task of the chaplain to enable children, as well as others, to play at the edge of knowing and being so that the positive aspect of this encounter can combine with the negative to create meaning and direction.

My discussion will be developed in six steps. First, the unique function of religious language will be defined by contrasting it to other communication domains. Second, the discussion will move to how religious language can meet the basic needs of children if it is put in the form of concrete materials and presented for use in a play mode. Third, adult resistance to giving religious language to young children will be examined. Fourth, a reframing of adult resistance will be presented that removes any need to feel such resistance or defend it intellectually. Fifth, a theological analysis will be presented to speak directly to chaplains as well as to the whole health care team. Finally, suggestions will be made about how this approach might be put to work in pediatrics.

The chaplain's special language

When a child dies the emotions of the health care team are complex and profound. This is especially true in the case of chronic illness such as cancer where the team may have grown to know the child and family well. At the boundary between life and death a strange shift in language and experience takes place.

When the child dies, the language and method of science, which have been coordinating the actions of the team, cease to function with the same power. Certainly, answers to scientific questions remain, but they can be explored by an autopsy or a team analysis. However, there are other questions that arise for which this powerful set of language tools seems inappropriate.

Why this child? Why does anyone have to die? Why me? What is life, anyway? How should I live my life if I am born to die? Such questions bring us to the very limit of human knowing and being. I believe that religious language is the most appropriate language system to use to cope with such questions, but the nature of this language system is so different from that of science or of everyday language that our first task is to set it in perspective by examining several other language systems.

Language systems do not come packaged in separate containers. They merge, get confused, and shed light on each other. I will briefly discuss five different systems to show how religious language relates to them.

A "communication domain" is the way we coordinate our actions when we are attempting to be specific and intentional about our language. For example, when you go to an attorney or physician, you need to translate your everyday language into language of the legal or medical system.

Science

The communication domain of science coordinates the actions of people who use terms in precise ways to identify particular entities, such as H_2O in chemistry. The term mirrors the molecular structure of the entity.

Science also puts such terms to work by combining them in agreed upon ways to make explanatory sentences. Models are constructed from experiments that explain how events in the experiment take place. Events in the world are inferred from such experiments and assigned a probability.

In science this coordination requires people to follow not only the narrow definitions of words and events but also the rules of observation prescribed by an experiment. Science, then, does not give us *the* reality but rather *scientific* reality from which inferences can be made with probability to the reality of everyday.

Ethics

The communication domain of ethics coordinates actions by agreeing to use language in an expressive way to say how life with one another and with the environment ought to be. Personal values are expressed, however acquired, and they are linked together into sentences based on a point of view identified with motives, acts in themselves, or the results of actions, as well as any combination thereof.

While science gives us the reality of the experiment, ethics gives us the reality of human values. The subjective aspect of value is joined with the objective aspect in the world to provide a well-developed statement of reasoning.

Art

The communication domain of art is also expressive. It re-creates life in another medium to express and identify the creator's relation to life. The medium might be stone, paint, words on paper, music, textiles, as well as other materials. This statement is more emotional than reasoning.

Politics

Politics coordinates our actions through law and power. Legal structures provide the linguistic structures by which we must live, and power backs up these structures to force this reality on us whether we like it or not.

Philosophy

Philosophy provides the analysis of each communication domain from within that domain's language. We have a philosophy of science, ethics, art, and politics, for example. This thinking about a particular kind of thinking is often joined with a history of the way that kind of thinking has been carried on over the centuries. This is a perspective-giving analysis, and when many of these domains are joined in a metameta system one has a philosophy of life.

Religion

The communication domains just discussed deal with the unknown by exploring beyond that boundary. There are certain boundaries to human life that cannot be pushed back without redefining that form of life. It is at these ultimate boundaries that the communication domain of religion coordinates the actions of people who agree to use it. Not only does it provide a way to speak about what is literally unspeakable, but it also is a way to place all the other communication domains into perspective by referring them to these limits.

We are limited by the genetic code with respect to our knowing and being. We are also limited by our need for limits in order to know or be. This paradox places humankind in a continual interplay between accepting and changing limits.

David Tracy stressed that there are both positive and negative experiences of the limit case.[44] The negative aspect is the despair experienced at the ultimate to our personal horizon. The positive experience of the limit is the ecstatic experience of intense joy, love, reassurance, and creation when one becomes aware of the presence of the limit as giving definition and shape to life as the Creator as Genesis calls this presence from the point of view of ultimate origins.

I would like to add a third response to the ambiguity of the limit's positive and negative aspects. It is the realization that both aspects are true. It is the awareness that the tragedy is comic and the comedy is tragic. It finds expression in the physical shrug of the shoulders or a half smile rather than actual laughter. In addition to this paradox there is also the paradox of attempting to speak of the limit when it is by definition beyond the power of speech to capture directly as if it were something in the world. It is the limit that gives things in the world their form for human beings. The limit is literally "no-thing." It is the limit to things.

To talk about no-thing and to speak of the unspeakable make the chaplain's language rather strange. It does not approach the empirical ground for its coordination of human activity directly but indirectly through sacred stories, rituals, and parables in the Christian tradition (and perhaps in similar linguistic functions in other traditions). In the indirect approach to the limit in these language forms one can discover the disclosure of overtones of ecstasy, anguish, and deep laughter.

This is not a call for enthusiastic irrationality. Rather, it is to say that the chaplain's special language is identifiable and that it plays a unique role. This is a call for rational analysis of this language so that the art can be better mastered to be put to work in pediatrics with children and families, as well as the health care team.

This analysis is not to be confused with the language itself. Religious language is not improved in its art by translating it into another communication domain anymore than science would be. This is thinking about the religious domain, a kind of philosophy. The question that is raised by this attempt to distinguish the religious domain is "What needs in children does it meet?"

Children's needs and religious language
Medical play therapy helps the child cope with anxiety about the unknown factors of health care as well as the child's feelings about medical procedures, such as shots, bone marrow biopsies, spinal taps, and surgery.

What happens when there is no object for the child to play with? What happens when there is no doctor's kit, needle, or operating room to focus this play on? The case of the limit is such a case.

Homo sapiens flourished from about 200,000 years ago. One type, the Neanderthal people, was able to live in northern Europe, because of a body specially adapted to survive intense cold. This group, who lived in caves, developed many different kinds of stonetools and also buried their dead. They began to die out about 30,000 years ago, but their legacy of tools and religious language still remains. A language to cope with human limits is as deep a need as tools, but while tools cope with limits that can be changed, religious language provides a set of tools to deal with the limits that cannot be changed and still remain human.

This is not to imply that religious language is a language in general. It is important to focus on a specific tradition. Children may learn many languages, but they learn languages specifically to speak to persons they need to communicate with such as parents, grandparents, or a nurse. They might all speak different languages and the child be able to speak three languages, but this ability is specific to particular people. The same is true with the language of numerals or music.

Children do not learn base systems in general or music in general. They learn what the culture teaches. The same is true of religious language. This does not mean that children are trapped in a religious language or that they will grow up to become religious bigots. If this language system is associated with the creative process with which to make meaning and find direction, then this malfunction is avoided.

Medical play uses the images and objects of the language of science. Children may find existential issues related to the limit case in their global reaction to such images and objects. The specific nature of the objects and images, however, will direct the play toward the specific medical aspects rather than the limit issues in these materials for play.

Theological play is more indirect in its use of images. Rather than a syringe one might work with sheep and the Good Shepherd. The images of theological language approach the limit indirectly to disclose the experience in sacred story, ritual, and parable. This allows the child to approach without the immediate threat either blocking the images as a means of coping with the limit case or coming too close to the limit itself to prevent the play from being able to be used to work through the existential anxiety.

Both medical play and theological play are helpful to the child. They are merely tending toward opposite ends of this spectrum that runs from immediate and specific threats to existential and limit-case threats.

What would a model of a religious tradition look like? At the Institute of Religion in the Texas Medical Center in Houston, the children can actually walk into the Christian symbol system at the Children's Center. Images of this communication domain are placed on shelves around the room. Children respond to presentations of the sacred stories, rituals, and parables in various art media and through their spontaneous, deep play with the materials.

I turn now to the need of the child to deal with the ambiguity of the limit case. I have already discussed the three aspects of this ambiguity. The positive aspect *is* the ecstasy of being in relationship with the Creator at the limit of knowing and being. The negative aspect of this relationship is knowing that one is personally limited. The oscillation between these two aspects creates "the logic of the moist eye" as Arthur Koestler called the link between weeping and laughter.[45]

This need is the need to deal with all limit as Ernest Becker spoke of dealing with the "death terror."[46] Becker's intuition was that the death terror was natural to the infant rather than acquired from the environment, but he concluded that neither the innate nor the environmental theory could be conclusively proved. His central point, however, was that whichever position one took, it was the quality of one's repression of the death terror that really matters.

Becker argued that repression of the death terror is not a negative force opposing life energies, but rather a force that lives on life energies. At the most basic level the living organism works actively against its own fragility by seeking to expand and perpetuate itself. To move toward life and death in this way is to use death creatively as part of life.

Becker was looking for a way to define a "hero" in modern terms. He contrasted the death-aware person who did creative "heroic" things to add to the world with the person who lived in flight from death. The person in flight from death does not have the freedom to create new life in the interplay of life and death, but is absorbed into the world by the compulsive avoidance of the limit.

Sacred story narrates the tale of people and individuals moving toward the Creator and then falling away. Ritual enables people to tie life together by means of a set of actions in community (L., *religio,* to tie, to fasten) when life has been torn apart or radically changed. The third function of this language system allows one to play with the interplay of presence and absence as well as the limit of language to speak of the ambiguity of the limit case. Only the paradoxical language of parable is equipped to provide such an experience of the tragic in the comic and vice-versa.

This theory of religious language draws on three main sources. The first is the recent parable scholarship represented by John Dominic Crossan.[47] The second source is the approach to personal knowledge and language represented by Michael Polanyi[48] and the studies of language by Walter J. Ong.[49] The third source of information is clinical. It is an approach to working with young children begun about 1970 that applied the Montessori approach to education to religious communication. This point of view was extended by Sofia Cavalletti to provide the basis for my own development of her work.[50]

The needs of children at different stages of development have been examined at the Children's Center. A tentative developmental model has been suggested to mark relative changes in the form of their use of religious language when presented to them in the mode of theological play.

We do not see children before the age of about two years. It is assumed that in the prelinguistic period the children coordinate their actions with primary others in a communication domain of private language such as gestures and sounds understood by the primary others. The main work of the child, however, is the absorption of the totality of life, often fixed first on the mother's face, which brings with it the child's ultimate horizon. Ana-Maria Rizzuto has demonstrated from the psychoanalytic point of view how related one's image of God is to the primary people of one's earliest ultimate horizon, although her method allowed her to draw no conclusions about the nature of God beyond that observation.[51] This image of God changes over a lifetime, but it remains rooted in these early images.

The dreaming innocence of Eden is broken about the age of two years by the use of symbols. This loss of pure action coordination in a sensorimotor way begins the long pilgrimage that overlays symbol upon symbol upon concept, etc. This overlay of symbols becomes especially complex and less playful with the onset of schooling.

Sacred story, ritual, and parable are used in the period from two to seven years in a way that involves the child in the valuing and sensorimotor experience of this symbol system. In the transition period from about five to seven years the ability to retell stories, consciously follow rituals, and respond to the parabolic develops.

Late in the period from about 7 to 12 years there is an interest that develops in a second level of abstraction to story, ritual, and parable. Laws and proverbs emerge from the sacred story function as a focus for interest. Rituals become known by their performance-commands (rubrics). The sayings of Jesus called "beatitudes" (the proverbs of the Old Testament turned upside down) emerge as points of interest out of the parabolic function. The comparison of different parts of the language system also begins to function in spontaneous ways.

The third level of abstraction dawns at the onset of adolescence. Theology and history as abstractions of the stories, rituals, and parables are noticed. If the child's experience is rooted in the nonreflective experience in a sensorimotor way and has developed through the primary use of story, ritual, and parable to the secondary abstraction of law and proverb, rubric, and beatitudes, and into the third level abstractions of theology and history, then this third level is able to function as a set of tools by which to organize the prior experience. If the child attempts to deal with life without such roots, theology and the history of the Church will not likely be of much help.

Certainly children and adolescents can memorize theological propositions. This has been demonstrated as long as there have been catechisms. What is critical, however, is whether the person can create meaning and find direction in the creative interplay at the limit by using the tools of religious language. To further examine this and other questions I turn now to a dialogue with those who distort religious language when they communicate with children and others and proposed limits to the child's ability to work with this language system. Both of these views present a resistance to presenting religious language to children in the form suggested here.

Resistence to theological play

There are two major kinds of resistance to theological play. One is based on adult distortions of religious language. The other is based on adult views of restrictions in the nature of the child that prevent this approach from being beneficial.

There are six adult distortions of religious language that are communicated to children and that also either by design or default contradict the definition of religious language proposed here as theological play. They are the tendency to trivialize, idolize, blaspheme, make magical, make antimagical, and limit to print.

Trivializing

This tendency stems from adult size and maturity of thinking compared with that of children. We literally and figuratively talk "down" to children with religious language. The core of a powerful image needs to be presented to the child to use rather than something simplified. If an adult cannot respect and use the image, then the unsaid message is that the said message is not true. This language system is not important. Adults do not really use it.

The key to avoiding trivializing is to cut away all extraneous material and adult interpretation and come to the heart of the matter. Although this is both difficult and threatening for adults, it is worth the effort, because the child not only has a more powerful tool in his or her possession, but also can avoid the contradiction between the said and unsaid messages from the adult.

Idolizing

The second way adults sometimes distort religious language is by turning it into an idol, something to be worshipped in itself. When sacred stories, rituals, and parables are presented to children as ends in themselves to be memorized and/or repeated back, we have an idol as surely as in ancient times one might worship a golden calf.

Theological play presents sacred stories, rituals, and parables to children as tools by which they can make meaning with God and the community of faith. This "community" might be the family or a wider range of social reference.

The way out of the idolatry trap is to avoid not only worshipping the language itself, but also the secular teaching model of transferring what is in the teacher's mind into the mind of the student. The religious communication model is more like art. It is a teaching of the ability to master the art to do it. One cannot learn to paint, sculpt, or play the piano without practice. Learning a description of this activity, its history, how to critique it, or the philosophy of it is not the same as doing it, especially becoming a master of it, although a master might be able to describe it, know its history, critique it, and philosophize about it, as well as do it.

Blasphemy

A third adult distortion of religious language is the tendency to blaspheme when presenting it to a child. This is to take the role of God. Adults sometimes do this by telling children how they ought to interpret a given sacred story, ritual, or parable.

The child has a dimly held, implicit, vague, partially conscious but deeply felt view that is emerging about these functions of religious language. Children are vulnerable to adult suggestions or commands about them, and adults can place them in a double bind. This double bind forces the child to choose between his or her own experience and its interpretation and the interpretation of the adult. To choose either to reject one's own experience or that of a powerful adult usually results in rejecting one's own emerging powers of interpretation, because the child cannot afford to lose the protection and affection of primary adults, especially when sick in the hospital.

This is not to say that dissonance is not sometimes helpful to encourage growth. It is. Blasphemy is done with such assurance of interpretation that the child is overwhelmed by the conflict between his or her interpretation and that of the adult's. Dissonance in the service of growth also depends on the child's developmental "ripeness" for structural change *as* well as his or her sense of safety to experiment with the conflict to allow the creative process to work through to a new view. The kind of presentation of religious language being described here does not have that kind of goal or sensitivity implied.

Magic

The fourth adult distortion of religious language is to consider this language system as magical. Magic is a way to control fate. If you perform the proper ritual and say the right words, you bind God or fate to your will. Of course, one century's science might turn out to be another century's magic as Walter Bromberg's book, *From Shaman to Psychotherapist*,[52] suggests. The same sort of distinction has had to be worked out in religion over the centuries, as George S. Worgul's book, *From Magic to Metaphor*,[53] suggests in its interpretation of Christian sacraments from a Catholic point of view.

A magical approach to religious language can arrest the child's natural period of magical thinking in the area of religious meaning, although being a magical child is not the same as using religious language as magic. The magical child tends to make associations that infer a magical explanation to events in the world. For example, faintly hearing the bell of the ice cream truck, wishing for an ice cream cone, and seeing the truck come around the corner allow the child to impute magical power to the association of the thought and the appearance of the truck by their juxtaposition in time. The use of religious language as magic would not by itself cause the child to remain magical as he or she enters the school years and Piaget's concrete operations period. It would, however, introduce a conflict that would grow worse as the child developed between religion as magic and the way the world of everyday works. Eventually, the child or young adult would need to decide whether or not to discard religion in this form.

Antimagic

People who discard the magical use of religious language present another distortion. Their distortion is to assume that all use of religious language is magical. Sometimes this distortion comes out of the disillusionment and related cynicism about religious language when it has been viewed *as magical.*

There are people who are as close-minded in an orthodox, fundamentalist atheism as there are in orthodox, fundamentalist theism. Both points of view tend to show evidence of acting out in unconscious anger toward its respective opposite. There is more in common between these two points of view than there are differences.

Children are sometimes vulnerable to a loss of a powerful language for expressing and identifying the limit by such adults. Ironically, the "religion-ism" is sometimes replaced by "science-ism" and science is given magical powers it never claimed. Such a view presents the child with inappropriate tools by which to make meaning in the limit case.

Print

The sixth and final distortion of religious language is not as ancient and classic as are the first five. It is a product of the invention of the printing press in the mid-15th century. One of the first books to be printed was the Bible, and in the following centuries catechisms and theological documents occupied much of the printer's time and labor. We are probably just now beginning to be aware of the power of print on our thought because we are entering a media shift to video and can now release somewhat from the domination of print to analyze it.

Print adds a nuance to the other five distortions. It trivializes the communication domain of religion by trapping it in a metaphor of editors and publishers for its sacred texts and gives priority by this metaphor to what was written and the writing process over the oral aspects of the tradition. When theologians think of research they usually also think of a library, the shrine of the print culture, and of typing and publishing papers and books. People no longer need to make a pilgrimage to a special context for hearing the sacred texts read aloud. This reading can be silent, private, and without supporting community and sensory stimulus.

One of the main points to be made about the power of print over religious language is that sometimes adults will read to children rather than internalize the sacred stories, rituals, and parables and speak them directly to the child. This is not done out of any intent to injure the child, but sometimes it is done because of reverence for The Book as distinguished from a more primary use of the communication domain. Books are also given to children to read rather than adults speaking to children directly, especially when the issues to be spoken about with religious language are vividly present as in the hospital's undeniable presentation of human limits.

Adult resistances to theological play based on distortions to the use of religious language are varied and classic in the centuries of Christianity. In addition to these classic distortions there is a resistance based on an adult view of the nature of the child and his or her ability to make use of this strange language of religion. I will explore this resistance by discussing the work of Ronald Goldman and more recently the work of Daniel Batson and Larry Ventis.

The main point of this objection is that children are not ready for religion. To give them religious language is to trap them in misunderstanding it because of a lack of experience and a lack of appropriate cognitive structures to identify and make analogies. There are many examples of malapropism when children make ludicrous mistakes with religious language. Two examples will illustrate this.

When I was about five years of age I came home from Sunday

school with a very positive attitude about Jesus. My reasoning caused a great deal of amusement among the adults in our family. I liked Jesus when I discovered he would "eat carrots for me." I hated cooked carrots and always had to finish them before I could have dessert.

What had happened was that the "memory verse" for that day had been "He careth for me." My experience did not include any knowledge of the word careth, so I used what experience I had to make that important phrase fit with the nice things people had been saying about Jesus with what I did know about, cooked carrots.

A second kind of misunderstanding was reported by Gordon Allport in his classic work on the psychology of religion.[54] A child has heard that God was "high and bright." He searched everywhere for God and finally saw him. There he was up on top of the barn, pointing the direction of the wind. The child had confused the weathercock, the highest and brightest thing he knew, with God.

Ronald Goldman brought the powerful model of cognitive development to the study of religious language. His concern was that these misunderstandings forced three choices on young children as they grew up. If they did not choose to be patient and grow into an understanding of metaphor, they would either continue to understand religious language in a literal way or reject religion as mere fantasy. He, therefore, argued that religious language should not be given to children before they could identify and make conscious use of analogies. His concern about literalism was based on his findings that children up to the age of 13 years gave literal interpretations to scripture in 80% of the cases.

Goldman's views were very influential in religious education circles during the 1960s and 1970s. His classic work was *Religious Thinking from Childhood to Adolescence* which described research done in English state schools. Copies of his test instrument and statistical model were provided for the reader in the book's appendix.

The definition of religion used by Goldman tended to limit it to a set of propositions to be learned from a school syllabus. He spoke of religion as the activity of thinking directed towards religion. He called this thinking "adult" and related to "ideas" and "concepts." Examples of what religious thinking is directed at are the concepts and issues of "the nature of God, his relationships with men in history, his dealings with men today, his revelation of himself through the inspired literature of the Bible and through the person of Jesus Christ."[55] (p. 4)

Goldman's view of scripture was that it required one to interpret it as an analogy. The term that is known links you to the unknown term of the analogy to explain it. When the unknown term is understood (The Good Shepherd), then the known term (sheep and shepherds) is no longer needed.

What is clear about Goldman's research is that when you define religious thinking as requiring the ability to make conscious analogies, then you relegate this thinking to the period of what Piaget called formal operations, which is achieved about the time of one's teenage years.

A more recent and also helpful book, *The Religious Experience,*[56] by Batson and Ventis, continues this line of thinking of how we coordinate actions in the communication domain of religious language. Their focus was not on thinking but on experience. They defined religious experience as the ability to ask "existential questions." These questions were conceptualized as those thinking about the nature of life itself.

All major world religions seem to have developed one or more "supreme synthetic symbols" that "conceptualize" a new vision. This new vision deals with a range of existential questions simultaneously. Christians, for example, focus on the cross and find meaning there simultaneously about personal death, relations to others, and history. The meaning is a dying to the self and becoming free to live for others.

Since synthetic symbols are the facilitators of religious experience, there are limits to how they can be used. One limit is when the speaker's (writer's) questions are not those of the listener's (reader's). A second limitation is when the language is taken literally rather than symbolically.

The authors found a great deal of research that examined the link between religious experience and drugs, but none that showed the relationship between religious language and religious experience.

This indicated the next step research needs to take and why there is so little understanding of how children use religious language to make meaning and find direction in life and death.

The work of Batson and Ventis rules out religious experience except that which is structured by adult philosophical questions. The youngest age for such question-asking is about 10 years, which is a very young dawning of formal operations, if that kind of thinking about thinking is implied.

Batson and Ventis do link religious experience with a process that follows a pattern of similar shape to the creative process. There is (1) an existential crisis, followed by (2) a self-surrender. A (3) new vision is experienced that is followed by (4) a new life. One wonders if a rudimentary pattern is experienced by young children that is similar to this one that has more adult connotations. I would suggest that they do, but they cannot speak about it to describe it to a researcher.[57] One needs access through art or the observation of play to estimate the progress of the process. In children this would function in their art response and in their play as they use religious language to play at the limit to knowing and being.

I turn now to a refraining of the questions raised by Goldman and the work of Batson and Ventis that will remove the need to prevent children from engaging in theological play. We will need to distinguish among the use of religious language and talking about it as well as the phenomenon of consciously identifying the way it functions through its metaphors.

Reframing research concerning religious language and young children

Three current research efforts suggest that the prevailing view among religion professionals about giving young children religious language can be reframed. One of these is Project Zero at Harvard, a second is the Religious Experience Research Unit at Manchester College at Oxford University, and the third is at the Children's Center at the Institute of Religion in the Texas Medical Center in Houston.

Howard Gardner and his associates at Harvard have been studying children's art and its relation to the art of adults. His book, *Art, Mind, and Brain*,[58] described the research and theory concerning drawing, music, and literature studies. Of special interest is the research on children and metaphor.

Gardner's research concerning the child's interpretation of metaphor was based on giving the child a metaphor such as:

After many years of working at the jail, the prison guard had become a hard rock and could not be moved.

The interpretation of the metaphor of the guard's becoming a hard rock (unfeeling) was found to have a developmental pattern.

2-5 years	The children turned to a magical version to turn the guard into a stone
5-7 years	The children did not equate the guard with the rock
8-9 years	The children began to assimilate the psychological state and the relationship with the rock
12+ years	Accurate definitions of the metaphor and its interpretation appeared

The situation was quite different when the children's use of metaphor was studied and compared with their ability to identify and interpret metaphor. Their speech patterns showed the following development:

3 years	Most children used metaphor.
4-5 years	Nearly all of these children had little difficulty generating metaphors based on appearance.
6 years	The ability to use metaphor declined from the onset of schooling.

By making the distinction between the child's ability to interpret and identify metaphors and the use of metaphors, the first step in the reframing process for this research is taken. Our concern is to put this powerful language tool into the hands of children to use, so the ability to interpret and identify metaphor consciously is not our primary concern. Furthermore, if children are presented a whole system of metaphors in a single room to distinguish this domain of communication, then there is more likelihood that these particular metaphors are at least implicitly recognized and associated with their creative use when met outside the room. A reference back to the sensorimotor experience can be made. Since in theological play the child associates the use of the language with the creative process, the danger of literalism is lessened at later stages of development.

The second body of research that helps reorient this discussion is that of Howard Robinson and his associates at Manchester College, Oxford University. This research was begun by Alister Hardy whose book, *The Spiritual Nature of Man*,[59] fills in some of the background to the project.

Hardy invited people to send the Research Unit first-hand reports if they "felt that their lives had in any way been affected by some power beyond themselves." No mention was made of childhood. In the initial response about 4,000 reports were collected. About 15% of these made reference to events that took place in childhood.

The Unit's present director, Edward Robinson, was struck by this indication that metaphors of this "power beyond themselves" had such a powerful impact on people's lives that they would both remember the metaphor and reinterpret as they matured. His book, *The Original Vision*,[60] details this study of about 390 responses of the 500 that mentioned childhood events.

At Manchester College, religious experience was defined in terms of "power beyond themselves," while in the Batson and Ventis study religious experience was defined in terms of existential questions about life itself. Goldman was interested in religious thinking directed at ideas and concepts. The Manchester College study, at least, presents us with the task to compare the definitions of religious experience. At most, it suggests that the use of metaphors to express and identify an experience of the limit in a positive limiting sense can take place in childhood, at least for about 15% of people in England.

The definition of religious experience as being identified by existential question-asking raises another question about the use of metaphor as distinguished from talking about metaphor. Among the existentialist school of philosophy were figures who chose to use metaphor rather than analysis when the discussion approached the limit case. Existential questions were posed in terms of the abyss, the boundary, the chasm, etc. Gabriel Marcel specifically spoke against the idea that life could be analyzed as a problem at all. His view was that the only way to know life was to participate in its mystery.[61] Philosophy became very close to religious language among this group with many shifting to novels and plays to express their experience of the limit case.

Participation in life as a mystery is a special capacity children have. They do not have the cognitive structures yet to turn life into a problem and analyze it. When philosophers turn to childlike participation to answer questions raised by analysis, then we must ask again if children might not be able to use religious language even if they are not able yet to analyze how they use it or say when they are using it. Martin Buber even spoke of children having a "spiritual instinct" and noted that when the child first speaks, he or she speaks in myth as early humans did.⁶²

Research at the Children's Center in Houston adds two additional features to this reframing. The use of metaphors is explored by two new means. One is the child's spontaneous play and the other is the child's art response and verbal response to this art response, both of which are linked to an original presentation of a metaphor from the religious language system.

Presentations are made following the Montessori approach to children usually sitting in a circle or in small groups of one or two, as well as to single children. Presentations follow a certain order of movement and speech. They can be made by either the adult or a child who has already had a presentation. Children are only supposed to take materials from the shelves that they have had presentations about.

The presentation guides the play. Spontaneous play with the materials that the child selects can be compared with the presentation. This gives some indication of whether the child is using this "materialized" metaphor to make meaning.

Children are asked to make something about how a presentation feels. The art response might be in any of the media furnished in the Center from wire sculpture to clay and paints. When the art response is finished, the child takes it into another room where he or she has a private talk with this author who listens carefully for an interpretation in words about the art without imposing significance or an interpretation to any part of the art.

The art response and the follow-up verbal response provide an opportunity for several kinds of observation. First, some children show no trace of the religious language system in their response. This typically takes place during the first few weeks of a child's introduction to the Children's Center. Second, there is a kind of stereotyped response where the child attempts to reproduce the physical appearance of the material. Neither of these responses indicates any use of the system.

A third kind of response is when the child begins to mix issues in his or her life with both the language of everyday and the religious language system in the art. A fourth kind of response takes place over several weeks and shows how a single image such as the Parable of the Mustard Seed can be returned to again and again in a spontaneous, self-selected way to work something through. Completion of this process is usually indicated by the returning of the art to a naturalistic representation or even a stereotyped response.

Research in Boston, Oxford, and Houston indicates that while children may not be able to indicate metaphors or interpret them, they can use them with profit. Even though they cannot ask philosophical questions, they can intuit how a metaphor can be used to work on a response to a limit case experience. This research is certainly not conclusive, but it does suggest that a reframing of the research about children and religious language needs to be done to show in more detail how children use religious language. It does seem conclusive that they do use it, and that when approached like the theological play described here there are safeguards against misuse both by the presentations and by keeping track of the spontaneous play and the art responses.

A theological analysis of children and religious language

Theology identifies patterns in experience as does any of the other communication domains. A theological system merely is an effort to think systematically about these patterns. My analysis will rely primarily on the thinking of Paul Tillich who used what he called a "method of correlation."[63] The questions arise from the coordination of actions in other domains or the language of everyday. These questions are correlated with "answers" put in the symbols of the Christian tradition.

I have been attempting to address the virtues of theological play in pediatrics in a philosophical and sometimes scientific way. There has been analysis of language and some reference to research based on the scientific method. What I will present now is a statement of how theological play works in relation to the theology of Paul Tillich and how this will fit into the care of the hospital team.

Your theological orientation may differ from this. Your religious tradition may be quite different from this protestant Christianity. But this is one of our human limits. No one is everyone, but we can still be in community despite our differences and various viewpoints. This theological orientation, however, is a conceptualization of my own roots in sacred story, ritual, and parable, so it is quite appropriate for me to speak this way to others who choose to coordinate their actions with this communication domain.

Tillich's system of theology is basically concerned with three aspects of a major pattern in existence. One is our unity with life (being). The second is our separation from life (existence). The third is the dynamic of being and existence in relation to each other.

Tillich's *Systematic Theology* has five parts. The first section is devoted to discussing reason and revelation to provide the reader with a view of his epistemology at the outset. The last section is devoted to the correlation of the experience of history with the symbol The Kingdom of God. Between these beginning and ending points is a trinitarian formulation that connects the issue of how we essentially are (or ought to be) with God. It connects the self-destructive and estranged existence we experience with the event of Christ (or the way we ought not to be). The third section correlates life (the complex and dynamic unit of being and existence that are abstractions in a human person) with the Spirit (which is not an abstraction).

The way that theological play is connected to this theological formulation of Tillich and the classic trinitarian pattern is by what we have called the three functions of religious language. Sacred story is related to questions of being and union. Questions of existence and separation are related to ritual, which heals the self-estrangement. Questions of the ambiguity of life and its creative process that involve being and existence are related to the Spirit. This is the realm of parable.

Disease, Tillich said, is a disruption of centeredness under all the dimensions of life. These dimensions are neither independent nor dependent but related to each other. The relation of these dimensions to healing is important to take into consideration theologically. Tillich said:

> The ways of healing do not need to impede each other, as the dimensions of life do not conflict with each other. The correlation of the multi-dimensional unity of life is the multidimensional unity of healing. No individual can exercise all the ways of healing with authority, although more than one way may be used by some individuals. But even if there is a union of different functions, for example, of the priestly and medical functions in one man, the functions must be distinguished and neither confused with the other, nor may one be eliminated by the other.[64]

A final theological clarification needs to be made. This relates to the distinction between faith healing and magical healing. It may be that healing through faith is so misunderstood that any attempt to clarify it is doomed, but I will make the effort.

Healing through the Spirit refers to the transcendence of the person's fragmented center to the Divine Center where it is made whole, Tillich said. In this sense salvation and healing are the same when one remains in the domain of religious communication.

The reality of New Being is received through faith. Tillich called this the "receiving function." The "actualizing function" is love. Such healing or salvation can be accomplished regardless of disease and decay at other places in the human system, but it can also enhance the scientific healing in the biological, psychological, and social dimensions.

When Tillich spoke of magical healing he did not do so in a pejorative way, nor do I. Acts of autosuggestion and placebo are used by many in both the clergy and medicine, sometimes without even being aware of it. It is the question of beneficial results that is the clarifying issue.

Spiritual presence is not healing through magic, as we have already discussed, and magical healing can be justified by benefical results. The problem arises when magical healing excludes other ways of healing in principle (as some faith healing movements and individuals do). It is then that this approach is predominantly destructive.

Putting theological play to work in pediatrics

Hospitals have their own folk ways. You will know best how to approach the introduction of theological play into your hospital system. What follow are merely some suggestions to stimulate your thinking.

The creation of a printed brochure is sometimes helpful. It ought to include pictures of children doing theological play with short explanations of the theory and practice. How to contact the chaplains also needs to be indicated. This brochure can be used as a calling card and given to all family members when a child comes into the hospital.

Television offers many possibilities to alert people that theological play is available to them and their children. It not only communicates this possibility, but it also can be a means to present this language domain to the children in a way that keeps them in control by holding on to the television's on/off switch or channel selector. They can be less anxious that way.

The pediatric chaplain can present a sacred story, ritual, or parable directly to the child through the screen. The child does not see the chaplain working with other children in the picture. Each viewer has a "personal" presentation. The focus moves to the material itself with the chaplain's voice in the background. If the children enjoy this experience, they can then call for the chaplain to bring them religious language in person, or they may continue to use this medium of television to encounter religious language in its secondary oral and visual medium.

The pediatric chaplain may need to consider using an art cart like those sometimes seen in pediatrics. This is to carry the materials of religious language and the materials for the art responses. This will enable the chaplain to come to rooms with more options or to go to meeting rooms where children might gather.

Children and/or their families might come to the chaplain's office. In the corner an area can be created for theological play. Psychiatrists and psychologists who work with children often have such an area in their offices so this is not without precedent in the medical setting.

Probably the most exciting possibility would be to set aside a whole room for theological play in the hospital. Space is usually at a premium so this might be difficult, but it is not without precedent since there are rooms set aside for medical play. With such a setting children could walk into the language system when they walk into that room. A part of the chapel in the hospital would accomplish this goal almost as well.

Although I have only discussed presenting religious language to children, such a focus should not be thought to ignore the family. In fact, one important approach to the whole family is to teach the parents how to present religious language to the child through theological play. If they become comfortable with this approach, it gives the family a tool by which to deepen their own unity and spiritual presence together in the limit case. The chaplain would still be available for the sacramental ministry *as* well as to support the parents in their support of the ill child.

Members of the health care team may also want to make use of religious language in the theological play mode. It reconnects the roots of what may have become almost completely conceptual to the sensorimotor experiences of childhood, and the power of the metaphors to function might be regained. In addition to this, the primary goal for presentations of theological play to the health care team members is to inform them of the activity of the chaplain, so they can be aware of it and support it as the chaplain does their work.

There is also information the chaplain will discover in the course of theological play that may be of help to the team. This will come from the children's art responses or the spontaneous play responses. Even if one does not coordinate his or her responses by means of the communication domain of religious language, the research of Ana-Maria Rizzuto can be followed to make interpretations about the child and the family from the images of God used in theological play.

Conclusion

The chaplain's contribution to the health care team is the reality he or she works in professionally. My focus has been on the language aspect of that synthesis of language and experience. The chaplain shares with other members of the health care team a spirit of open and flexible cooperation as well as a commitment to a comprehensive understanding of the patient.

On a team one shares knowledge but also ignorance and frustrations. This self-exposure can be contributed when it is assumed such an act is professional honesty and maturity rather than incompetency or insecurity.

The chaplain and the health care team members need to recognize the interdependence they share and the limits of their partial views. This makes the need to work together clear. The multidimensional unity of life can be matched with the multidimensional unit of healing. Such a vision is made present and personified on a smoothly working and creative team.

Original Source:

Berryman, J.W. 1985. "The chaplain's strange language: A unique contribution to the health care team." Pp. 16-39 in *Life, Faith, Hope and Magic: The Chaplaincy in Pediatric Cancer Care*, edited by J. van Eys & E.J. Mahnke. Austin, Texas: The University of Texas Press.

5

The Illusive Use of Religious Language in Childhood

This chapter primarily describes a series of pictures made by Bobby who is age 6 and Jimmy who is age 7 during 8 Saturdays of a 12 week term in the fall of 1981. This series changed my attitude and approach toward research about the function of religious language in child development and committed me more than any other event to follow its winding track wherever it might lead.

This research could be an important complement to the work of Professor Kalevi Tamminen and his associates. What is described, however, comes more from an angle that is like the spiritual direction of children than research done within the scientific model.

There are two major reasons for operating from within the theological model. First, any study of a child's use of religious language assumes that the child needs to learn the art of using that language system in an appropriate way. To teach that appropriate use of language one needs to authentically model it, especially for children. Secondly, it is very difficult to predict and control for what existential issue a child needs to work on and what "piece" of the religious language system a child will use to work through that issue. The researcher, then, needs to be "in" the religious language domain with the children both to teach it and to be able to respond to the child's existential needs with that language.

The definition of the function of religious language has been clarified over the last 50 years. Much of this work was done in England by those such as A.J. Ayer, Anthony Flew and Ian Ramsey in a process that began somewhat hostile to religion and concluded (at least for me) with Bishop Ramsey's description of religious language use as (1) an "odd discernment". It is "odd" in the sense of not being a function ruled by the canons of the scientific method. It also involves (2) a total commitment, and (3) having universal significance.[65] The latter two aspects of the function refer to what I would like to call having an existential grounding in the limit to human knowing ("total commitment") and being ("universal significance").

The concept of the limit case has also been helpful. David Tracy outlined the "limit" concept in his Blessed Rage for Order[66]. This places the empirical reference for religious language in the limit case. The function of religious language becomes a way to cope with this limit which has two aspects, a positive and negative boundary experience.

The negative experience of the limit is a sense of how we are defined as human beings by our need for meaning, our aloneness, our death and the threat of freedom which forces us to take responsibility for our actions. Tracy's summary has been further filled out by the practical experience of the therapist, Irvin D. Yalom, whose Existential Psychotherapy[67] refuses to reduce existential issues to manageable pathology and maintains a strong developmental point of view so that children's involvement in such existential issues can be better understood.

The positive experience of the limit is a presence, a Holy Presence, that enables one to transcend human limits by a relationship with the Creator and by the use of an appropriate kind of language. In this study the piece of religious language used by the two young boys is the Parable of the Mustard Seed.

The origin of the research

This research project began in Houston, Texas, in 1975 when I was Director of Christian Education at St. John's Presbyterian Church. We used this approach for educational purposes in our church school for children (1975-1977). It was first used with adolescents as well as children at Pines Presbyterian Church (1977-1980), where I also served as Director of Christian Education. At Pines a special Saturday morning class also was begun in 1978. Research rather than purely educational goals was the primary focus. These three years (1975-1978) were needed to learn how the materials, method and environment worked best.

In 1979 the focus of this work narrowed to research and moved to the Institute of Religion in the Texas Medical Center. Results of the research there were primarily used to develop an approach to the pastoral care of children in hospitals. In 1985 the Children's Center (the name of the research project) moved to Christ Church Cathedral, The Episcopal Cathedral in Houston, where both the research continued and a major adaptation for religious education involving about 250 children was begun.

The research setting

The children were self-selected and came from a variety of socio-economic, religious and school groups in Houston. When Bobby and Jimmy were attending the Children's Center in the Fall of 1981 the group included about 12 children from age 3 to 10 years of age and expanded during that fall term into two groups. The next year's classes went to 20 per class, 2 to 7 and 7 to 12 years of age. This is relevant since the approach uses much of the method of *Montessori* [68]and materials adapted for that method by *Cavalletti*.[69]

The research environment has materials for the children to work with on shelves. The children are literally surrounded by parables, sacred stories and liturgical symbols of the Christian language system.

The children are invited into a circle for a lesson at the beginning of the class. After the lesson they are invited to "get out their work" which means that they can choose something to work on from the shelves, make an art response to the lesson presented by the teacher, or work through the days' lesson again.

The "art responses" involve drawings, paintings, clay forms, wire sculpture, and other art forms. The "play responses" use the materials to respond to the lesson of the day or to work on their own interests. As you will see constructive wandering is also supported. (Note Bobby on the fifth Saturday.)

The material the two boys found so useful and interesting was the Parable of the Mustard Seed in a gold box. The yellow, oval underlay was taken out of the box and spread out on the floor. The figure of a person planting the tiny seed was placed on the underlay and the parable was told. When the shrub "grows" a green felt tree[70] is unrolled. Birds and nests are placed around it by the teacher and the children. The children and the teacher then wonder about what the parable might "really be". The children are then excused one at a time from the circle when they are able to choose their first bit of work.

The research classes are two hours long. The lesson and wondering with the teacher take about 30 minutes. The work period is about 60 minutes and the final 30 minutes are devoted to putting things away, gathering again in the circle, getting ready for the feast, saying our prayers, sharing the feast and then saying good-by.

The structure of classroom time is shaped by the deep structure of the Holy Eucharist. There is first an approach through the Liturgy of the Word: (1) A Greeting, (2) The Lesson and (3) A Response. The Liturgy of Holy Communion continues which includes: (4) Setting the Table, (5) Sharing the Feast, (6) Blessing, and (7) Dismissal.

The reason for using the deep structure of Holy Eucharist as the pattern for the class is that the language of religion, a linguistic domain people can learn and choose to use like any other linguistic domain such as science or law, is grounded in a special kind of experience. This experience is the relationship with God in community. This relationship which we call "worship" has taken the classical shape of the Eucharist in the Eastern Church, the Church of Rome, the Anglican Tradition, and in various Protestant denominations and national churches.

The theological control for this research is an attempt to steer between blasphemy (thinking that I know in advance what the children can and will do in this situation) and idolotry (turning religious language into an object of worship in itself rather than seeing it as a tool to make meaning and find direction in life with God and each other). The caution about steering a path between these two dangers in the religious journey is as ancient as is the religious journey itself.

Some 20 articles have been written by this author describing the theory and practice of this method for pastoral care in hospitals, for religious education in the parish and for research. The most complete but now somewhat dated statement of this position can be found in *Scriptura: Journal of Biblical Studies*[71]. Two book-length essays are now in process.

The description of the pictures

The series of 13 pictures made by the two boys in response to the Parable of the Mustard Seed were done over a period of eight weeks during a term of 12 Saturday classes. They began on the second meeting of the term and concluded in the ninth week. The classes met on Saturday mornings from 10:00-12:00 a.m. until the sixth week when we divided the groups into 2-7 and 7-12 year old sections. The older children began to come in the afternoon. Bobby and Jimmy remained in the morning group.

Bobby and Jimmy were present at every class during the period of the pictures. The size of the groups ranged from 8-14 children and on the days Bobby made the paintings there were 8, 7 and 9 in the class. The times in between these Mustard Seed Parable pictures Bobby generally responded to the lesson of the day or wandered.

The first Saturday the lesson was the parable of the Good Shepherd and both boys responded with pictures related to that. Bobby made one picture and Jimmy made two. The second week was when the series of pictures under study began. Our description will move week by week. A discussion will then follow.

The second Saturday the lesson was the Parable of the Mustard Seed. Bobby made two large paintings with tempera paint and large paint brushes. The first one had a large, thick vertical shaft, rounded at the top in the middle of the page. On the left side was a large, black bird and above it were two smaller birds, but they were pale blue. On the other side of the tree were several other pale blue birds.

I sat down with Bobby and enjoyed the painting. I did not say anything except, "Hmm. I like your painting" and then I waited. He sat quietly and finally began to tell me about this picture. The large bird on the left side he said was an "eagle flying to get the others". I asked, "How did they feel about the eagle?" He said that they were "happy and sad about the big one." I nodded my head that I understood and took what he was telling me seriously. Bobby continued. "Coming to get the babies to eat them..." He did not say anything else. We sat there a few minutes more.

When it was apparent that Bobby was not going to say any more I said, "I like your painting. It is important. May I keep it here and take a picture of it?" (This is a standard request and the children usually give their consent. Their permission is also gained before I write their comments on their pictures.)

The second painting was also tempera and on big paper (12 inches x 18 inches). It also had a large cylinder in the middle of the paper but this one had an oval at the bottom of it. Birds were flying on both sides and this time they were a variety of colors rather than just pale blue. In the first painting the eagle was the largest figure but this time it is smaller than most of the other birds.

Bobby said, "The birds are many colors now. Here is the eagle (He pointed to the figure on the left side of the tree)". He was matter-of-fact about the second painting and kept referring back to the first one as he talked about the second one. He paused and then said, "No stuff happening. All happy. Bited him all up (He pointed to the eagle). Laughing at him (referring to the eagle)." We turn now to Jimmy's first response of this day. In the circle I said, "I wonder where this could really be (and swept my hand over the whole Parable of the Mustard Seed that was laid out on the floor)?" Jimmy said, "It's in Houston."

Jimmy also made a painting response to the Parable of the Mustard Seed. It looked much like the second painting he had made the week before in response to the Parable of the Good Shepherd. He continued the sun motif that connected the point of emphasis, first the sheepfold and now the tree, with the sun. Five out of eight children including Bobby and Jimmy responded to the Parable of the Mustard Seed on this Saturday with a painting about it.

The *third week* Bobby made another picture of the Parable of the Mustard Seed. On this particular day the lesson was about the Seven Days of Creation. When it came time for him to get out his work he chose to get the Parable of the Mustard Seed in its gold box from the shelf and present it to himself. He then made an art response in tempera on the large paper.

In the center of this painting was another large cylinder. There were little birds all over the head of the tree which was larger than the shaft of the trunk. More birds were flying toward the tree from the left side of the paper. At the ground level stood a man. A line went from the gun he was holding up to a bird flying toward the tree. Red dashes fell down to the base of the tree into a container. Not all of this was obvious until Bobby and I began to visit together about the painting.

"I like your painting", I said. I then waited. Finally I touched the bird gently with my finger. "The bird got shot," Bobby said. He then pointed to the figure on the ground and said, "Man with gun". His finger traced the red dashes down to the container and he said, "blood dripping down into nest".

Another dimension was introduced as Bobby went on. "Other page (picture) don't have names (for the birds). These do. All are coming to nests."

Bobby went on. "It's like Jimmy's. He was going to write (paint) a lot of birds. My tree is bigger." He had been watching Jimmy as he worked and even looked over at Jimmy's picture while he was talking.

On this third Saturday Jimmy first made a painting of "the sixth day" (of creation) which continued his theme of the sun linking to the primary focal point in the picture.

The second picture Jimmy made was a tree related to the Parable of the Mustard Seed. His primary comment was that the birds could all fit into the nests because the birds were small and the nests were large. This picture which Bobby had been watching him make did not look at all like the one Bobby made. It looked much more like a tree than Bobby's did.

The *fourth week's* lesson was the circle of the liturgical year. Jimmy and Bobby worked together again on the Parable of the Mustard Seed despite the lesson. Both made pencil drawings of the tree. Unfortunately the originals were both lost, so I do not have slides of them. There is only the notation that this was done. They did not comment on them.

The *fifth week's* lesson was the Parable of the Pearl. Bobby wandered about the room that day, unable to choose a piece of work and concentrate on it. He watched others work and visited with the other children, but he did not make an art or play response to any piece of religious language. Jimmy, on the other hand, made a response to the lesson. Telling about his painting, he said, "these little things are the parables – no the pearls".

At the end of each two hour class there is a time we call "the feast". It takes about the last 30 minutes. When the napkins are laid out in front of the children sitting in the circle the bread is placed on them. The juice is then placed also on the napkins. When everything is ready, including the children, we say our prayers.

Each child is invited to pray, but there is no pressure to do this so many of the children signal that they "pass" by shaking their heads "No". I also tell the children that there are all kinds of prayers. There are prayers that are their own words, like normal talking. There are also prayers that use other people's words that they remember. Sometimes prayers don't have any words. They are feelings. You can say your prayers out loud or say them inside so only God can hear.

The handling of the prayers is important to mention now because up to this point Bobby had always shaken his head "No". Jimmy on the other hand always indicated his desire to say a prayer. His manner of prayer was to pray intently but silently.

On *the sixth Saturday* the lesson was the Parable of the Good Samaritan. Bobby did not want to get any work out. When this happens in the circle the child remains sitting so he or she can have more time to choose. When we go around the circle the children who choose work leave one by one. We then go around again until all have been able to get up and move with intention to some task. Bobby stayed a long time this day. Finally, he did get up and make an art response. This was a response to The Parable of the Good Samaritan, the lesson for the day. He made almost no comment at all.

Jimmy made three pictures this Saturday. The first and second ones were about the Good Samaritan. His pictures focused on the violence of the Parable and he said, "They jumped out on that guy" and "the guy got hurt". The third picture he made was about the Parable of the

Good Shepherd, the lesson of the first week, now 42 days ago.

Noah and the Flood was the lesson on *the seventh Saturday*. Bobby made no response to it or anything else. He wandered. Jimmy made four pictures. The first two were about Noah and the Flood. The third one was about the Parable of the Good Shepherd. The last one was about the Parable of the Mustard Seed. Jimmy made the first with ink markers, the second with tempera paint, the third with markers and the last he made with a pencil. I asked him, "Where is the mustard seed?" He said, "It is the tree."

Before we shared the feast Jimmy again said a prayer. I am the last one in the circle to decide about praying and I usually pray the same prayer out loud. I say, "Thank you, God, for these wonderful children and for our feast." On this day when I finished by saying "Amen" Jimmy spoke up and said, "That's what I said, same as Mr. Berryman." Again, Bobby did not say a prayer.

On *the eighth Saturday* I had to be away to attend a professional meeting in Canada. The children did not come to the Children's Center for class.

The ninth Saturday's lesson was about Advent which would begin the next day. The Advent Lesson first presents the Holy Family since these wooden figures are sitting on the focal shelf on top of a cloth which is the color of the liturgical season. A small circular board is set on a rug in front of the presenter and each person and animal is named and valued as it is placed upon it. The cloth is changed to the color of the new season and then each piece is carefully replaced on the new color.

Additional lessons about Advent use a set of cards with symbols for the Prophets, the Holy Family, the Shepherds and the Magi on them. An abstract replica of Bethlehem is placed in the center of the circle of children. The motif is that we are all on the way to Bethlehem during Advent with the Holy Family. The cards are laid out, one per

Saturday during Advent, and a large candle is placed by the card. It is lighted and in turn we enjoy the light of the Prophets, the Holy Family, the Shepherds and the Magi. The last Saturday we remember the Christ Child and the last candle is lit. This candle is white and comes from the lesson on Baptism, leaving a clue for the children to discover that the Light of Christ, the Paschal Candle and Nativity share the same Light.

On this day when the shepherds were being placed on the wooden circle on the rug one of them fell over. Bobby said, "looks like that shepherd's dead". He grew agitated. I set it up. Bobby smiled and relaxed again.

On this day Bobby made three art responses. The first was in crayon and it was on a small piece of paper 9 inches x 6 inches. It was the most tree-looking "tree" Bobby had yet made. It was the first one with branches, for example, and they were green. It also looked rooted in the yellow ground and Bobby wrote his name along the contour of the earth. Blue birds were flying away from the tree to the right. On the top of the tree there was a half circle in which sat a bird a little bigger than the others. It seemed to be nesting and was more formed than the rest. It was yellow.

I sat quietly beside Bobby and waited for him to speak. I showed nonverbally how much I liked his work and how important I thought it was by touching it with care. I decided not to touch any specific figure in the picture. I waited. Finally, Bobby said, "The Mustard Tree". I shook my head, "Yes". "These are flying away (the ones on the right). They are going to get some food for the baby." He pointed to a little speck on a branch at the lower left of the tree's branches. He said, "a little ...". Over on the right side of the lower branches he pointed and said, "a new bird". He then brought his finger up to the top of the tree and pointed to the yellow bird nesting there. He said more firmly, "a new bird".

The second picture Bobby made on the ninth Saturday was about the Parable of the Good Shepherd. The sheepfold was in the upper middle of the picture with black rocks on the lower left showing a place of danger and a blue pond on the lower right. The figure he called "The Good Shepherd" and what appeared to be another figure he did not identify were standing in the middle of an open gate. There was one sheep inside the sheepfold and there were no other sheep in the painting. Bobby said, "The Good Shepherd." I nodded. He pointed to the figure in the gate and said, "He's letting the sheep out." He paused and then said, "There's just one."

The third picture Bobby made was on the smallest paper (9 inches x 6 inches). It was in chalk. He worked very rapidly and came over to me in a decisive way, as if he were finished with the theme he had been working these 49 days since the second Saturday of the term. Birds were flying away in all directions from another naturalistic tree. Even the yellow bird had taken flight. He merely put down the picture and walked away without comment.

This Saturday Jimmy made four pictures. The first one was about the Advent lesson. Jesus was in "his bed". There was a candle and a wreath. The second picture was about "the parable of the guy who's half-dead" (The Good Samaritan). The third picture was about the Parable of the Pearl. The fourth picture was a small pencil drawing of the Parable of the Mustard Seed. His only comment was to say "the Parable of the Mustard Seed".

Bobby shook his head "Yes" when it was his turn to choose to pray. He prayed silently. Jimmy also prayed as he did every Saturday that term. This turned out to be the only time Bobby prayed.

On *the tenth Saturday* the lesson was about the second week of Advent. The Holy Family card was laid down and the wooden figures placed upon it. The candle was lit and we enjoyed the light of the Holy Family as they and we made our way toward Bethlehem.

Bobby made his final Mustard Seed picture that day. It was a small pencil drawing. The tree in it shifted back to being non-naturalistic again. The two sides of the trunk in the center of the page swept up in concave curves from each side and a ball sat on the top. Three birds flew away to the right from the trunk. I sat quietly. Bobby seemed ready to sit a long time with me without speaking. Finally, I said, "Where is the bad bird?" He did not respond. I tried again. "You know, the one that was hurting the other birds." Bobby said, "He's gone." He then sighed a deep sigh. "All the others are asleep."

Jimmy did three pictures on that tenth Saturday. The first one was related to the presentation of the day. He made a picture of Bethlehem and a path going towards it. The second picture was about the Parable of the Pearl. The third picture was the Parable of the Mustard Seed. I sat down beside him to appreciate his picture. We sat there for some time and then I asked, "Are the birds coming or going?" He said, "Coming."

On *the eleventh Saturday* Bobby was away traveling with his family for the Christmas holidays. Jimmy made six pictures, all related to the Advent lessons. They were candles, wreathes, prophets, and Bethlehem. On *the last Saturday* of the term, both boys were away with their families.

Discussion

The primary focus of this study is on Bobby, but the interaction between Bobby and Jimmy and their respective interactions with the Parable need to be discussed. The first point of interest is that Bobby usually produced pictures of The Mustard Seed on days when Jimmy did (Classes 2, 3, 4, 9, and 10) although Jimmy made a picture of the Parable one time when Bobby did not (Class 7). Days five, six, and seven were wandering days for Bobby, despite Jimmy's brief work on Day seven with the Mustard Seed Parable. This suggests the powerful influence and importance of children learning how to use religious language in community.

Secondly, it is important to note that the juxtapositions between the Parable and other lessons had an influence on the work with the Parable. The lessons about Advent on Day nine seem to have linked the images of birth and new life to the "eating of babies" by the eagle when the series began. Bobby said that the birds in his first picture of Day nine were flying away, "going to get some food for the baby". This was also the day when the trees became more naturalistic and the image of the "new bird" was introduced. One easily could make too much out of this, but the link is suggestive. The idea of "food for their babies" also came up in Bobby's last picture on Day ten. What this suggests is the importance of having the whole context of religious language present in the room, as it is in the worship process, the architecture and in the lections of the Church Year in the classical Eucharist liturgy and setting.

The whole series of seven pictures for Bobby and six pictures for Jimmy done over a period of eight weeks suggests the importance of being able to return again and again to an image that has special significance for the individual. This means that in teaching the art of using religious language this opportunity needs to be given and supported by allowing the children to choose their work whatever the daily lesson is.

When we look at the pictures of the two boys side by side we see how different they are despite their interaction around the same image. Bobby's images such as eating the babies, "biting" the eagle on Day two, the hunter's shot and dripping blood on Day three, the death concern about the shepherd on Day nine suggest the existential issue of death. Even the tree itself seems very dangerous before it turns into a more tree-like tree and becomes a place of nourishment.

Jimmy seems to have felt the tree was a place of nourishment all through the series of his pictures. At the end he decided to stay flying toward the tree while Bobby decided that he could fly away from this nourishment to new and other positive things now that the "bad bird is gone" (Day ten).

Both boys appear to be using the same process which is natural to human beings when they are permitted and can find a safe place in which to create new ideas or new frames of reference. The creative process has been widely studied[72] and was applied to religious studies especially by James E. Loder in *The Transforming Moment*[73]. What is agreed on in this literature is the general sequence by which the process flows.

The first step is a disruption of ones circle of meaning. A break begins the process. We have a natural tendency to complete broken units of meaning like when we complete figures visually that look like a circle, triangle or some other figure when in fact they are broken lines. In Bobby's case there was some disruption in his life's meaning that was expressed in the early pictures as the threatening tree and the eagle. Jimmy did not seem to have such a disruption. His circle of meaning seemed to remain complete during the whole series and the tree remained a source of nourishment and "nesting".

The second step in the creative process is the scanning for a new frame of meaning to cope with the disruption that has been experienced. The scanning began at once for Bobby on Day two with his second picture and continued to the nineth Saturday when the lessons on Advent began.

The third step is the insight. A new energy is experienced by the person when the sense of a solution becomes evident whether it is explicit yet or not. The energy used for the scanning is converted into energy to create the new frame of meaning. On both Day nine and Day ten this solution was worked out in terms of nourishment and the ability to fly away to new things despite the danger and threat of death and separation in life.

The existential ground for the process

If a child can learn the art of using religious language to create meaning and appropriately place that language in its existential ground at the boundary of our knowing and being, then, the possibility is open to cope with his or her existential limits by means of this language to transcend these limits. This transcendence is accomplished by participation not only in the negative sense of the limit which stimulates the creative process but also in the positive sense through the relationship with the Creator.

If this art is learned and if it functions to cope with ones existential limits as in the case of Bobby, then, a pattern is revealed that correlates with the creative process used at all levels of human functioning – biological, psychological, social and spiritual. It is when this process, religious language, existential issues and the Creator are involved in community with other human beings that changes in ones perceived world can take place. Even the threat of death and separation can be reframed so that one can "fly away" to take up new challenges with faith, hope and love.

If we perform an operation of distinction which makes the focus of observation the biological aspect of human interaction, then, we might discuss such issues as how Bobby's pictures are "really" about an intuited biological threat such as cancer. Such a biological discussion presumes certain rules of observation, a technology for investigation and a particular way of making conclusions about Bobby's health.

If we were to look at the psychological aspect of human interaction the unit of observation might be personality function and such things as how Bobby's new male teacher, myself, might be a phallic threat to his development. This discussion, too, would have its own rules of observation, "instruments" of investigation and ways of making conclusions to show what Bobby's pictures "really" mean.

If we were to distinguish the social world as the unit of observation we might want to discuss the fact that Bobby's weekly school experience during this period included the threat of a schoolyard bully whom Bobby experienced as having specially picked him out to harass. (This information came from Bobby's parents.) We might further want to compare Bobby's experience in school with that of Jimmy who attended another school. This discussion, too, would have its own rules of discourse to decide what Bobby's pictures "really" mean.

When we choose to study the theological world in which Bobby functions we distinguish that unit of observation and enter into the language appropriate for that realm. One might just as well enter an ethical, aesthetic, legal or other language domain to discuss Bobby's pictures but the discourse of science with its interacting systems of biology, psychology and sociology are more customary. These languages and their realities are not self-authenticing unless one enters their systems of interaction and obeys their rules.

When Bobby entered the Parable of the Mustard Seed and the world it created we refused to reduce his interpretations to biology, psychology, sociology or any other secular language game so we could discover more about how religious language functioned for him in this case. This is why I said at the beginning of this paper that what is being studied here is closer to careful spiritual direction than science.

Both boys seemed to be seeking coherence in the largest possible terms when they meditated again and again on the Parable of the Mustard Seed through involvement in their art responses. Their sensorimotor knowing and expression engaged their theological cognition at this stage of development in a powerful way. Of course, they do not make distinctions or think about their thinking like older children would do, but when they are "in" the Parable and their art response how can we say that we as adults could express what they know better. We can only talk "about" it more conceptually and with greater differentiation. The question remains do we know more in terms of theological experience?

Bobby and Jimmy seek meaning, but that is not all. Other existential issues merge with this one. Both boys are involved with the issues of death and separation and both are involved with the threat of freedom. Bobby finally risks death as separation to accept the responsibility of freedom while Jimmy continues to seek nourishment and the status quo, perhaps, later to take such a risk and continue to grow when he is ready or a crisis presents itself and he must grow or be trapped in his retreat. Jimmy flys back to the tree while Bobby flys away a "new bird". It is very Christian to speak of Bobby's "new Birth" and his "turning". This is a turning that responds to the Creator and creates a new life.

Conclusion

It is complicated to develop a rich environment and to become adept at teaching the art of the use of religious language through sensorial materials and relationships, but all research is complicated. What this approach does do is complement the monumental work of Professor Kalevi Tamminen and his colleagues by suggesting some of the process by which the creative spirit in creatures and the Spirit of the Creator interact. The language of religion and the language of science can, thus, become more open to each other as they interact to know more about the illusive use of religious language in childhood.

Original Source:

Berryman, J.W. 1988. "The illusive use of religious language in childhood", in *Kasvatus ju Uskonto*, edited by M. Pyysiainen. Helsinki, Finland: Werner Soderstrom Osakeyhtio.

6

Silence is Stranger than it Used To Be[74]

Introduction

Silence is stranger than it used to be,[75] but it still has deep religious roots. The *Encyclopedia of Religion* calls silence "one of the essential elements in all religions," and the *New Catholic Encyclopedia* adds: "Silence is a familiar phenomenon in the history of religion and is employed in both private and public worship." Religious educators should, therefore, take more responsibility for its teaching in their daily tasks.

To explore the strangeness of silence and its role in religious education, I will begin by saying why silence is stranger than it used to be. I will then discuss three levels of "referencing," as described by Terrence Deacon, to explain how postmodern communication has been severed from its roots in silence.

Third, I will acknowledge and reflect on the relentless ambiguity of the cluster of words – *silence, quiet,* and *still* – by which we refer to the experience and fact of silence. This ambiguity further demonstrates why the teaching of silence must show what silence is, rather than speaking about it.

To "show" silence, teachers need what Paul Ricoeur called a "second naivete." Howard Gardner's concept of aesthetic development and James Fowler's faith-development theory will help elaborate this point. I will then link silence with the creation of existential meaning.

Meaning is more than verbal coherence. It also includes an

awareness of presence. Presence reveals itself generously in silence, whether the relationship is with God, others, the deep self, or nature.

The capital-T truth is known first in the silence of ontological appreciation and only later in words. We are too often blinded by "logo-centrism" in the West, as Jacques Derrida has warned. We too often begin with words and end with words. The antidote to this is silence.

I will conclude by suggesting the importance of silence in one of the daily tasks of a religious educator: the telling of sacred stories.

The strangeness of silence

We often think of silence as the lack of sound, movement, or communication. In nature we say there is silence when the forest is still or the lake is calm. The forest or lake, however, does not disappear because it is still. We can still know what is present if we can be silent and receive it.

Silence is present as an opening and as a waiting for knowledge. Human silence is also present when there is nothing to say, as well as when there is too much to say.

Some people are silent because they are physically unable to speak or because they have been forced not to speak. This does not mean that we cannot know them. We can know them well if we approach their silence with our silence.

Today such silence is in danger of disappearing as a way of knowing. It is being "silenced" in at least four ways:

1. The presence communicated by silence is considered to be a "text" for deconstruction, a focal point for endless interpretation, whether the silence is in nature, among people, with God, or within one's deepest self.
2. Everyone is paying attention to something else. Some can only "focus" if there is opposing noise on which to concentrate.

Others focus on being unfocused. They are tuned in and turned on to multiple channels. Sound is reversing its ground. It is becoming the symbol of nonpresence, noncommunication, and nonmeaning. Postmodern "silence" is noisy!
3. The postmodern grand narrative undermines the ability to be aware of silence. It is as totalitarian as any other grand narrative, but does not prohibit silence by the power of legislation, argument, or threat. It works more subtly, by an unrelenting analysis of silence.
4. Today's evaporation of silence has disrupted the creative process, the crowning achievement of *Homo sapiens*. There is little brooding silence left in which to scan our inner and outer worlds for new ways of being and communicating.

Each of the four modes of silence suppression raises questions about our capacity for referencing what is real. Let us therefore ask first how homo sapiens do their referencing. This will help us better understand nonverbal communication, and enable us to show why silence is necessary for human beings to create meaning adequate for living and dying.

Silence and the levels of referencing

The disenchantment and mathematization of nature that began in the seventeenth century has shifted in our time to an appreciation for what is elusive and indeterminate. This perspective and the development of new technologies have brought about vast changes in science. The cognitive revolution, which is part of this change, has been described in Howard Gardner's *The Mind's New Science* (1985).

New ways of thinking and the use of new technologies to explore the mind and brain have sharpened the discussion about how human beings make references. I will use Terrence Deacon's theory about the coevolution of language and the brain to explore this idea.

Deacon identified three levels of referencing (1997, 69-101) and used the terminology of C.S. Peirce to name them. He also borrowed

Peirce's idea that referencing is not an invariant relationship with the world but an ongoing interpretation of that relationship. The three kinds of referencing are *iconic, indexical,* and *symbolic.*

To illustrate *iconic* referencing, let us suppose that a moth, whose wings resemble the graininess and color of a particular tree's bark, is at rest. The moth, depending on the interpretation of a bird looking for food, is like or unlike the bark of the tree. If the moth moves, but the bird is inattentive and does not notice the difference between the moth and the bark, then the bird's iconic interpretation of sameness remains, and the meal is missed. An iconic relationship, therefore, is one we notice as likeness (moth-to-bark, portrait-to-person).

The second kind of relationship is an *indexical* relationship, which exists when we interpret the experience of something, such as smoke, as indicative of something else, like fire. Suppose a small, furry, black-and-white creature – a skunk – crosses our field of vision. The sighting stimulates the memory of a very disagreeable odor. Wishing to avoid the stench, we avoid the skunk.

The third kind of relationship, *symbolic,* is what makes us the "symbolic species." Language is a collection of social conventions called symbols. Either a tacit or explicit cultural code establishes the relationship between a symbol and what it represents, such as a wedding ring that symbolizes a marital agreement. As I have said, no particular object is intrinsically an icon, index, or symbol, but is interpreted in that way. In the case of symbolic referencing, the token of the relationship is a sound or mark that suggests nothing about the relationship until social convention establishes the connection.

Deacon argues that language did not supersede or replace the two other forms of referencing. Language evolved in parallel, and depends on the other two forms of reference to create meaning. For example, innate calls and gesture systems, such as those available to primates, still exist in humans, along with an ability to use symbolic language.

Innate calls and gestures, however, involve different regions of the brain from those that control speech production and language comprehension. This explains physiologically why it is impossible to translate smiles, grimaces, laughs, sobs, hugs, kisses – and all "panhuman nonlinguistic communications" – into words. They are part of a communication system, which is unlike although parallel to symbolic referencing.

The three referencing levels are also related hierarchically. Symbolic relationships are composed of indexical relationships among sets of indices. Indexical relationships are composed of iconic relationships among sets of icons. To construct an interpretation which is symbolic, a person must build from lower-order forms and replace or represent them by higher-order forms.

The dependence of symbolic referencing on indexical and iconic referencing helps explain what is meant by the phrase, "There is silence in the saying." The silence of nonverbal communication provides the context and ground for what we have to say. Without nonverbal communication words lose experiential richness and depth.

Crossing the threshold into symbolic referencing takes both learning and unlearning; symbols are not learned one at a time. A logically complete system of relationships among symbol tokens must be learned before the symbolic association between a symbol token and its object can be determined. As Deacon says, "It's hard to get started."

The shift that takes place when crossing the symbolic threshold is the result of having built prior associations of indexical experiences, which in turn were built from iconic distinctions. Over time, tokens of indexical references are built up, until suddenly the implicit pattern in the indexical associations is recognized. No one can do this for us. It must be discovered personally (Deacon 1997, 93).

The "discovery" that Deacon identifies, it seems to me, can be described as an application of the creative process, usually associated only with discoveries in language. In this case the creative process moves a person from one kind of referencing to another.

Symbolic referencing takes place the moment we let go of one associative strategy and "grab hold of another higher-order one to guide our memory searches." This is the moment in the creative process, I would suggest, when nonverbal and often-unconscious scanning forms an insight that can then be put into words.

We might call the use of the creative process to develop a new level of reference a *vertical use*. A *horizontal use* involves making discoveries through use of a single level, although creating in upper referencing levels is also rooted in those below.

In this learning-unlearning process we are at times in danger of unlearning better than we learn. This is dramatically illustrated by Williams syndrome (WS). WS is represented in highly verbal individuals who seem adept at storytelling and in reciting verbal information, but who also exhibit major cognitive deficits in analyzing thematic-level language processes. They also have poor problem-solving abilities and impaired spatial reasoning.

Although children with WS may have IQ scores in the range of 50, their vocabulary and speaking skills at early ages may test above normal. Despite this mix of abilities and disabilities they are intensely social and gregarious and display a "constant wide grin" (Deacon 1997, 268). WS children are like people who memorize entries from a dictionary or encyclopedia but who have never had the experiences to which the words they memorized refer. The words they use are not rooted in indexical or iconic referencing experiences.

WS is a case in which indexical learning abilities are poorer than normal. As Deacon argued, "Discovering an alternative mnemonic strategy to hold together a weak network of indexical associations may lead them to rely more heavily on higher-order combinatorial patterns than do normal children. But lacking indexical support, they are far more trapped by word-association logic alone" (1997, 271). In my terms, they are trapped in words about words. Their speech is not enriched by the silence of the nonverbal iconic and indexical referencing.

Language cannot "make sense," then, without the involvement of our senses. Our speech must be enriched by silence to carry adequate meaning.

Why? Let us take as an example the words we use for the experience of silence. What is unsatisfactory about them? To answer this question our focus must shift directly to the tokens of symbolic reference themselves. They are the words *silence, quiet,* and *still.*

The ambiguity of language about silence

No single term seems to exhaust the meaning of "silence." In German, for example, the word for "quiet" is *die Ruhe* or *die Stille*. The word for "still" is *die Stille*. The word for "silence" is *das Schweigen* (or *die Ruhe* or *die Stille)*. This complex of stillness, quiet, and silence is interlocked in many languages, including English.

The *Oxford English Dictionary* states that *still* comes to us from Germany, Friesland, Norway, and Denmark, but that *quiet* and *silence* entered the language from Latin. In Latin *quietus* means to be at rest or quiet. The verb *quiescere* means to come to rest. *Tranquillus* means "still," and *silentium* means "silence."

The verb *to still,* however, adds the connotation of motion to what the noun and adjective signify. There is also an added emotional association, for the *OED* associates *to still* with calming, relieving, keeping back, pacifying, lulling, soothing, and inducing one to cease from weeping, or, as the *OED* elegantly states, "to check the turbulence of a person."

When examining the verb *to silence,* we find the sense of causing or compelling one to cease speaking, or to overcome another in argument. It is also used as a military term to indicate a cease-fire, or disabling an enemy's cannon by superior fire.

The imperative use of these words is also interesting. The command "Silence!" shuts down public sound. "Quiet!" calls for an absence of disturbance or tumult, but it is not merely other-directed. Reaching this more peaceful condition requires inner activity. Finally, the construction "be still" is not as forceful as a single-word command, and refers to motion as well as sound.

Further ambiguity results when *still* is used as an adverb, because the word also means "in addition to" or "in further degree," as in the phrase "still alive." The word also is used to indicate a contrary sense, such as in the phrase "different and yet still alike." These meanings, suggesting duration, add the quality of time to what we find in the noun and adjectival forms, while also reinforcing the link between being still and in motion.

As said above, much of the interpretation of symbolic speech is determined by parallel systems of nonverbal communication. In the case of silence this can be shown by the following:

Stillness
(as movement)

Quiet   **Silence**
(as inner motivation   (as outer motivation
or cause)   or cause)

Stillness
(as sound)

Silence compelled from the outside sits to the far right on the horizontal quiet-silence axis. If generated from within silence is located toward the left. The range of meaning encompassing the stilling of the body to quiet the mind, or the quieting of the mind to still the body, is shown on the vertical stillness axis.

Two forces in combination, such as stillness-as-sound and motivation-from-within, can be located in the lower-left quadrant. Where the meaning should be positioned depends on the relative strength of the two forces.

To take another example, silence as the result of a physical inability to utter sound is caused by something "outside" one's will. This combination of vectors will appear in the lower right-hand quadrant, because it involves two forces, stillness-as-sound and silence-imposed from-the-"outside."

Much of what we experience as silence is communicated at the levels of iconic and indexical referencing, as illustrated by the above graph. This is why our symbolic tokens referring to silence are so confusing. Borrowing a couplet from Robert Frost, we might paraphrase:

Our words dance around in a ring and suppose
while silence sits in the middle and knows.

Ideally, this section should have produced a neat definition of *silence,* with no verbal remainder. As you can see, however, this task has proven impossible. What I have done instead is to construct a rough graph showing modes and vectors of the connotations in meaning.

What follows from this ironic, not iron, logic of language is that when it comes to teaching silence, who is communicating is more important that what is said. This is because much of the verbal meaning of silence is carried by nonverbal connotation read parallel to the symbolic referencing.

The second naivete, and showing silence

How can we show the "is-ness" of silence, since symbolic referencing does not clearly convey its meaning? Someone needs to show us, but who? It might be another adult, but nature often uses an intergenerational approach: children show adults and adults show children.

When adults and children are segregated or silence is not identified or valued in their relationships, then the mutual learning between children and adults breaks down, as it often does in our culture. Adults need to model the correct approach to other adults, so they can model it to children and support their valuing, identification, naming, and use of silence.

In *Godly Play* (Berryman 1995) I discussed the two great gates into our humanity. They were the gate of relationships, discovered in infancy, and the gate of language, which is passed through around our second year. There is a third and related gate. It is the doorway into the second naiveté, at which point we regain sensitivity to the kinds of knowing we had before language. People who have passed through this gate, I would like to suggest, are especially qualified for teaching silence.

The term "second naivete" was coined by Paul Ricoeur (1967) and used by James Fowler to define his fifth stage, conjunctive faith (1981,187-88). Fowler found that this stage occurred late in adulthood; however, most of us have moments of such knowing much earlier. These isolated experiences are not pervasive enough to be called a "stage," that is, a global way of interpreting the world.

Ricoeur became interested in the second naivete because of his interest in interpretation. As he said, "Whenever a man dreams or raves, another man arises to give an interpretation" (1967, 350). We live in a sea of interpretation in which, as Ricoeur said, "Symbols give rise to thought."

If a symbol is to give rise to thought one must enter into the symbol and believe in it. During life's early years we have a natural ability to dwell in symbols and to believe in them. Later, critical reasoning takes over, and the first naiveté evaporates. At the time of the second naivete, however, one enters by conscious choice into the circle of believing to know and knowing to believe.

Some have argued that Ricoeur's idea is a vicious circle, empty of meaning, but Ricoeur has called it "a living and stimulating circle." Ricoeur continues: "[T]he second immediacy that we seek and the second naivete that we await are no longer accessible to us anywhere else than in a hermeneutics; we can believe only by interpreting. It is the 'modern' mode of belief in symbols, an expression of the distress of modernity and a remedy for that distress" (1967, 352). It is by entering this circle that the tools of interpretation, which modernity gave us, can help us "transcend" modernity. "The second naivete aims to be the postcritical equivalent of the precritical hierophany" (352).

I would like to add that children are naive only from an adult perspective. As children, they are open and able to participate deeply in the world around them, to connect with the world and to know it personally. As adults we learn how to be critical and to distance ourselves from the world to get perspective. The second naïveté is not a return to childhood. It is a choice to be open and to participate in the world, at appropriate times, in a childlike way, so that we can give symbols adequate interpretation.

Adults who act like children, unconsciously or consciously, are childish. They fool no one except, perhaps, themselves. The second naiveté is something else. It is the reawakening of what Edward Robinson called the "original vision" (1977). To pass through this gate may require a shock: a profound loss, the experience of stunning beauty, the arrival of grandchildren. One's cognitive and developmental situation is overwhelmed. Distance dissolves. The urge to control softens. Intimacy and synthesis, rather than analysis and distance, come to be preferred.

Fowler refers to this experience as a way of knowing that moves beyond the dichotomizing logic of either-or and that sees all sides simultaneously. He writes: "Conjunctive faith suspects that things are organically related to each other; it attends to the pattern of interrelatedness in things, trying to avoid force-fitting to its own prior mindset" (1981, 185). The tools of the previous stage are no longer trusted except as "tools to avoid self-deception and to order truths encountered in other ways" (188).

The second naivete is a return to valuing the body-knowing of the child rather than words about relationships or words about words about relationships. The need to achieve symbolic coherence dissipates, and words lose their linking power in favor of unspoken connections with life. The value of iconic and indexical knowing is reevaluated and once again given credibility.

In the realm beyond the third gate our relationships count for more than words. At this "place" in life, one knows that this is true, but people who know do not need to speak about it. (As children, we could not speak about it and had no other way of knowing to compare it to.) Silence as a way of knowing and being steps into the foreground; symbolic referencing steps back.

Here is an example. In the summer of 1998 my mother was diagnosed with cancer. There was no longer a possibility of medical help. Mom said to me quietly on the back porch, "There is really nothing more to say, is there?" When people entered a room where she sat, she would get up, frail as she was, and move toward them, usually in silence, to receive a hug, and then return quietly to her chair.

This process continued when she went to the family cabin in Colorado a few days later. By this time her children and their spouses, grandchildren, and three great-grandchildren had arrived to be with her. She tired easily, so she often moved into the back bedroom to rest. One evening, a few days before she died, her six-year-old great-granddaughter kept going silently in and out of the bedroom, bringing flowers she had picked on the mountainside and carefully arranged into bouquets. The two one-year-old twins also kept coming back to see her, one in the early stages of exuberant walking and the other still crawling. Mom said, "I just love to hear their voices." They, as yet, had no words, but their sounds and movement, their presence, carried them close to her and her close to them.

Such vectors and modes of being are not symbolic language, yet this kind of knowing and communication is profound. It is this kind of knowing that we regain when we pass through the third great gate and enter the second naivete. Nothing can overwhelm such knowing at this stage. It is too well-tested, too real, too connected.

Such knowing also refreshes creative energies, because much of the work of the imagination takes place in silence. Given the loss of silence, some postmodern thinkers have foretold the demise of the imagination in our species. These statements lead to the realization that the loss of silence and the demise of the imagination are connected, and that both have a bearing on our future.

Silence and the imagination

An ability to know in silence and to communicate silently enables appreciation of the silent aspects of the creative process in other living creatures. This is what I think Richard Kearney means by the "ethics of the imagination" referred to in the conclusion of his book, *The Wake of Imagination* (1988). In this postmodern age of words about words, it is a matter of ethical importance to slow down, to listen until we hear, and to respect the silence in other people, in our own deep self, in nature, and in God.

The ethics of the imagination is a matter of respect for "the other," but it is also an ethic of emergency. The ability to hear silence may be dying out. If that happens, then the imagination will disintegrate. It is true that what humans do with our imagination often endangers the world, but without it we lack even the possibility of coping with destructive tendencies.

Hearing silence, then, is of broader importance than passing on the tradition of silence through religious education. It is also a way for religious traditions to take the lead in helping to heal our hearing, so humans can know silence and its value for communication and meaning. Religious language often functions to maintain the status quo, but when it comes to silence we are running out of time. It is time for religious educators to lead the way back to the roots of our words and creativity. Both are deeply grounded in the nonverbal stuff of life.

I have already suggested that silent knowing and the creative process are grounded in the modes and vectors of our earliest knowing. It is now time to fill out that statement in greater detail. I will follow primarily the work of Howard Gardner. In Gardner's first book, *The Arts and Human Development* ([1973] 1994), he traced three themes in aesthetic development: *perception, emotion,* and *making.* Awareness of these themes is important, because, as Gardner writes, the arts "lie in a middle ground between mundane experience, from which it is difficult to maintain one's distance, and scientific practice, which generally avoids subjective qualities" ([1973] 1994, 35).

Gardner's view of modes and vectors is at the heart of his work:

> Let me try to flesh out what I am proposing. Initially the modes are limited to a few aspects of bodily functioning – the young infant feels openness or closedness, emptiness or fullness, particularly at the regions of the mouth, but perhaps also throughout his body. Two trends occur during the first year of life. First, he becomes increasingly able to transfer these modal experiences, which occur initially within his body, or in relation to objects in contact with his body, to the perception and making of objects external to himself. Second, he becomes sensitive to subtle nuances within each mode and to a multiplicity of modal and vectoral properties. The modes and vectors become a set of categories that he can bring to bear on the full range of his experience; in addition they come to combine with one another in diverse ways, giving rise to distinct emotions, styles, aesthetic categories, and temperamental strains. A basic set of modes and vectors, founded in bodily experience, interact and coalesce with one another to form a much larger set of general categories through which the child comes to know the world. The child at the threshold of symbol use conceives of the world in significant part as a flux of these different primary and secondary general

properties, which have their origin in his organismic experience and which now pervade his experience of objects and persons. ([1973] 1994, 108)

No appreciation of object permanence is necessary for modal/vector sensitivity, so the modes and vectors are more primitive than objects. Pre-verbal children and artists have a heightened sensitivity to this aspect of knowing and communication. Sometimes this "heightened sensitivity," it seems, returns to those who are not artists when they enter the second naiveté. In a way, we all become artists at that time, and our art is life itself.

Some of this sensitivity is always with us. When an object in the world is the focus of our interest, we call that *denotation*. When we meditate on what that object means to us, we shift to the modal/vector aspect of the experience, the *connotation*. The language of everyday is a mixture of connotative and denotative tendencies. In some specialized language domains, such as the language of science, art criticism, and so on, the denotative tendency rules. In art the connotative tendency takes over. The symbolic referencing we do after entering the second naïveté also shows deep appreciation for the connotations of words.

Gardner expanded his study of the making process – the third of three themes discussed in *The Arts and Human Development* – in *Creating Minds: An Anatomy of Creativity Seen through the Lives of Freud, Einstein, Picasso, Stravinsky, Eliot, Graham, and Gandhi* (1993). An individual's second naivete, it seems, will follow a natural preference for one of Gardner's seven ways of knowing and the style of creativity that each entails.

Gardner notes that creative breakthroughs are more likely to take place when the creator is surrounded by people with whom he or she is comfortable. The creative process apparently shuts down when people feel unsafe. A creator also must deal with what Gardner called a "Faustian bargain," the decision to preserve his or her unusual gifts at the cost of a well-rounded personal existence. Unless the bargain is compulsively adhered to the talent may be compromised, or even lost.

Given these discoveries, we can predict that it is easier to enter the second naivete when there are people around us who support this way of looking at the world. Second, some people move through the gate earlier than others, because they are no longer interested in what society may consider a "well-rounded personal existence." The creativity it takes to enter the third great gate cannot be overestimated. It requires a huge shift in the way meaning is made. In some sense the shift carries people beyond modern and postmodern points of view into a more timeless and less culture-bound realm.

Kearney writes that there is an ethical summons "lodged at the very heart of our postmodern culture," a "poetic summons" to see that "imagination continues to playfully create and re-create even at the moment it is announcing its own disappearance" (1988, 397). The imagination is nourished by silence, and in the early stages of the creative process works mostly in silence. This is where iconic and indexical referencing thrive, giving flower to insights later coded into symbolic referencing.

If a discovery has been nourished by silence it will remain informed by and inform our modes of being and vectors of movement. It is, after all, in the silence of the brain's right hemisphere that we orient ourselves in space and time. When creativity takes place only at the level of symbolic referencing, as in the extreme example of Williams syndrome, then referencing is severed from body-knowing. The disembodied words seem superficial and remain mostly irrelevant to the fundamental issues of existence such as aloneness, freedom, death, and the need for meaning.

It is not enough, then, to make a rational compromise between the modern search for certainty and the perpetual suspicion of postmodernism. A balancing act or wager is not enough. What needs to be done is to help people pass through the third great gate, and to enter their second naiveté. This is so they can engage in silent knowing and show its value to others, especially the young. Children need to be around people who know what W.B. Yeats discovered late in life and wrote about in his last letter:

> I am happy and I think full of an energy, of an energy I had despaired of. It seems to me that I have found what I wanted. When I try to put all into a phrase I say, "Man can embody truth but he cannot know it." I must embody it in the completion of my life. The abstract is not life and everywhere draws out its contradictions. You can refute Hegel but not the Saint or the Song of Sixpence.

This brings me to a conclusion: Silence is necessary for human beings to communicate and create existential meaning. Religious education must, therefore, be deeply concerned about what it shows about silence. To conclude I will apply what has been discovered to the daily task of telling sacred stories.

A concluding application of silence

I was relieved to discover that when Gabriel Marcel first read Max Picard's classic, *The World of Silence,* he was "disconcerted" (Picard [1948] 1988, 9). Marcel had trouble thinking about silence as something positive rather than as the lack of something. I had the same reaction, but am now ready to say that silence is not only positive but necessary for human beings if they are to find meaning and to be creative. Picard, too, went further than calling silence positive. He called it "an autonomous phenomenon," which is positive, even creative, and wrote that it belongs to the "basic structure of man" ([1948] 1988, 15).

Religious educators have many tasks in which to show silence, but a primary task is the telling of the sacred stories of their tradition.

These narratives invite people to become acquainted with silence so they can approach The Silence, the Source of life. The great narrative of the Christian people, for example, needs to be told in a way that is soaked in silence. The storyteller needs to disappear so as not to distract the participating listener from the depth of the stories, which is physically present in the modes and vectors in which the words are rooted. Such meaning is bound neither by space or time.

At the silent level of modes and vectors Christianity is about moving toward and away from, about wholeness and breaking, about being empty and full. Those who enter the Christian story pass through religious language into the nonverbal. It is only in the silence of presence beyond the language that one can build an interpretation of adequate depth and usefulness for one's life and death.

Storytellers also need to trust their own silence to receive and absorb the noise of those trying to learn, or trying to avoid learning, how to enter the story. If we cannot take in and defuse such noise, listeners will not be able to learn how to hear the silence. This shows those who are distracted and distracting that they are missing something powerful and tangible.

The story's depth is the connotation that connects the words with iconic and indexical referencing. This depth is intuited because it is true nonverbally, although we are accustomed to trying to verify it verbally. God is known first and most directly in the silence of the iconic and indexical referencing.

Teaching silence, then, is a game of high stakes, but the answer to the question of how to teach it is simple. We must show it. This is because there is much more to words than more words. Words, in fact, can become like "so much straw," as Saint Thomas said at the end of his life after a profound, nonverbal experience of convergence in the Mass.

References

Anderson, W.T. 1990. *Reality Isn't What It Used To Be.* New York: Harper San Francisco.

Berryman, J.W. 1995. *Godly Play: An Imaginative Approach to Religious Education.* Minneapolis: Augsburg.

Deacon, T.W. 1997. *The Symbolic Species: The Co-evolution of Language and the Brain.* New York: W.W. Norton.

Fowler, J.W. 1981. *Stages of Faith: The Psychology of Human Development and the Quest for Meaning.* San Francisco: Harper and Row.

Gardner, H. 1985. *The Mind's New Science: A History of the Cognitive Revolution.* New York: Basic Books.

_____ 1993. *Creating Minds: An Anatomy of Creativity Seen Through the Lives of Freud, Einstein, Picasso, Stravinsky, Eliot, Graham, and Gandhi.* New York: Basic Books.

_____ [1973] 1994. *The Arts and Human Development.* New York: Basic Books.

Kearney, R. 1988. *The Wake of the Imagination.* Minneapolis: University of Minnesota Press.

Picard, M. [1948] 1988. *The World of Silence.* Washington, D.C.: Regnery Gateway.

Ricoeur, P. 1967. *The Symbolism of Evil.* Boston: Beacon Press.

Robinson, E. 1977. *The Original Vision: A Study of the Religious Experience of Childhood.* Oxford: Religious Experience Research Unit, Manchester College.

Original source:

Berryman, J.W. 1999. "Silence is stranger than it used to be: Teaching silence and the future of humankind." ***Religious Education,*** **94 (3): 257-272.**

Part Three

Children, Spirituality and Religious Education

Preface to Part Three

For Berryman, the purpose of religious education is to enable both children and adults to create and find meaning in their lives by using religious language to confront and cope with existential issues and limits so as to know intimately the Creator. The means through which this is achieved is play – play with the deep self, with others, with nature and with God. This also represents Berryman's understanding of spirituality. The confronting of issues at the edges of knowing and being – death, the threat of freedom, aloneness, and the need for meaning – and the relationship one has with the deep self, with others, with nature and with God accords with the scholarly literature's understanding of what spirituality entails. All people are spiritual. While spirituality can be located outside of a religious tradition (that is, one does not have to belong to or practise a religious tradition to be spiritual), for Berryman, the acquisition of religious language provides a common language for a community to speak about and explore existential issues, and to enter into relationship with others and the Creator.

Children are especially spiritual. They already have a relationship with their deep selves, with others, with nature and with God. They live at the edges of knowing and being, and so have a deep concern for the existential limits to their own lives. However, their spirituality is largely nonverbal. What they do not have is a language to express their relationship with the Creator, or to speak about and confront the edges of knowing. The purpose of religious education is to support the child in the acquisition of such a language.

Each of the contributions in Part Three serves to develop Berryman's understanding of the spirituality of the child, and how this may be nurtured in religious education. In the first contribution

Berryman draws on a simplification of the epistemology of Richard of St. Victor to distinguish the knowing of the spirit by contemplation from the knowing of the body by the senses and the knowing of the mind by reason in order to indicate the primary kind of knowing that makes religious education unique.

People may recognise spirituality when they encounter it, Berryman argues, but cannot define it because it is primarily a part of humankind's non-verbal communication system. In the second contribution, Berryman clarifies the difference between verbal and non-verbal communication in terms of "referencing". He then proceeds to describe and apply the mode-and-vector method to various non-verbals calls that humans use to express spirituality. The modes-and-vector method also highlights the negative aspects of spirituality – the dark side, which Berryman also explores. Some fundamental conclusions about spirituality and religious language are then drawn.

7

Spirituality, Religious Education, and the Dormouse

Introduction

Spirituality usually refers to what animates or makes us vital. It is about consciousness, as distinguished from the purely physical. Often spirituality is considered to be a universal characteristic of human beings. The distinction between spirituality and religion for this discussion is that spirituality is treated as a general potential. When it is expressed in a tradition of language, practice, morality, and by a group of people of any size to support and evaluate it efficacy, then, it becomes actual and specific. Spirituality becomes religion.

This author's references to religion will be to the Christian Tradition which he knows best. It is true that at times, Christians, as other traditions, have stunted and distorted children's spirituality by religious education. This, however, is neither logically nor empirically necessary and this author has spent most of his life trying to understand why that happens and how to teach in a way that helps open children's spirituality to expansion and deepening through religion – all their lives long (Berryman, 1991).

Sometimes the meaning of spirituality is reduced to what makes someone alive instead of dead. Anyone who has been present at the death of another human being knows what a powerful distinction that is. The focus here, however, is on the meaning of spirituality which is concerned with the quality of one's life while the body is still functioning.

The discussion that follows explores the connection between spirituality and religious education, because it is this connection which makes religious education unique. This is because spiritual knowing by contemplation is so different from the knowing of the body by the senses or the knowing of the mind by reason which we are more accustomed to using. When these three kinds of knowing become confused in the actual practice of religious education children can get lost and lose their motivation to find out what kind of knowing is appropriate for spiritual matters. They get lost like Alice did when she went beyond the looking glass. Suddenly, Alice saw the Cheshire Cat sitting in a tree. It kept grinning, but it also had long claws. Finally, she got up the courage to ask the Cat a question:

> "Would you tell me, please, which way I ought to go from here?"
> "That depends a good deal on where you want to get to," said the Cat.
> "I don't much care where ..." said Alice.
> "Then it doesn't matter which way you go," said the cat.
> (Carroll, 1960: 87-88).

If religion teachers are to be good guides they need to know the territory and how to use good maps, but they also need to know how to help children make the journey and that involves the knowing of the spirit by contemplation. This is as important for religion as knowing and using the right method is for science education.

Showing which way to go

To distinguish the knowing of the body, mind, and spirit for a more adequate understanding of religious education, we need to return to a time when clarity about this was given a much higher priority than it is today. In the twelfth century both monastic and scholastic theology attracted the great minds of the age, and the two approaches were still in conversation to complement each other's strengths and weaknesses.

Jean Leclercq used the friendship between Peter Lombard, master of the Sentences, and St. Bernard, abbot of Clairvaux, as exemplars of this mutual understanding and complementarity (Leclercq, 1982: 3).

The schools were in the cities and the monasteries were in the country. On the boundary between these two locations and approaches to theology were the monks of St. Victor, who lived at the gates of Paris. They were a cloistered group under the Rule St. Augustine. They practised contemplation, did works of charity, and yet maintained a vigorous intellectual life in the disputations of the Paris schools.

Richard of St. Victor (d. 1173) expanded the work of an earlier master, Hugh of St. Victor, who died in 1133. It was Hugh who said: "Learn everything: you will see afterwards that nothing is superfluous and that there is no joy in a knowledge that is cramped and narrow" (Vandenbrouke,1982: 230). Hugh and Richard argued that induction and deduction were important kinds of knowing, but that spiritual truth only could be reached by contemplation.

In Paris during the next century Bonaventure wrote *Itinerarium mentis ad Deum*. It was greatly influenced by Richard, whom Bonaventure called the "modern" master. The *Itinerarium* helped form the spirituality of Bonaventure's brother Franciscans who provide us with a living link to the masters of St. Victor apart from their few writings that have been left to us.

The emphasis of our century has been on the masterly use of science to explore the material and mental world, but Richard was a master of the experience of God as well as the science of his age. This enabled him to clarify and integrate three distinct kinds or contexts or ways for knowing: knowledge of the material world by the senses, knowledge of the mind by using reason, and knowledge of the spirit by contemplation.

It is contemplation that gives the appropriate context for both mind-knowing and body-knowing. Richard wrote: "Contemplation is the free, more penetrating gaze of a mind, suspended with wonder concerning manifestations of wisdom" (Richard of St. Victor, 1979: 157). The spontaneous, penetrating gaze, the suspension with wonder, and the focus on God's presence are what still distinguish this act today.

The act of contemplation does not exclude the knowing of children, because, as Piaget has shown, young children do not yet have the ability to put their experience "on hold" mentally for analysis, much less to think about their own thinking. Thus, it seems to me, also following Maria Montessori (1967) that they cannot help but absorb the world about them naturally by contemplation.

Children, really then, have no choice about "connecting" with life by their spiritual knowing through contemplation, but this kind of knowing can be lost, especially when they arrive at school, where the values the body and the mind are most appreciated. We cannot give children spirituality, but we can take it away.

Adults often have to consciously choose to learn again how to do what they did as children spontaneously. We seek what Paul Ricoeur has called a "second naivete", something Wordsworth and others have despaired of ever finding.

Richard's three "levels" might also be thought of as three potentials. When the potentials are stimulated they develop three different logical types for communicating with ourselves, others, nature, and God. Our body-knowing and our spirit-knowing develop first. The potential for knowing by the mind also is present from birth, but it needs language to flower. When the mind develops it attempts to conceptualize what we know by the senses and contemplation, as we are doing now. This kind of knowing is powerful, but it can also distort our appreciation for body-knowing and block the knowing of the spirit.

When the knowing of the spirit by contemplation is overlooked by our child-rearing and educational practices the spiritual potential is not acknowledged and nourished. We put human beings at risk. Existential limits tend to be avoided rather than embraced as part of our identity. This diverts energy from all three kinds of knowing in an impossible attempt to ignore our existential environment, especially our mortality.

The larger and more differentiated view of knowing which Richard described gives us a way to keep clear where we are going with our religious education. This standpoint can help us avoid making a category mistake.

A category mistake?

After seeing the Cheshire Cat Alice went to the Mad Hatter's Tea-Party, where the sleepy Dormouse finally began to tell his story about three girls who lived at the bottom of a treacle-well. They were learning "to draw":

> "But I don't understand. Where did they draw the treacle from?"
> "You can draw water out of a water-well," said the Hatter; "so I should think you could draw treacle out of a treacle-well – eh, stupid?" "But they were in the well," Alice said to the Dormouse, not choosing to notice this last remark.
> (Carroll: 102).

Alice had identified a category mistake in the Dormouse's discourse. Russell and Whitehead examined this also in their *Principia Mathematica*. (Whitehead and Russell, 1910-1913) The objects in a class (chairs 1, 2, 3, and 4) are of a different logical type than the class itself (the class of all chairs). We can't "draw" spiritual knowing from the well of the body or mind if we are stuck deeply in those kinds of knowing.

The spiritual context can be intuited implicitly by the senses and the mind, but those logical types are not useful to know explicitly what the spirit knows by contemplation. For example, in *Either/Or*

Kierkegaard (1944) argued from his own existential experience that one can move from the aesthetic life to the moral realm by reason, but to move from the realm of the moral to that of faith takes a "leap". It is beyond reason, as knowing is conceived of before one leaps. After one leaps and lands then a new perspective on the kinds of knowing is established.

After breaking with the world, as Kierkegaard might say, one is returned to the world, although the person of faith is outwardly indistinguishable from others. What is different is that inwardly the ability has been developed to combine the sublime and the mundane, the unconditional and the relative, without making a category mistake.

If we approach the teaching of religion from a point of view that is the wrong logical type, the result will be confusion at best and at worst children will dismiss the knowing of the spirit by contemplation because it does not work. It does not work, because it is assumed it can't work and there is no permission to try to discover whether it works or not. A category mistake also can lead to confusion about what kind of evidence is appropriate to determine the success of our teaching and to develop the foundational theory which helps us to understand our teaching better.

For example, psychology has a tendency to reduce the spiritual to pathology. Religion is not rational from the point of view of the mind using reason. Religion is trimmed by that logical type to become an illusion, a projection, an hallucination, or some other reduction of the spiritual to the reasonable or the biological.

There are exceptions. In the second act of T.S. Eliot's *The Cocktail Party* Celia says: "... I want to be cured/ Of a craving for something I cannot find/ And the shame of never finding it/ Can you cure me?" (Eliot, 1952: 363-365).

The unusual psychiatrist, Reilly, responds by saying that the condition is curable, but one must choose between being reconciled to the human condition or something more. Celia says that adjustment to the normal leaves her cold. It does not satisfy her craving.

Reilly then told her about the other way: "The destination cannot be described;/ You will know very little until you get there;/ You will journey blind. But the way leads towards possession/ Of what you have sought for in the wrong place."

Another example of a category mistake is the use of physics to validate the spiritual. The fact that physics is no longer conceptualized as being about solid matter does not change the kind of knowing used to understand the "material" world. The elegant mathematics of physics remains quite different in purpose and method from spiritual knowing by contemplation, although the contemplation of God in nature by the spirit may stimulate one to know more about nature by the means of physics and indirectly more about the complexity of nature's Creator.

Knowing God has its own logic, but it is like trying to picture day and night at the same time. The non-dual reality of the spiritual realm cannot be understood by making distinctions. It is known by a logic of bringing-together. It is about presence in relationship and not concepts. It keeps focused in the present and is silent.

The spiritual realm is beyond reason, but it is not incoherent. The same general pattern for knowing is used for all three levels. The core of this pattern is the creative process (Berryman, 1991: 110-135) - whether we seek to know the moon by our senses, the meaning of *Don Quixote* by our reason, or the experience of the presence of God by contemplation.

The result of spirit knowing by contemplation is complicated to express. Distance from the experience is needed and a shift takes place from the present tense to the past tense for such communication to be possible. The memory, Richard tells us, is like remembering through a veil or through the middle of a cloud so that "...we do not remember, and not remembering, we remember" (306). Still, we know what we know.

This brings us back to the problem of the category mistake. When reason attempts to conceptualize the spiritual reality it generates contradictions such as God being a "coincidence of opposites" as Nicholas of Cusa suggested, a God-Man as Christine doctrine tells us, or praying that we be "... made one body with him, that he may dwell in us, and we in him" (*The Episcopal Church*, 1979: 336). One must live through such paradoxes of the mind to enter the spirit's unitive kind of knowing.

Living through logical paradox by presence

When I was about five years old I was staying with my grandmother. My grandfather was away on business, so I got to sleep in his bed by the wall. My grandmother had arthritis, so when she got into bed she did so with difficulty but grace and I peered out from under the covers to watch this mystery.

She turned out the light. It was dark. High up on the dresser, the clock ticked. I stretched out under the clean sheets and warm covers. My skin tingled with pleasure. I stretched again. Suddenly an enormous door opened up where the wall had been. There was no light, no sound, no movement, no scent coming from within, only the huge opening. It was nothing itself.

I cried out, "I don't want to die," or something like that. I don't know where the words came from, but I do know what happened next.

My grandmother spoke to me. Her words have faded, but I still remember vividly her presence in the dark which put me in touch with a larger presence. The system of relationships, then only faintly differentiated, with God, self, others and nature was restored and helped me to feel at home again. I relaxed and fell asleep.

My Grandmother had shown me a different kind of knowing. It had carried me through the ultimate paradox of life into a larger unity of relationships, at least for a few moments. It was a matter of presence, not concepts.

When Alice went through the silvery mist of the looking-glass she did what adults had taught her to do to find her way. She looked for the principal rivers, mountains, and towns, but she found none. Instead she found a Gnat about the size of a chicken.

> "Crawling at your feet," said the Gnat (Alice drew her feet back in some alarm), "you may observe a bread-and-butter-fly. Its wings are thin slices of bread-and-butter, its body is a crust, and its head is a lump of sugar". "And what does it live on?"
> "Weak tea with cream in it".
> A new difficulty came into Alice's head. "Supposing it couldn't find any?" she suggested.
> "Then it would die, of course."
> "But that must happen very often," Alice remarked thoughtfully.
> "It always happens," said the Gnat.
> (Carroll, 1960: 223).

The Gnat then made a joke about Alice losing her name and then punned how she might "miss" her lessons, then two large tears came rolling down its cheeks and it sighed such melancholy sighs, it sighed itself away, and disappeared.

Nourished or not nourished we die. Humpty Dumpty has had a great fall, and there is no power of body or mind that can put the world back together again in a different way for children or adults. The fundamental paradox of being born to die is what makes our spiritual knowing so important and difficult.

We must be realistic about spiritual knowing. It can take a long time to discover the knowledge it offers. Yeats, for example, struggled all his life with his spirituality. On 22 January 1939, he wrote in his last letter: "... I am happy and I think full of an energy I had despaired of. It seems to me that I have found what I wanted. When I try to put all into a phrase I say 'Man can embody truth but he cannot know it'. I must embody it in the completion of my life. The abstract is not life and everywhere drags out its contradictions. You can refute Hegel but not the Saint or the Song of Sixpence." (Ellmann, 1948: 285) Six days later he was dead.

Presence does not logically refute the lethal questions raised by the limits to our being and knowing. It does not solve life completely like a jigsaw puzzle is solved by fitting all the pieces together with none left over. What a larger presence does is help drain away the toxicity from our existential anxiety so that our boundaries can become a matter of deep identity rather than dreadful threat.

The German poet, Rainer Maria Rilke, was sure that the mind alone cannot help us feel at home in this strange place, so he wrote about what to do in the meantime:

> Be patient towards all that is unsolved in your heart and try to love the questions themselves like locked rooms . . . Do not now seek the answers, that cannot be given you because you would not be able to live them. And the point is, to live everything. Live the questions now.
>
> Perhaps you will then gradually, without noticing it, live along some distant day into the answer.
>
> (Rilke,1986: 34-35).

Edward Robinson followed up on this notion in 1978 with a book called *Living the Questions.* He wrote: "paradoxes that cannot be resolved must be held in suspense, as a note in music may be, suspended to form a temporary discord" (Robinson, 1978:1). It may take another kind of knowing for this resolution to take place.

It is important for religious educators to avoid making a category mistake, because the paradoxes fundamental to religious growth cannot be done away with by the mind or the body. One can only take them in and make them part of life by the spirit. A sense of presence available through spiritual knowing by contemplation is what gives one the means to do that.

Research and the sense of presence

Kenneth E. Hyde's *Religion in Childhood and Adolescence* (1990) covers many themes of research. It includes children's ideas about God, how parental images shape the idea of God, religious beliefs and their development, understanding religious language, studies of religious attitudes, personality and religion, the development of religiousness, surveys of religious beliefs and practices, and other kinds of studies. These are primarily descriptions of people talking about ideas of God and religious practice, but the experience of spiritual knowing itself, that which this thinking and remembering is about, is difficult to study directly, because it is silent and, as we said above, one can present only a kind of hearsay evidence about one's own experience.

One series of studies about religious experience is especially noteworthy, because of its effort to stay close to the words of the people who have had the experience, however faulty their expression of it may be. Sir Alister Hardy invited people who had "felt that their lives had in any way been affected by some power beyond themselves", to write an account of that experience and say what it had meant to them.

First-hand accounts of religious experience began to arrive in Oxford in June of 1969. During the year that followed about 1,000 accounts were received and in one of the resulting studies Timothy Beardsworth began to classify the experiences according to dominating sense used, much as a naturalist might classify different kinds of butterflies. His early classification was published in 1977 in the book, *A Sense of Presence* (Beardsworth, 1977).

This study sacrificed a good bit of cleanness and control to allow the connotative language of the participants' reports to shine through. The value of this rather messy way to work is that the personal metaphors involve what Gardner (1994) calls the modes and vectors of body-knowing, as well as by the knowing of the mind by reason to gesture towards what happened in the silence of the knowing of the spirit by contemplation.

One type of response, described by Beardsworth, was visual. The illumination of one's surroundings, a light or lights, a feeling of unity with one's surroundings, out-of-body-experiences, and the transformation of one's surroundings were described.

A second classification was auditory, such as voices reassuring one or giving commands. A third type was tactile, ranging from a slight touch to a blow that knocks one down. Beardsworth also noted a kind of religious experience reported as "inward sensations", a kind of vibration or feeling like electricity.

The most interesting classification was called a "sense of presence". There were only 113 such cases in the first 1,000 reports. Presence was defined as the sense of a relationship that came before objective perception and sometimes without any objective perception. The experience was like someone was there but no specific sensory evidence could be identified as the cause for the experience.

Beardsworth proposed that this sense of presence was the key to his whole classification system, because it underlies the more specific "sensory" categories. It is what gives such events their significance and arouses a serious response. The sense of presence was *filled out* by the visual, auditory, tactile, and inward sensations, so it was actually the most pervasive category, involving far more than the 114 cases that exclusively identified it.

Children may move away from or towards this presence and the language that identifies, names, and values it. Other children may shrug their shoulders and be agnostic. What is important is that all children have a real choice. Such a free choice is often not allowed, even in religious education. School is usually ruled by the reasoning and science-only fundamentalisms of mind-knowing.

Being fundamental without closing the mind

There may be a general potential for spirituality in all of humankind, but to be actualized and communicated, spirituality needs the language of a specific religious tradition to be communicated. This is because we do not learn any means of communication "in general".

Our "mother tongue" is learned to communicate with our primary caregivers when we are infants. Young children might learn additional languages to speak to others or to use in other settings, but language-learning itself begins with the primary caregivers. We also learn base ten from our culture and then learn other base systems rather than math in general. In music we call random or general sound "noise". Sound becomes music when it is ordered by a tradition such as the music of the East or the West. The same is true of religion.

It does not follow that one must teach the art of using religious communication, such as the communication system of Christianity, in an imperialistic way. When the use of such language is associated with ultimate issues of life and death it connects all of us in the most fundamental way.

When religious language is associated with the creative process as well as the ultimate environment it does not arrest growth or perspective-taking but contributes to both. This avoids creating bigots by our teaching and encourages life-long learning and expansion of one's spirituality.

Teaching the language of the spirit without "spookism"

One of the problems about teaching the knowing of the spirit by contemplation is that one risks falling into a theory of teaching that James Michael Lee has called "sham mystery and eerie spookiness" (1973: 174-180). It obscures rather than describes how to teach and evaluate one's teaching.

To avoid this we will close with an effort to show in contemporary terms what the knowing of the spirit by contemplation is like. We will make analogies to play and to "flow", a term used by Csikszentmihalyi (1990) to describe creativity, to guide our teaching and evaluation.

First, let us look at play. The interest in play by psychologists has been growing in recent decades. During the late 1970s some twenty research-oriented books were published about play. This was more than the total number published in the previous fifty years (Rubin, 1980: vii-viii). This interest has become deeper and broader.

In 1977 the subject of play was included in the Harvard University Press series, *The Developing Child*, edited by Jerome Bruner. The volume about play, called simply *Play,* was written by Katherine Garvey.

Garvey's view of play was that it is "a product and a trace of man's biological heritage and his culture-creating capacity" (1977: 1). She balanced her debt to Huizinga's ideas about play with the advances that science had made since his classic *Homo Ludens* (1955) was published in 1938.

When Garvey described the phenomenon, she summarized five characteristics usually found in theories about play:

1. Play is enjoyable
2. Play has no extrinsic goals. It is played for itself.
3. Play is spontaneous and voluntary. It is freely chosen by the player.
4. Play involves active engagement on the part of the players.
5. Play has certain systematic relations to what is not play. For example, play has been linked with creativity, problem solving, language learning, the development of social roles, and a number of other cognitive and social phenomena. (1977: 4-5).

Huizinga's assertion that play extends beyond human beings also has been given additional credence. What appears to be useless movements, not contributing to survival, are often observed among wild mammals. About 20% of the energy that could be used for survival is consumed by such playful acts as upward springing, twirling around, or tumbling over and over (Brown, 1995a: 9).

We may not know what play is for, but we know what happens when it is absent. Stuart L. Brown's question makes that decidedly clear, "what is shared by mass murderers, felony drunk drivers, starving children, head-banging laboratory animals, some anxious students, most upwardly mobile executives and all reptiles? They don't play" (Brown, 1995b: 2).

The sheer variety of play activities is amazing: a cat chasing its tail, a child shaking a rattle, a chimp advancing in mock-attack, a child running from her mother and laughing, children skipping rope and chanting rhymes, a game of marbles, an adult stepping over cracks in a sidewalk and smiling, a 1,200 pound polar bear who has not had a major meal in three months engaging in mouthings, tossings, wrestling and cavorting with a loosely tethered sled dog near Churchill, Manitoba. The list could easily be extended almost without limit, perhaps, even to contemplation.

Play's variety, however, is not what makes it difficult to define. It cannot be defined by a class of actions, because any activity that can be done in a playful way can also be done in a way that is not playful.

When Garvey concluded her book she observed that children's play discloses what they really know, but she cautioned that this is not easily discovered in the more literally-minded, clinical settings used for scientific experiments. We, therefore, need to be on our guard against being too reductionistic in our desire to understand play. The evidence, accumulating from many fields during the last few decades, suggests that play is, indeed, a distinct form of behaviour like sleep or dreaming, and it is not only important for our quality of life but also survival.

Let us now compare play and contemplation:

Richard of St. Victor (Contemplation)	Garvey's Play Summary
1. Contemplation is the free	1. Play is voluntary
2. More penetrating gaze of mind	2. Involves active engagement
3. Suspended with wonder	3. Has no extrinsic goals
4. Concerning manifestations	4. Is related to creativity, of wisdom learning languages, and developing social roles
5. (Is pleasurable, ecstatic)	5. Is pleasurable

We will use the work of Howard Gardner (1994) to show why creativity is integral to our growth and development. The themes he chose to study the arts and human development were perceptions, feelings, and making.

All three kinds of knowing identified by Richard of St. Victor are better differentiated as well as integrated by Gardner's developmental scheme than in those, such as Fowler's (1981) and Oser's (1991) which are dependent on Piaget (Berryman, 1992), whose masterful work was focused primarily on logical-mathematical knowing.

The child's first experience of the world is physically bound by the senses and by an interest in particular parts of the growing body. This guides the child's co-ordination of physical analogies for making meaning about the world before language. This is body-knowing.

Gardner's theory of modes (kinds of action) and vectors (the direction of the action) suggests that initially the child's meaning is limited to a few aspects of bodily functioning such as openness and closeness or emptiness and fullness. These sensations are particularly at the region of the mouth but may extend throughout the body.

A basic set of modes and vectors, founded in bodily experience, interact and coalesce with one another to form a much larger set of general categories through which the child comes to know the world. The child at the threshold of symbol use conceives of the world in significant part as a flux of these different primary and secondary general properties, which have their origin in his organismic experience and which now pervade his experience of objects and persons.
(Gardner, 1973, 108).

Usually by the second year the world is no longer perceived directly as a coordination of actions. It becomes mediated by symbols. The child can now construct a complex world of permanent objects. This is mind-knowing.

The three developing systems of making, perceiving, and feeling are integrated in an increasingly fluent way if, indeed, they did not originate as a single system. Two kinds of communication become available, denotation (grounded in mind-knowing) and connotation (grounded in body-knowing) to be used by the making system.

In *The Arts and Human Development* (1994) Gardner did not expand much beyond the four steps in the creative process identified by Graham Wallas in 1926, but in *Frames of Mind* (1983) he proposed a much broader view of knowing than Piaget's focus on the logical-mathematical way. In *Creating Minds* (1993) Gardner combined his seven frames of knowing with a more developed view of creativity and provided 20th century exemplars for seven kinds of creativity: logical-mathematical (Einstein), intrapersonal (Freud), interpersonal (Gandhi), visual-spatial (Picasso), music and rhythm (Stravinsky), bodily-kinesthetic (Martha Graham), and verbal (T.S. Eliot).

Gardner's *Creating Minds* has been joined by Mihaly Csikszentmihalyi's *Creativity* (1996) to enlarge the theory of creativity. In addition Csikszentmihalyi's concept of "flow" suggests how this process feels, the conditions needed for its continuity, and why it is intrinsically motivated.

Following Gardner, Csikszentmihalyi, James Loder (1981), and others, a six step process opens (1) because of surprise, wonder, a crisis, boredom or some other disruption of one's assumed circle of meaning. A scanning of the horizon (2) for possible patterns to replace what was lost begins which is often unconscious. When insight comes (3) a new pattern has formed, usually in the unconscious, and the connections fit so well that the pattern is forced into awareness. A shift of energy can be felt, as Loder has suggested, sometimes even before one is aware of what the insight is.

After the insight is recognized the process of articulation and evaluation (4) begins. In addition the insight is often elaborated (5), making the new pattern more and more conscious, differentiated, and available to others. Finally, I would like to add, an intentional act of will (6) is sometimes needed, because the originator is drawn to elaborate indefinitely. This "will to believe", as William James called it, brings a pragmatic closure to the process, and a new pattern of meaning is established to be relied on.

As you can readily see, steps 1-3 may not manifest themselves in the language of one's preferred frame of knowing, although steps 4, 5, and 6 probably will. This means that the only behavioural signs that creativity (or contemplation) is in process may be children with puzzled faces, frowns of concentration, the twisting hair of doubt, a tapping of frustration, and the look of amazement when insight comes.

The creative process constructs not only what is now for an individual but also what is new for larger groups. It also is at work to create new ways of knowing such as those identified by Richard of St. Victor. Both the micro and macro use for this process draws into its making all of our perceptions and feelings as well as our thinking. This is why Gardner's developmental scheme is so useful for guiding religious education.

We turn now to the elements Csikszentmihalyi used to identify flow, so we can compare this experience to the experience of contemplation described by Richard of St. Victor and the experience of play as described by Garvey:

Contemplation	Flow	Play
1. Contemplation is the free		1. Voluntary
2. More penetrating gaze of a mind	1. Concentration is deep 2. Self-consciousness disappears 3. The sense of time is altered	2. Active engagement
3. Suspended with wonder	4. The experience is "autoelic" (worth having for itself)	3. No extrinsic goal
4. Concerning manifestations of wisdom	5. Feedback is immediate 6. Goals are clear 7. Skills match challenges 8. Control is possible 9. Problems are forgotten	4. Links to creativity, learning languages, social roles
5. (Is pleasurable, ecstatic)	10.(Is pleasurable)	5. Is pleasurable

A few observations will help clarify these comparisons. First, it is clear that all three are pleasurable even if contemplation and flow do not make pleasure or ecstasy one of their explicit tenets. This implication is suggested by the parentheses in the diagram.

Csikszentmihalyi began his study by wondering why artists continue to practice their art when there were no extrinsic rewards. It was because they loved creating. Mystics in addition to Richard also speak of pleasure in the extravagant terms of ecstasy. Play is universally engaged in by humans and other mammals because it is great and deep fun. It gives pleasure.

A second observation is that flow is as voluntary as contemplation and play are freely engaged in. Force alone will not cause creativity. As the challenge goes up so do worry and anxiety, when skill is low. If skill is a bit higher, then arousal replaces anxiety. When skills are high and the challenge can be met, then flow begins.

A third observation is that flow fills in rather than conflicts with the rest of the points of description about play and contemplation. The clear goals (you know every moment what you are going to do, like carefully placing your body when mountain climbing), immediate feedback (you know how you are doing each moment), skills matching challenges (the challenge and your ability are balanced which draws you forward), deep concentration (your focus is on the task at hand.), forgotten problems (irrelevant stimuli are excluded from your consciousness), control is possible (success is in your hands), self-consciousness disappears (the limits of your ego are transcended), and the altered sense of time (usually it passes faster but slow motion is also possible) add detail to Richard's more penetrating gaze of a mind, his suspension with wonder, and the involvement with manifestations of wisdom. Garvey's active engagement and the related activities of creativity, language learning, and the learning of social roles (which is the rudiments of ethics) are also added to by this comparison.

The fourth observation is that all these experiences are self-motivating. They are done for no other reason that for themselves.

The points of analogy among these three descriptions of experiences suggest an overlap if not an identity. This provides some assurance that in modern times we can get a sense of what Richard of St. Victor was talking about by looking at the creativity and playfulness by which we teach the knowing of the spirit by contemplation to children.

Conclusion

When teachers are experiencing flow or play when they present the knowing of the spirit by contemplation, then they can have some confidence that the nonverbal communication which undergirds the lesson matches or shows what the lesson is about in terms of relationships.

If the children being taught show signs of play or flow, then, you know that there has been a meeting of the spirits and not just the minds or bodies concerning the knowing of the spirit by contemplation.

Richard's three ways of knowing are not only helpful to clarify a primary way to evaluate teaching and learning in religious education. These distinctions are also useful to elaborate the epistemology that ought to be taught in religious education as distinguished from that taught in science education.

Waking up

When Alice awoke from her Looking-Glass adventure she found that the Red Queen she was shaking was actually her cat.

References

Beardsworth, T. 1977. *A Sense of Presence.* Oxford: The Religious Experience Research Unit, Manchester College.

Berryman, J.W. 1991. *Godly Play: A Way of Religious Education.* San Francisco: Harper SanFrancisco.

_____. 1992. "Faith development and the language of faith." In D.E Ratcliff (Ed.). *Handbook of Children's Religious Education.* Birmingham, Alabama: Religious Education Press.

Brown, S.L. 1995a "Through the Lens of Play." *Revision,* 17 (4).

Brown, S.L. 1995b. "Introduction." *Revision,* 17 (4).

Carroll, L. 1960. *The Annotated Alice,* Introduction and notes, Martin Gardner. Cleveland and New York: The World Publishing Co., 1960.

Csikszentmihalyi, M. 1990. *Flow.* New York: HarperCollins.

Csikszentmihalyi, M. 1996. *Creativity.* New York: HarperCollins.

Eliot, T.S. 1952. *The Complete Poems and Plays: 1909-1950.* New York: Harcourt, Brace.

Ellmann, R. 1948. *Yeats: The Man and the Masks.* New York: E. P. Dutton and Co., Inc.

Fowler, J.W. 1981. *Stages of Faith.* San Francisco: HarperSanFrancisco.

Gardner, H. 1983. *Frames of Mind.* New York: Basic Books.

Gardner, H. 1993. *Creating Minds.* New York: HarperCollins, Basic Books.

Gardner, H. 1994. *The Arts and Human Development,* With a New Introduction by the Author. New York: HarperCollins, Basic Books.

Garvey, C. 1977. *Play.* Cambridge: Harvard University Press.

Huizinga, J. 1955. *Homo Ludens.* Boston: Beacon Press.

Hyde, K.E. 1990. *Religion in Childhood and Adolescence.* Birmingham, Alabama: Religious Education Press.

Leclercq, J. 1982. *The Love of Learning and the Desire for God: A Study of Monastic Culture.* New York: Fordham University Press (first English 1962; original French 1957).

Montessori, M. 1967. *The Absorbent Mind.* New York: Dell.

Oser, F and P. Gmunder. 1991. *Religious Judgment.* Birmingham, Alabama: Religious Education Press.

Kierkegaard, S. 1944. *Either/Or: A Fragment of Life.* Princeton: Princeton University Press.

Lee, J.M. 1973. *The Flow of Religious Instruction: A Social-Science Approach.* Dayton, Ohio: Pflaum/Standard.

Loder, J.E. 1981. *The Transforming Moment.* San Francisco: Harper and Row.

Robinson, E. 1978. *Living the Questions.* Oxford: The Religious Experience Research Unit, Manchester College.

Rilke, R.M. 1986. *Letters to a Young Poet.* Trans. and forward Stephen Mitchell. New York: Random House, Vintage Books Edition.

St. Victor, Richard of. 1979. "The twelve patriarchs, the mystical ark. Book Three of The Trinity." In *Richard of St. Victor* in New York/ Ramsey/Toronto: Paulist Press.

The Episcopal Church. 1979. *The Book of Common Prayer.* New York: Oxford University Press, 336.

Vandenbrouke, F. 1982. "The Schoolmen of the Twelfth Century." In *A History of Christian Spirituality,* vol. 2, Jean Leclercq, Francois Vandenbroucke, Louis Bouyer. New York, The Seabury Press.

Whitehead, A.N. and B. Russell. 1910-1913. *Principia Mathematica.* Cambridge: Cambridge University Press. The context for this discussion may be found in William Kneale and Martha Kneale (1964) *The Development of Logic.* Oxford: Clarendon Press, Chapter XI.

Original source:

Berryman, J.W. 1997. "Spirituality, religious education and the dormouse." ***International Journal of Children's Spirituality*, 2 (1): 9-22.**

8

The Nonverbal Nature of Spirituality and Religious Language

Why do we know "spirituality" when we meet it, but can't define it? Why do our explanations fail to satisfy? Perhaps, the answer is that spirituality is part of our non-verbal communication system. If this is so we cannot hope to make a point-to-point translation from its way of communicating into symbols. This chapter, then, can only gesture towards the non-verbal nature of spirituality to better understand religious language, which refers to it.

Gesturing towards spirituality's non-verbal nature is useful for four reasons. First, spiritual directors (including religious educators and those charged with the responsibility for worship) need to be more aware of spirituality's non-verbal nature to be better guides. Secondly, those who help children make the transition from non-verbal spirituality to religious language need to find ways for this powerful language to be constructively rooted in the non-verbal. Thirdly, we all need to be better informed about spirituality's dark side, so the misuse of religious language can be detected and remedied. Finally, researchers need a way to describe the non-verbal aspect of spirituality to test this hypothesis about its nature.

I shall begin by clarifying the difference between verbal and nonverbal communication in terms of "referencing". Secondly, the method of modes and vectors for depicting spirituality will be described. Thirdly, the mode-and-vector method will be applied and elaborated. The fourth step will be to examine the primary, non-verbal "calls" used to express spirituality. I shall then turn to spirituality's dark side. A synthesis will then be made in terms of complexity emerging out of chaos. Finally, the four reasons why this speculation is useful will be revisited and fundamental conclusions about spirituality and religious language will be drawn.

Referencing and spirituality

The basis for the following discussion of language and spirituality is Terrence W. Deacon's *The Symbolic Species: The Co-Evolution of Language and the Brain* (Deacon 1997). Deacon's work has been chosen because it deals with the co-evolution of the brain and language in terms of what Deacon calls "referencing". He follows Charles Sanders Peirce to distinguish three categories of referential associations.

Many great philosophers of the mind have used such categories to describe the fundamental forms of knowing, but what Peirce did was reframe the problem of "mind" as a problem of communication, i.e., sign production and interpretation. The three kinds of referencing are termed iconic, indexical and symbolic.

Iconic referencing can be shown by thinking about a bird searching for food in the bark of a tree. The bird registers only "bark" and "not-bark". If a moth is the same texture and colour as the bark and the bird is not attentive, then the interpretation will be "bark" and the meal will be missed. If the moth moves and this is interpreted as not-bark then the moth is eaten. No language is necessary for such interpretations.

Indexical referencing links memories. Suppose a dog is prompted by nature to chase the small furry creatures we call "cats". The "cat" or "not-cat" interpretation is complicated when a small, black and white, furry creature that looks like a cat is encountered. This cat-like creature stands instead of running, raises its tail, and sprays one with an unforgettable, foul, stinging, vapour. The two iconic references of "cat" and "not-cat" and this "not-cat" and "aversion" are coupled in the dog's memory to make an indexical reference. The next time a small, furry, black and white creature stops and raises its tail the dog will link these memories and retreat. No language is involved here either.

Both iconic and indexical referencing relies on relatively stable physical correlations. There is no *necessary* mental linkage. If a parrot stops being fed when it squawks "Wanna cracker!" it probably will stop producing the sound. This is not true of human language. The symbols chosen to carry specific meanings do so as long as the community continues to use them in a particular way.

Our non-verbal system developed independently and alongside language and uses different parts of the brain. The smiles, grimaces, laughs, sobs, hugs, kisses, and all the rest of our non-linguistic communication system are, therefore, not "words without syntax". This is because gestures and vocalizations cannot explain, describe, command or ask. You can neither argue, disagree, bargain, gossip, persuade or change tense with non-verbal communication. Still, calls, grunts, gestures, social grooming, etc., are needed to understand our symbolic referencing. The referencing of symbols is completely different from non-verbal referencing. It takes a shift in learning strategy to move from indexical to symbolic referencing. This difference must be "discovered". It is a "restructuring event". We must make an effort to suppress one set of associative responses, the indexical, for another strategy derived from symbols. Referencing is also hierarchical. If I fail to grasp the symbolic reference for any reason I could still interpret the indexical or iconic relationship, as many of our pets do when we talk to them.

To summarize, then, iconic referencing is an interpretation based on form. Indexical referencing is based on correlation. Symbolic referencing relies on a socially agreed upon set of relationships among symbols. (A wedding ring references a marriage agreement in some cultures but not in others.) This is why we can only hope to gesture in symbols towards the realm of indexical and iconic referencing and yet our symbols owe some of their meaning to the non-verbal context.

Gesturing towards the non-verbal by connotation

A definition of spirituality cannot be as clear and distinct as we might like. This task is not like defining a triangle. Instead of verbal precision we need to apply as much connotation as possible to show the nonverbal nature of spirituality. This is because vestiges of the non-verbal can be found in the verbal by noticing such connotations. There are two groups of human beings which are especially sensitive to connotation. One group is adult artists. They retain a special interest in their iconic and indexical referencing and are adept at playing with words, movement, stone, colour, sounds, numbers, social situations, and other media. The second group is children. They have no choice but to be in tune with their non-verbal system of communication, since their symbolic referencing is just developing. I will use the work of Howard Gardner (1994) to develop this idea.

Connotation is rooted in our pre-object-formation way of knowing and continues to influence our language all our lives. It communicates by what Gardner calls modes and vectors, a kind of deep body knowing. This probably begins in a global way and then develops more specificity at canters of sensitivity such as the mouth. A summary follows (Gardner 1994, 101):

Zones	Characteristic Modes	Vectoral Properties
Lips & Tongue	Passive and Active incorporation – take in, or bite, grasp, investigate	Speed – quick or slow Time – regular or irregular Space – wide or narrow & curved or angular
Sphincter	Retention – hold onto Expulsion – let go, release, push out	Facility – ease or strain
Penis	Intrusion – stick into,	Repletion – hollow or full Density – thick or thin
Vagina	go into Inclusion – take into, envelop	Boundness – open or closed Also: directionality, force, depth, comfort and texture

Gardner's work is based on that of Erik Erikson (Erikson 1963, 72-97), who attempted to bridge the gap between the child's physiological functioning and psychological processes by describing the psychological implications of organ modes and zones, building on his psychoanalytic background. Gardner then applied this connection to the transition from non-verbal into symbolic, placing the roots of connotation in the non-verbal. This is why our definition of spirituality uses connotation as a pairing of related axes of modes and vectors to show the non-verbal nature of spirituality. The resulting pictures of spirituality are detailed below.

Picturing spirituality

I shall begin by considering a physical operation not spoken about by Gardner. It is the rhythm of life, our breathing in and out. The connection between life and breath is this reflex. It is one of the few we come equipped with at birth. Babies fight for their air. Their bodies know its importance. The Bible begins by God breathing life into us. The Hebrew term *ruach* has deep connotations in our cultural memory, as do the words "animate" and "inanimate". They entered English from the Latin *animare,* which means to fill with breath.

A second experience we are in tune with before language is being globally full and empty. If we are full we are happy. If we are empty we cry to be filled. (Later this global sense will be distinguished from specific zones of fullness and the need to empty them.) One axis for our basic picture of spirituality, then, is the polarity of being full and empty. The other polarity is being animate or inanimate.

The relationship between the two pairs of polarities shows us by the directional force of the vectors pushing towards one or the other pole that sometimes people who are alive can be empty of spirituality. This is shown in the lower-left quadrant of the figure 1 By contrast we find that people who are almost dead can be full of spirituality. This is shown by the upper-right quadrant (Figure 1):

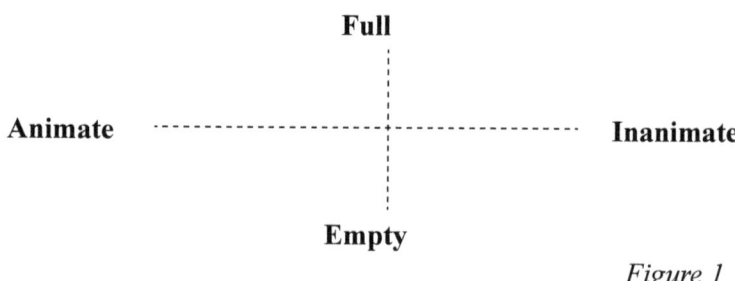

Figure 1

To further develop our view of spirituality, let us now examine the vertical spectrum of full and empty more closely. There are different qualities of being globally full and empty. This intuition also has been coded in English with a Latin heritage. *Anima* refers to a current of air, to wind, to breath, and to the soul as a vital principle of life. When the Latin noun becomes masculine, however, as *animus,* the dark side of the polarity becomes evident. *Animus* also refers to the soul, but in contrast to *anima* it points towards intellect and reason. It is also about thought, memory, consciousness and self-possession. There is in addition a hint of character, courage, heart and spirit in its Latin usage, but when the Latin term for spirit becomes masculine it adds the qualities of haughtiness, arrogance, pride, passion, vehemence and wrath. It is this sense, which is the origin of our English word, "animus", which means a feeling of animosity. "Animosity" is the feeling of bitter hostility or hatred towards another person.

There is another breath-related term in Latin for spirit. It is *spiritus*. It refers to breath, air, breeze, spirit, soul, mind, inspiration and courage, but it also refers to haughtiness and pride. It is no wonder that *spiritus* needs to be qualified by the adjective *sanctus* to give it an unqualified sense of the sacred – that which is inviolable, venerable, august, divine, virtuous, holy, pious, innocent, pure, chaste and just.

The polarity of *anima* and *animus* is used to show the quality of spirituality we are full or empty of. The second and related polarity pair shows action in relation to *anima* and *animus*. It ranges from movement towards, to movement away from, another's spirituality. If one moves towards another in a positive way there is pleasure and connectedness. If one moves with *anima* away from such pleasure and connectedness there is loss and sadness. On the other hand, if one moves towards another with animosity the movement is aggressive and unpleasant. Moving away can also be negative if it is done with haughtiness and pride. To capture this complex sense of spirituality the following pairs of modes and vectors are proposed:

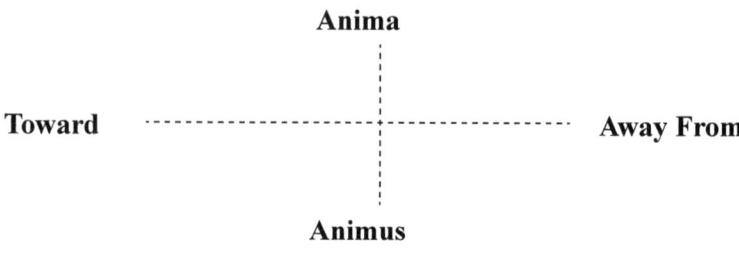

Figure 2

I shall now attempt to fill out the meaning of spirituality beyond the above two pictures. A third aspect of spirituality involves an awareness of one's personal life and death. This is spirituality's existential dimension. Existential awareness allows the edge of our knowing and being to come into our consciousness. Such boundary awareness is complicated by a breakdown of language's ordinary usage. Let us take four limit cases to illustrate this. They are existential aloneness (not mere loneliness), freedom, death and the need for meaning.

Let us imagine that these four ultimate issues define the "space" in which we live. These boundaries limit and yet define us and, in addition, all four sides (and there are probably more nuances of our ultimate issues than these four) are related. As we approach any one of the boundaries there is also a kind of oscillation that can be felt between being consumed (thus disappearing and being out of control) and consuming (taking the boundary into one and controlling it).

The consuming aspect of this paradox involves both passive and active incorporation. Passive incorporation involves being taken in. Active incorporation involves biting, grasping and investigating. Other physical connotations jostle us at these boundaries. There are the physical aspects of retention (holding onto) and expulsion (letting go, releasing, pushing out). From the next stage of development there are physical memories of intrusion (stick into, go into) and inclusion (take into, envelop). All of these experiences, felt before we had language or just as it was developing, provide the physical connotation for our words about the above existential issues.

When our ordinary use of language breaks down into the equivocation of existential paradox we stutter and stammer since what we have to say is part of our non-verbal communication system. Some examples will help clarify this. The first example is the case of existential aloneness. I sense that I am alone and crave joining others, but if they begin to incorporate me I oscillate back to aloneness in which I soon begin to crave company again. A second example is our need for meaning. If I create meaning I am comforted by it until I realize that I am the one who created it. It can't define me, since I defined it. We oscillate between seeking and rejecting the meaning we make. With respect to death we rest and then, fearing death, become active, only to rest again. The case of freedom is our fourth example. Freedom is craved by those who are not free until they realize that they *are* free. They then flee to the safety of limitations to avoid taking responsibility for their actions and because of being overwhelmed by the formlessness. Such equivocation is likely to continue all of one's life.

The oscillation described above is entailed in the consuming – consumed axis of Figure 3, which gestures towards the existential aspect of spirituality. The other axis is the spectrum between the polarities of control and letting go. This is how we often attempt to deal with the consuming-consumed aspect of spirituality.

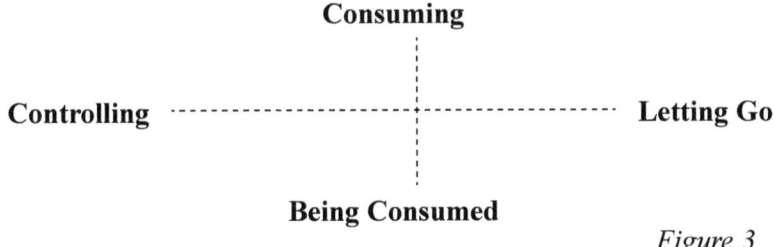

Figure 3

With the above three diagrams of spirituality in mind we turn now to three fundamental calls, which alert us further to the complexity of human spirituality. They are laughing, crying and silence.

The calls of human spirituality

In this section we will look at three of the calls used by human beings to signal aspects of their spirituality. They are laughing, crying and silence. By a call I do not mean a simple language without words, because such calls convey very important and complex information. They also have an echo effect, which has benefits as well as dangers. To give an example of a danger related to the mimic effect of laughter, let us suppose children grow up hearing only sarcastic, put-down laughter from living people and the electronic media. They are likely to mimic this sarcastic sound which stimulates the state it references. If their repertoire of laughter does not include the laughter of delight, which references creativity, their creativity is likely to atrophy. If creativity disappears among *Homo sapiens* the ability to adapt is lost and the whole species is in danger of extinction.

The warning call of the vervet monkeys is a further example of audible but non-verbal communication and its echo effect. Once the call is sounded the whole troop picks it up and continues until long after the danger is past. There are three such calls. One signals the danger of eagles and sends the monkeys racing down from upper regions of the trees. The second call sounds the danger of leopards, which sends the troop scampering into the small branches in the upper parts of the trees. The third alarm alerts the monkeys to the danger of snakes. They begin peering into the grass and bushes around them. Such communicating and recruiting arousal is more than predator information. It refers to things in the world and to internal states (Deacon 1997, 59) as language does, but although it grew up alongside language it is independent from it. Despite this, such communication influences our language. For example identical words said with a smile, a sneer, a wink, or tear can mean different things. Our depiction of calls, signalling states of spirituality, will begin by pairing laughing and crying. This is because we sometimes laugh until we cry and cry until we laugh. Both polarities can result in tears. The laughing – crying axis will be related to ecstasy (overwhelming delight) and devastation (overwhelming annihilation). The vague discrimination of these sounds is learned as one grows up, but for researchers and spiritual directors becoming connoisseurs of their nuances it is important to be able to better communicate and monitor the mimic affect.

To give an idea of the kinds of laughter we usually intuit but need to become connoisseurs of are the categories defined for my own Laughter Scale: derision, sardonic, ironic, neutral (from tickling), comic, mirth and delight laughter. Seven such distinctions are about at our limit for ongoing conscious analysis, but Baldasar Castiglione, who counselled one to do everything with *sprezaturra* (graceful ease), identified 35 different kinds of laughter in his *Book of the Courtier* (translated into English in 1528) and illustrated them with jokes taken from Cicero (as referenced by Sanders 1995).

The analysis of tears also invites verbal distinctions, none of which can exhaust the meaning of the non-verbal communication any more than our laughter distinctions can. In *Crying: The Natural and Cultural History of Tears,* Tom Lutz discusses tears of pleasure, theological grace, heroism, mourning, revenge, seduction, escape, empathy and fiction (Lutz 1999). Our relational display is as follows:

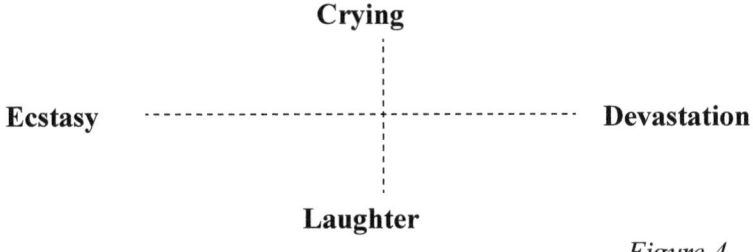

Figure 4

When the vectoral force on the horizontal axis of ecstasy and devastation moves one near ecstasy as overwhelming delight we can become "beside ourselves". If the direction of the force moves us towards "devastation", the overwhelming annihilation can also make us beside ourselves. In either case a person may not return from such extreme states. There may be no self to return to. It is no wonder, then, that crying and laughing can become signs of madness when one goes beyond delight and annihilation.

If the force vectors carry us into the upper-left quadrant we find the tears of overflowing fullness. If we are carried into the lower-left quadrant we find the laughter of delight. If we are carried into the upper-right quadrant the tears signal painful loss. Experience in the lower-right quadrant is conveyed by cynical, sarcastic laughter.

We turn now to the third kind of call. It communicates as a call but involves no sound. Silence can signal as well as sounded calls. The clue for its depiction is in the ambiguity of the language we use to refer to silence. In many languages there is a cluster of words which refers to communication without sound. In English they are "stillness", "silence" and "quiet". All three are needed, because no single one contains all that is meant by the whole cluster. Our task, therefore, is to depict this complexity to gain access to its non-verbal nature.

One axis shows stillness, which refers to both movement and sound. For example, when the lake or woods is still, it is not moving. It is also silent. Movement and sound are related. The relationship in terms of physics has to do with movement in the medium of light (waves or quanta) as it stimulates our eyes and in the medium of air as sound waves stimulate our ears.

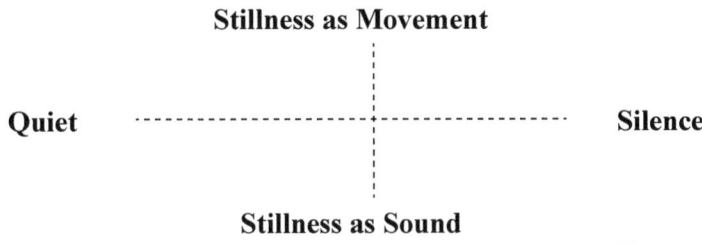

Figure 5

The distinction between quiet and silence is on the basis of motivation. Quiet's motivation is inward while silence is imposed from outside. For example, public silence can be imposed to force an outward calm while at the same time increasing inward agitation.

Discussion of the calls and their references adds to the complexity of spirituality. I turn now to its dark side.

The dark side of spirituality

Each of the above pictures of an aspect of spirituality has a negative as well as positive tone to it. Being Empty (Figure 1), *Animus* (Figure 2), Being Consumed (Figure 3), Devastation (Figure 4) and imposed silence (Figure 5) are examples. The religions of the world have built up treasuries of wisdom about how to cope with this dark side. They have also warned followers to be aware that even the positive side of spirituality can be dangerous.

I turn now to a primary polarity of the dark side not yet examined. It deserves special attention, because it comes disguised as play, another aspect of our non-verbal communication system. Play is pleasurable, has no extrinsic goals, is spontaneous, requires engagement, and has formal links to creativity, language learning, and learning social roles. It is an indicator of people who are full of spirituality. Pseudo-play is associated with empty people, who become spirituality sponges. Pseudo-players are parasites. They attract people full of spirituality by their personality or by being so powerful in their social positions that they can compel victims to come close enough to be robbed. Their obsession to control others is motivated by the need to suck their spiritual vitality from them. They are detached, clever and assume disguises for this exploitation. Satan in Milton's *Paradise Lost* is a classic example.

Play and pseudo-play make up one axis to depict this danger. The related polarity is the creation – destruction axis. A few words need to be said about the creative process to show what this polarity is about. The creative process operates on many levels – from biology, to psychology, to sociology, to spirituality. It provides the means to create a menu for supper or articulate one's destiny. It is also the non-verbal process by which the body, mind and spirit carry out their repairs and regenerate.

The creative process at the level of words begins with a disruption of the status quo. This disruption may be a "soft" one that dissolves one's assumptive world by wondering or as-if play. Disruption may also be a "hard", such as the death of a loved one. Once this disruption takes place we begin scanning for a way to repair it by finding a larger meaning to encompass the change. The scanning often takes place in silence and without words. It usually prompts one's preferred way of creating. Gardner has identified at least seven of these ways: words, music, movement, intra-psychic musings, social activity, visual expression such as painting, or mathematics (Gardner 1993).

Insight comes when a new synthesis has taken form. The formation of this synthesis is often felt before it enters consciousness, because the energy shifts from scanning to insight before it is coded in a preferred creative means. The working-out of the insight in terms of one's preferred way of creating is tested by the canons of the particular form. This is as true for mathematics and the scientific method as it is for music, poetry, social action, dance, painting or psychology. Finally, a decision is made to halt the process, which could go on forever, especially if one is a perfectionist. The insight is considered complete enough to furnish one with a new assumption, which then awaits a new disruption.

The reason that this axis has the mode Putting-Together at one end and Taking-Apart at the other is that the creative process always involves both opposing poles. One tears down (or has the status quo broken or dissolved) to build up better, but one might also tear down what is better for the sake of irrational destruction. The diagram of these polarities in reference to each other looks like this:

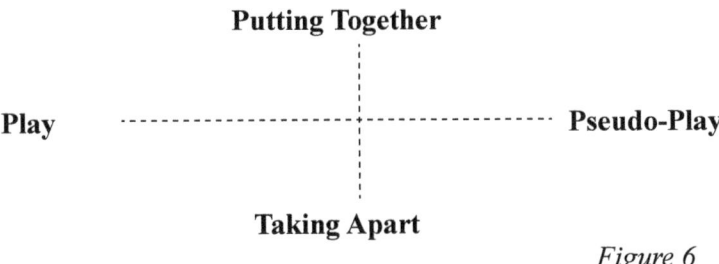

Figure 6

I have now presented six figures to show various aspect of spirituality's non-verbal nature, as much as can be shown in symbols and pictures. I now turn to a different kind of presentation, one more dynamic and metaphorical.

The deep channel of living spirituality

We now need to synthesize the rather static figures above into a dynamic picture of the experience of complexity emerging out of chaos, which makes living systems, human as well as others, "alive". How this feels to human beings is what needs to be conceptualized at this point to guide our recognizing and fostering this positive dynamic in human spirituality.

Complexity emerging in the turbulence of a river is our visual metaphor. On either bank of the river we find the limits for the turbulence, although the river can reshape the banks that give it shape. On both banks we find the collapse of emerging complexity. On one side there is locked-in chaos and on the other bank tightly controlled rigidity.

Laughter/Tears of Madness	Two-Dimensional Chaos	Nothing is Serious

THE BOUNDARY OF COMEDY IN OPPOSITION TO TRAGEDY

Laughter/Tears of Delight	Creativity	Disjunction	Process as Stability	Becoming
Serious Laughter/Tears of Play	Complexity	Emerging Game	Comedy–Tragedy in Interplay	Meaning
Laughter/Tears of Wonder	Contemplation	Conjunction	Connection as Stability	Being

THE BOUNDARY OF TRAGEDY IN OPPOSITION TO COMEDY

Laughter/ Tears of Scorn	Rigidity	All is Serious

Figure 7

At one limit is madness, a meaninglessness where nothing matters. On the other bank is the trap of inflexibility where meaning is wound too tightly. The effort to completely control life at this extreme ends in the breaking of the person, heroic as the person may seem. Complexity is found emerging in the interplay of comedy and tragedy, which holds a person in the turbulence of the deep channel. Within the turbulence we can hear the river's sounds. They are the laughter and crying of delight and wonder, which converge into the serious but joyful laughter and tears of play. This is the human sound of complexity as it emerges in the ultimate game, played for the sake of playing without end.

It is in that emerging game within the interplay of comedy and tragedy that we can find our non-verbal meaning for life. It is this dynamic that signals the definition of spirituality at its best, cumbersome and imprecise as the language may be.

Conclusion

The use of the above diagrams will increase the awareness of the nonverbal nature of spirituality for the spiritual director (including religious educators and those charged with the responsibility for worship). They also provide a useful guide for pastoral care. Parents, religious educators and others charged with the responsibility of guiding children from non-verbal spirituality into religious language can find here an appreciation of the child's spiritual complexity, which needs no language. This complexity is important to keep in mind when searching for ways to keep the child's religious language rooted in the creative spirituality they come to us with. We cannot give such spirituality, but we can take it away, even with the best of intentions.

The dark side of spirituality is important for us to know in order to guard against its danger. The traditions of wisdom coded in religious language take on an increased importance when this is understood. It is especially important to be aware of pseudo-play, since it often passes as a way of spiritual direction. Researchers can use the above diagrams to begin to quantify the modes and vectors to make more measurable what is pictured here. Nevertheless, the conceptual work is begun.

It is especially interesting to note the complexity of spirituality shown here. This is one reason why it cannot be translated into a language of spirituality-in-general. It is not an "oblong blur" of good feelings, as is sometimes naively imagined. This means that specific traditions and nuances of religious language are necessary to evoke, guard and nurture our spirituality. Furthermore, since children cannot learn any language in-general – whether it is the language of mathematics, music, a mother tongue, a way to pray and live, or any other language – we are forced to make compromises. Our non-verbal spirituality must be rendered in specific language traditions despite misunderstanding, misapplication and our inability to translate all that we know, because we are the symbolic species, as Deacon has observed. This is our unique way to make meaning.

Finally, and most importantly, whatever religious tradition of communication we use, we need to ground it in the fullness of a living and creative spirituality. When religious language is uprooted from this source it becomes full of animus and destruction, as all "religious wars" – usually in the name of peace, truth, and love – have shown.

References

Deacon, T. 1997. *The Symbolic Species: The Co-evolution of Language and the Brain.* New York: W. W. Norton.

Erikson, E. 1963. *Childhood and Society.* New York: W. W. Norton.

Gardner, H. 1993. *Creating Minds: An Anatomy of Creativity Seen Through the Lives of Freud, Einstein, Picasso, Stravinsky, Eliot, Graham and Gandhi.* New York: Basic Books.

_____. 1994 [1974]: *The Arts and Human Development,* New York: Harper Collins, Basic Books.

Lutz, T. 1999. *Crying: The Natural and Cultural History of Tears.* New York: W. W. Norton.

Milton, J. 1957. "Paradise Lost." In *Complete Poems and Major Prose,* edited by M. Hughes and J. Milton. New York: Odyssey.

Sanders, B. 1995. *Sudden Glory: Laughter as Subversive History.* Boston: Beacon Press.

Original source:

Berryman, J.W. 2001. "The nonverbal nature of spirituality and religious language." Pp. 7-21 in *Spiritual Education: Cultural, Religious and Social Differences,* edited by J. Erricker, C. Ota, & C. Erricker. Brighton, UK: Sussex Academic Press.

Part 4

Play, Imagination and the Creative Process

Preface to Part 4

The concepts of play, imagination and the creative process lie at the heart of Berryman's approach to religious education with both children and adults. For Berryman, play is at the heart of creativity, and creativity is at the heart of all creatures created in the image of the Creator. Play is rooted in smiles and laughter, which are the key signals of play for human beings. Yet play is a serious business. Play with the language of God and of God's people is the means by which children and adults enter the creative process and so confront their existential issues and limits. The role of the imagination in play and the creative process cannot be overstated. Rather than enabling us to retreat from reality, the imagination is at the center of the creative process and takes us deeper into reality. Therefore religious education for both children and adults must be grounded in play and imagination, and must enable the participants to engage freely in the creative process.

Berryman's contributions in Part 4 develop the notions of play, imagination and the creative process. The first comes from an entry in *Harper's Encyclopedia of Religious Education* (1990) in which Berryman describes what is meant by the term "imagination" and its centrality in religious education. This short entry prepares the ground for the subsequent contributions which follow in Part 4.

In the second contribution, Berryman focuses on theological play as an approach to working with children in hospitals. Theological play is not therapy; it is a game. In this contribution, Berryman describes the goal, rules, pieces, the players, the place and time of this particular type of game. Theological play is important. In the context of this particular contribution, it potentially integrates the pastoral care of children in the hospital with their experience of worship and education in the parish context.

The third contribution is unique in that it explores the role of laughter and intrinsic motivation in religious education. Berryman is troubled by Christian attitudes towards laughter, and how these attitudes have distorted the use of power in Christian education. In this contribution, Berryman reminds us that "serious laughter" is what arises with delight from the complexity of life. Using the metaphor of a river, Berryman posits that religious educators need to become connoisseurs of laughter in order to guide children through the turbulence of the river in which we live and move and have our being.

In the final contribution Berryman argues that what appear to be two opposing tendencies in religious education – teaching for the closure of orthodoxy, and teaching for the openness of the seeker – are in fact actually parts of a larger whole, the creative process. In terms of play, Berryman refers to this as exploring (wondering play, the opening tendency) and conserving (role-play, the closing tendency). The opening and closing tendencies of the creative process have become separated as religion has shifted its experience base from the creative process to power. Power-based religion is so pervasive at the present time that our language has conformed to this separation as though it were normative. In this contribution, Berryman seeks to address this issue by re-grounding the teaching of religion in the creative process. The term "playful orthodoxy" is used by Berryman as the result of such a reconceptualization of the teaching and learning process in religious education.

9

Imagination

The word "imagination" refers at times to remembering something already seen (reproductive imagination) and at other times to creating an image that is entirely new (productive imagination). There is also a range of meaning that stretches from having critical distance on images so that they can be distinguished and critiqued to being so fascinated and involved with them that one becomes confused about what is real and crosses over into the realm of illusion. The use of the term shifts about along these two lines of possible meaning suggested by Paul Ricoeur. What is most important is that the imagination at the center is the creative process taking us deeper into reality. Illusion is a defence to avoid reality.

Before the seventeenth century, the imagination was thought to be located in the brain and to regulate visual phenomena, including both dreams and hallucinations, as well as emotions. Then when French philosopher Rene Descartes (1596-1650) redefined the soul as "immaterial substance," imagination's role in the disease process and in revelation was denied by physicians and theologians. It seemed impossible for "immaterial substance" to get sick or to know God.

Theologians became especially suspicious about the imagination when Ludwig Feuerbach (1804-1872) said that religion was a projection of our own nature onto the screen of the heavens. God, therefore, was an illusion. Nietzsche, Wagner, Marx, Freud, and others attacked religion on this basis. Today religious educators may still be reluctant to stimulate the imagination because of its association with this attack or the possibility of confusing illusion with the deeper reality of the creative process.

But hostile attitudes towards the imagination in theology began to change in the 1960s or even earlier. In 1976 two popular books by major theologians marked this change, *Ministry and Imagination,* by Urban T. Holmes, and *Introduction to Theology,* by Theodore Jennings. In 1981 appeared *The Transforming Moment,* by James E. Loder, on the structure of the creative process and its relation to religious education and pastoral care.

Loder enlarged the view of the creative process from involving just the mind to involving one's whole existential being. He identified five steps in the process: (1) conflict initiating a need for a knowing response; (2) an interlude for scanning possible resolutions to the conflict; (3) transforming the terms in which the conflict was first felt into ones that can yield a new and constructive way of looking at it; (4) a release of tension and an opening of the knower to this new way of seeing the situation; and (5) interpretation.

While Loder's scheme provides a good working analysis, we know from others how imagination is fundamental to the nature of being human. Perhaps no one has looked more carefully at mothers and babies than psychoanalyst D.W. Winnicott (1896-1971). He found that the mother and child work together to affirm the infant's imagined reality. The imaginative process of the infant conjures up the mother, who sustains the infant's capacity for imagination.

Psychoanalyst Christopher Bollas called the mother a "transformational object" to underline the infant's experience as a process. The first image of the mother is a source for transformation, not as an organized image of a person. The interplay between mother and infant effects the process of development by means of imagination and play.

Ultimately the mother does not respond completely and the child discovers that the reality of the mother is other than him- or herself. This begins the other side of development, the testing of limits of newly imagined realities. Religious education needs to help guide, nourish, and celebrate this process.

In analyzing the work of the two halves of the cerebrum in adults, however, two kinds of thinking were isolated by researchers – the verbal and analytical versus the visuospatial and intuitive. The use of images might be said to be "located" in the right hemisphere of the brain, while the left hemisphere uses language to articulate them. The full process of the imagination requires the complementary function of both realms. Teaching "both sides of the brain" is a priority, then, for religious educators, because of the need to balance both kinds of knowing for the imagination to function fully in all aspects of the religious life.

Both therapists and educators have been interested in how people can impoverish their experience and imagination by deleting the use of one or more of their representational systems. These systems are primarily the kinaesthetic system (feeling and touch), the visual (seeing and picturing), and the auditory (hearing and listening, telling and saying). Not only does awareness of these systems help identify a primary communication match in education, but it also helps people change and engage life more fully. This has implications for a multisensorial approach to religious education that stimulates the motivation and will as well as thinking and feeling, so that people will be more likely to do what they think or feel they ought to do.

Unless religious language is learned while using it in creative ways, there is a danger of placing artificial limitations on the development of both children and adults, because it becomes associated with processes other than this constructive one. In addition, the imagination is needed to envision ways of moving beyond where one is developmentally. If one's religious education's goals is to help foster faith development, then the imagination is of paramount importance. The imagination does not deserve mistrust, but consciously creative and faithful stewardship of our freedom to be creatures created in the image of God, the Creator. *See also* Aesthetics; Affective Development; Creative Activities; Creativity.

For Further Reference

Gardner, H.1982. *Art, Mind and Brain.* New York: Basic Books.

Jennings, T.W., Jr. 1976. *Introduction to Theology.* Philadelphia: Fortress.

Lindbeck, G.A. 1984. *The Nature of Doctrine.* Philadelphia: Westminster.

Lowenfield, V, and W.L Brittain.1975. *Creative and Mental Growth.* 8th ed. New York: Macmillan.

Miles, M.R. 1985. *Images as Insight.* Boston: Beacon.

Original Source

Berryman, J.W. 1990. "Imagination." Pp. 320-321 in *Harper's Encyclopedia of Religious Education*, edited by I.V. Cully and K.B. Cully. San Fransisco: HarperSanFransisco.

10

Caring for Sick Children: The Parish, the Hospital and Theological Play

Theological Play, an approach to working with children in the hospital, was developed in The Children's Center at The Institute of Religion in The Texas Medical Center in Houston. Designed for work with children in the parish setting, it has the great advantage of integrating the pastoral care of children in the hospital with their experience of worship and education in the parish.

Three advantages for the child's religious life result from using theological play in both parish and hospital. First, children are already comfortable with this activity before they are involved in a health crisis and in the strange world of the hospital. Second, theological play engages many levels of communication. Pastoral care in the hospital and worship and education in the parish are two independent realities in the child's faith world. The larger concept of church into which both of these kinds of ministry fit is a construct which young children cannot yet build with their minds. Using the same approach in both places comes as close to integrating what happens in the two places as can be expected at this stage of development. Much of this integration will, of course, be non-verbal.

The third advantage of theological play is that the sick child brings the experience back to the parish when he or she returns to the group. By his or her presence in the group the issue of illness is present and can be dealt with in the context of religious play. The hospital experience of the formerly sick child with the materials of theological play arises in discussions and through art responses to work with the materials, and in the deeper ways of communication that go on constantly around our more conscious pathways of relationship in groups.

For children play is serious. It is how they learn about reality and language. It is also how they participate in their own biological development.

The seriousness of play

It does not demean theology to relate it to play. Play is at the heart of creativity, and creativity is at the heart of creatures created in the image of the Creator.

Adults are just beginning to discover how serious play is. In the late 1970s over twenty research-oriented books on play were published – twice the total number of such volumes in the previous fifty years[76].

Play is rooted in smiles and laughter which, for the human being, are the main signals for play. Like many other mammals we use the activities of "regular" life in our play, but we re-frame them within the play context. The awareness of this context "clicks" when we know its limits.

The "click" delights us and brings an old problem into new focus – and it is fun. Researchers such as Garvey[77] have discussed the natural history of the smile and laughter in relation to play. Koestler[78] spoke of the relationship of spontaneous mirth to the creative act. Playing and creating are associated with well-being. Maslow's last work[79] made this integral to his concept of health. For him, the inability to create playfully trapped one in pathology.

To play requires safety. The game limit gives us that safety, and the signal from another player that this is a game calls the limit into play. When safe a player can risk deep involvement in the game.

Play can be very powerful in non-verbal ways. This is implied in the discussion above, but here I specifically refer to the play of children. Both the reality of the self and the reality beyond the self can be re-created.

When children play mommies and daddies they *become* mommies and daddies. This is the result of an over-accommodation which Piaget calls "imitation." It is a powerful kind of identification process.

When children play with objects such as a match box, the match box can *become* a boat. Piaget says this is done through a process of over-assimilation and limits his use of the term "play" to that process.

The power to change and be changed in play and the power to make meaning through play are certainly serious matters. They nevertheless remain playful. We must, therefore, be careful to distinguish superficial, adult escape, play-like activities from the deep play of children. Their play is their work, for in their play they are constructing not only meaning but their own means to make meaning. This continues to be true for childlike adults.

Certainly Hugo Rahner took play this seriously in his *Man at Play*[80] when he recovered the ethic of the "grave-merry" person. The single Greek word *"spoudogelows"* contained this unlikely association of the two apparently opposing contexts of being serious and being playful.

Rahner traced the long history of human interest in play from classical humanism to Christianity. He found Aquinas using Aristotle's *Nicomachean Ethics* to associate play with the ability to live in the tragic-comic world and to go beyond it through the experience described by the doctrine of redemption. Such an experience enables one to live an "easily turning" *(eutra'pelos;* versatile, witty) serious-serene life.

Theological play

In theological play there is no therapist as in psychology's play therapy. Before life's ultimate experiences and before God we are equal and the healing is in the *mutual* play.

People at different stages in their lives interpret life's experiences differently. Experiencing death, pain, joy, justice, evil, ultimate meaning, beauty and the other mysteries of life are also equalizing. It is not sick or well to die or be in pain. It is not sick or well to experience joy or do justice. The smallness of the medical model for therapy becomes apparent when faced with the categories of theology.

Theological play is not therapy; it is a game, something that holds together to give a structure which can be "played". It is no single game nor class of games. We use the word, "game", to indicate a structure of relationships in which neither winning nor losing is constant. Possibility and consistency are built in. This is different from a so-called game that is too easy to lose. It destroys itself. A so-called game that is too difficult to win destroys the player. A game balanced between winning and losing can be counted on, so the player can relax without having to make a constant analysis of the game's structure or be suspicious about its ability to be played. When the game's existence is trusted then the player can lose himself or herself in it, and deep play can take place.

The authentic person is someone who knows what game he or she is playing. This is necessary to prevent cross-gaming with the self or between the self and others. Such authenticity is especially important in the health care situation, because the games of science and religion can be played at the same time, in the same place, and by the same players. Authenticity allows one to hold such games in juxtaposition and play them appropriately rather than to blur them and, thus, disorient the self or the gaming. This authenticity prevents one from shifting by degrees into either a religion of science or a science of religion.

Science plays with the reality of nature to gain knowledge about it. Religion plays with the reality of God; it awakens us to the being of God in, with, among, and beyond us and makes us aware of all the relationships in this game. The relative value of the games of religion and science cannot be determined by comparing them with each other.

The value comes from their authentic use for appropriate needs.

To become more authentic about the use of theological play in the hospital and the parish, we turn now to its description in detail as a game.

The goal of the game

The goal of theological play is to awaken to the game itself and its value. This awakening or rebirth process leads one to find meaning and direction in life and also to experience changes in both life's meaning and direction. The game's structure gives a measure of security and so does one's relationship with the other players. The relationship, with God, the other players, and the self changes as one's life journey progresses. These changes can be roughly correlated with the stages of faith development described by Fowler.[81]

Rules to reach the goal

The rules to play the game of theological play are five, and they define the way that religious language ought to be presented and used by young children or by adults whose own faith journey has become arrested. The major resource for these rules is the Montessori Method, but they are also influenced by the tradition of play therapy.

The best resource for play therapy can be found in a book, *Emotional Care of Hospitalized Children*[82], which includes a chapter "Play in the Hospital." This book is recommended over many excellent works, including the classical ones, because it places play in the context of the hospital and this serves our needs here.

The best resources for looking at the application of the Montessori Method to religion are Standing's book, *The Child in the Church*[83] and Dr. Sofia Cavalletti's book, *Il potenziale religioso del bambino*[84]. This theme is elaborated in my introduction to the English translation of Cavalletti's book.

There are many misunderstandings about the Montessori tradition and insights. This method was selected for theological play, however, for several reasons. First, it employs an indirect approach that prevents the adult from telling the child how to think and feel. Second, as this method developed in a cross-cultural experience it is aware of the universal child and thus the universal aspect of the child's religious nature. Third, it has enjoyed nearly eighty years of consistent development; most educational or psychological "movements" are not that long-lived. Fourth, its open access to the environment for learning allows one to observe the spontaneous use of materials by the children. What is not used by the children is revised or discarded as inappropriate. Fifth, the balance in this method between structure and creative openness is flexible and used to encourage growth in the individual child according to his or her needs. Sixth, the curriculum is designed in a spiral and is related to the developmental abilities and concerns of children. These are the six major reasons for the selection of this method.

We should also mention Montessori's complex attitude toward religion[85]. Her family was Italian and Catholic, but she traveled widely during her life and lived for many years in India. Her view of religion was broadened as it matured, although it remained rooted in her Italian childhood experiences. Paradoxically it was further strengthened by interaction with her scientific colleagues. Montessori was the first woman to earn a medical degree in Italy. This was in 1896.

Montessori was not only religious, but she also did experiments using her method to teach religion, especially during her twenty years in Barcelona, Spain. After 1936, and for over a quarter of a century, Dr. Sofia Cavalletti continued Montessori's work in Rome[86]. My own work has been influenced by Cavalletti. It extends her pioneering efforts in the two areas of faith development[87] and the hospitalized child.[88]

We turn now to the way religious language is used in theological play. The first rule is that the form of this language needs to be translated and essentialized from its written or spoken medium to a medium in which children can work in a sensorimotor way as well as verbally. Parables, sacred stories, or liturgical acts are "essentialized," not simplified, when the unessential elements are cut away.

Such "essentializing" enables us to put parables, sacred stories, and liturgical acts into concrete form for the children to work with. Then they are placed on the open shelves around the room. Once a presentation has been made about how to use one of the materials anyone can work with it on his or her own or with a small group.

Some people are concerned about imposing a prescribed use of the materials on the child. Others are concerned about imposing specific religious images. We do not, however, teach young children language-in-general, math-in-general, or music-in-general. We teach a native tongue, a decimal system and an eight note music system as something to grow with. We need to teach likewise a specific religious language. Then, in the later stages of development, this orientation can be related to other traditions.

The way a specific symbol system is presented and used gives the child emotional roots as well as an openness to future growth. This attitude combines the security of having roots with an open creative attitude that prevents an artificial ceiling that might stunt one's religious growth or narrow one's perspective.

The second game rule is that once a piece of religious language has been presented to a child or a group of children they are allowed to work with it by themselves or among themselves. Religious language can begin at once to do what it is supposed to do while it is being learned.

Biblical stories, parables, and liturgical acts are not taught to children as ends in themselves. They are taught as tools for the art of making meaning and finding direction in life. The way to use religious language is taught by modeling how this art of play is done. This is like the art of any other kind of game. One learns it by doing it.

The third game rule is that the child needs to make a response in some art form to his or her initial work. This promotes a synthesis of the child's concerns, the child's personal symbol system, and the religious language presented for deep play.

The fourth game rule is that once the art response is made the child and the game-master wonder together about it. The child now has an opportunity to make a further exploration and synthesis. The adult and the child can indirectly discuss this through mutual storytelling or in some other appropriate way to see what issues might still be bothering or invigorating the child.

The fifth and final rule for this game is to review all the children's communication in whatever form it takes, verbal or non-verbal. The adult who directs the theological play area needs this for his or her own evaluation as a player and for the evaluation of the materials and the environment.

The game pieces

The pieces by which one plays this game are the symbols of religious language that have been "materialized". An example of turning religious language into an object by which the game is played is putting a parable into a gold box.

Inside the gold box there is a cloth upon which the parts of the parable are moved. In the parable of the mustard seed there is a person who plants the seed and a green felt tree that unrolls as it grows. Birds' nests and birds are also provided so that children may experience how the "birds of the air" come to make their nests in the tree's branches.

Parables, sacred story, and liturgical materials are all present in the theological play area. The materials are designed to be used by adults also; hence, no artificial ceiling is placed by default on their use by children. This also means that people, adults and children, at any stage of faith development might use these materials together despite their stage differences.[89] Since the adult can be authentic in his or her own involvement with the materials as it is presented to the child, no non-verbal double message is communicated about the real value and usefulness of this game. It is not demeaned by default.

The players

The players are the children, the adults, and God. One of the distinctions between religious symbols and secular signs is that religious symbols participate in the reality to which they point. A diagram will be useful to illustrate the relationships involved in theological play:

Religious symbols not only unite and expand levels of meaning, but they also unite the inner and outer realities of persons. Religious symbols also unite the self and the community which in turn is also related to God. This kind of communication is much more involving and complex than the kind of communication that is used or attempted in the scientific method. Recall that the Latin roots for our word, "religion", are in *re-ligio,* which means something like "to tie" *or* "to fasten".

Figure 1

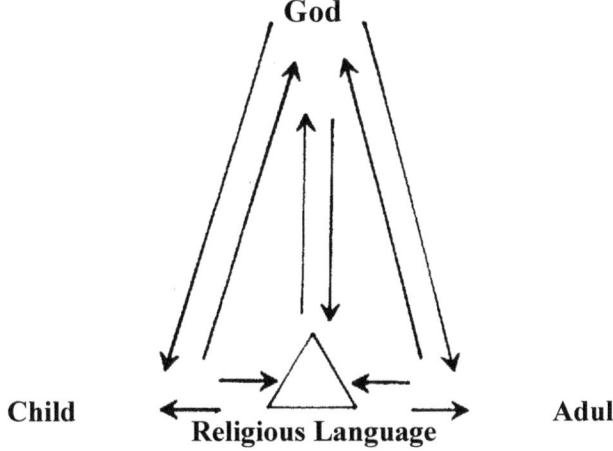

The place for playing

The game space for theological play might be anywhere, but we will limit our discussion to the hospital setting. Like the chess pieces moved on the chess board, the pieces of religious language need an area in which to be moved to make meaning and find direction.

An optimum area for theological play is a room where religious language literally surrounds the child. Our "lab" area at the Institute of Religion's Children's Center has shown that the presence of such a total environment enables the child to make links between the mythic materials, the liturgical materials, and the parable materials. This adds to the total meaning that can be made in the room. It would not be possible to make these links unless the materials were physically present for the young child. The structures by which they put the world together are not yet so flexible or developed that they can do this abstractly.

It is not always possible to set aside a whole room for theological play. A corner of a chaplain's office or a part of the hospital chapel might serve as a less than complete environment.

The children's chaplain also needs to carry the materials with him or her when visiting the bedsides of children who cannot travel to another place. The best general introduction to this whole approach of theological play is the parable of the good shepherd.

When the hospital has access to a video system it can become an electronic "place" for theological play. The television screen is often the only "window" out of the room or out of the child's sickness. It is important to have at least an introduction to theological play present in the window and sound of the television day.

Television changes the three-dimensional art of theological play into a two-dimensional picture of it. This reduces but does not extinguish its impact and usefulness. Certainly, the ability to move the parts of religious language around and to hold them close while wondering about them is gone. On the other hand, television provides the opportunity to introduce theological play to children. The people in the hospital who can engage in this sort of play with the children can also be introduced through television. All the children need to do then is call or have another call by phone for someone, to come play in person.

The time of the game
We have just discussed the game's relation to space. We must now talk about its relationship to time. Some games are strict about time and others are not. In theological play time is a limit structure, but it is also something to be played with. Different kinds of time are used within its structure and they all differ from customary, chronological time-keeping.

The three kinds of time involved in theological play are related to the three functions of religious language embodied in it. The parabolic materials use a self-contained time. The liturgical materials involve one in circular time and tie parables to myth. The mythic materials are linked together by linear time.

The three time frames within theological play operate within a larger view of time. This larger view makes the outside frame for time the boundary between significant time and chronological time, the *kyros* and *chronos* of the New Testament. Inside this boundary significant time collapses the chronology of history. Past events become present and project into the vision of the future through their symbolic meaning. This gives the child a way to construct the future and also to enjoy the security of the past at the same time. It gives a way symbolically for the child to be able to re-center without de-centering during growth.

Conclusion
It is not really possible to understand deep play and how it works in theological play without becoming involved in it. Perhaps this sketch

of the game's structure will enable the readers' imaginations to picture what it would be like to some degree. I hope it will do this sufficiently so that one can envision the possibility of integrating a parish and pastoral care approach to hospitalized children.

The use of theological play as an integrating link between the worship and education experience in the parish and the pastoral care experience in the hospital is not an easy one to make, but it might be a very, very good one. Our experience at The Children's Center suggests that it is.

Original source:

Berryman, J.W. 1982. "Caring for sick children: The parish, the hospital, and theological play." *Liturgy: Ministries To The Sick,* **2 (2): 47-53.**

11

Laughter, Power, and Motivation in Religious Education[90]

Some say religion is dangerous when laughter disappears, but which kind of laughter? Laughter can signal the haughty scorn of the dictator in a repressive power struggle. Other laughter can express the delight of discovering something for yourself. Teachers of religion need to become connoisseurs of laughter to guide their teaching.

This author, who is an Episcopal priest, is troubled by Christian atttitudes toward laughter and how these attitudes distort the use of power in Christian education. Perhaps readers from other traditions will have noticed something such as this in their own teaching as well. To investigate the connections among laughter, power, and motivation for religious education we will look briefly at the history of laughter and then at four philosophical models for laughter. We will then discuss complexity and the laughter of complexity. Finally, we will take a new look at intrinsic motivation and conclude that the laughter of complexity can guide us toward the appropriate use of power by using intrinsic motivation in the teaching and learning of the Christian way.

Freedom and the history of laughter
Barry Sanders begins his book *Sudden Glory: Laughter as Subversive History* with these words: "In the nineteenth century, the Russian philosopher A.I. Herein made the following tantalizing statement: 'It would be extremely interesting to write the history of laughter (1995, x)'". Sanders took up the challenge.

Of course, the laughs have long since evaporated, so such a history must be one of recorded attitudes and theories about laughter. Unfortunately, the writing of theories has been done by people in positions of power. How can we know about the connection between laughter and freedom, then?

Rabelais will be our standard by which to measure laughter and freedom in history. The person who will teach us how to use this measuring device will be Mikhail Bakhtin. His *Rabelais and His World* (1984) was finished by 1940 but not published in Russia until 1965 after much danger and many adventures. The subject of Bakhtin's book was understood to be dangerous. Laughter cannot be tolerated in a totalitarian regime in any century.

In 1932, all Soviet authors, no matter what their style or politics, were forced to join the new Union of Writers. In 1934, stylistic unity was added to institutional unity. The Socialist Realist novel was required. There was now one leader, one party, and one aesthetic.

Bakhtin's study of Rabelais was an indirect way to help prevent the idealization of the Soviet people and the Stalinization of Russian folklore. Bakhtin wanted to promote the exuberance and "corrosive laughter" of ordinary people so that it could be reintegrated into the official view of the world to make public life more open and livable. Like Rabelais, Bakhtin understood the primal force of laughter and wanted to help "carnivalize" Russia. He did this out of hope for the future, because freedom and creativity had been nearly extinguished in his homeland.

To better understand Rabelais, Bakhtin had to locate him in the history of laughter, and so he also took up the challenge of Herzen.

What Bakhtin discovered was that the acknowledgment and respect for laughter as a worldview in the West had been declining since the time of Rabelais to the present.

Bakhtin's history of laughter began as the Christian church became more important politically during the fading of the Roman Empire. This was when the official church view of laughter was worked out. Tertullian, Cyprian, and John Chrysostom condemned ancient spectacles, mime, mime's jests, and laughter. Chrysostom preached that jests and laughter are from the devil.

During the Middle Ages, however, laughter among Christians still flourished in a tradition that ran parallel to the official view. It was used to suspend one's concern with the official "eternal, immovable, absolute and unchangeable" view of reality that the church required. The laughter tradition was complementary, not antagonistic at first.

Bakhtin discovered that until about the twelfth century, medieval parody was not concerned with the negative or imperfect specifics of the church itself or political rule. It had not yet been narrowed to being used to critique these institutions. Instead, everything was considered to be *sub specie ludi*. All was fundamentally and seriously playful.

Hugo Rahner traced the intertwining of the parallel traditions in his *Man at Play* from the classical Greeks to St. Thomas in the thirteenth century (1965). Rahner found an attitude that was "poised between gaiety and gravity, between mirth and tragedy, and which the Greeks designated by the inimitable expression ... the 'grave-merry' man" (9).

Exceptions then began to develop. In fourteenth-century England, for example, the tradition of sacred play came under attack. In 1370, Simon Sudbury, soon to become archbishop of Canterbury, declared that the indulgences granted at Canterbury possessed no spiritual value (Lindahl, 33). This forced a difficult choice between playing and praying.

Lindahl, a student of folkloric patterns in the *Canterbury Tales,* observed that the split in the "play-and-pray ethic" left its mark on Chaucer's work (34). Pilgrimages were dividing into anti-play and play-only groups about this time. The seriously pious turned pilgrimages into acts of self-torture and the non-pious journeyed for completely irreligious ends.

Johan Huizinga noted that there was also a "failure of the imagination" in the fourteenth and fifteenth centuries. His classic *The Autumn of the Middle Ages* (1996) described how European culture began to lose its ability to play (249-267).

When the symbolizing function disappeared or became merely mechanical, all thought became a "barren cataloguing." In the church the "concrete embodiments of the idea and the colorful garb of symbolism" lost their power.

The reaction of the mystics was to attempt to climb to "the absolute imagelessness of the deity" but the mind is not satisfied with speaking only in negation of that which is highest and most fervently desired (257). In addition to those who had, so to speak, been struck by lightning, there were also those who were more sober and more down to earth in their mysticism and daily practice.

These people in the Fraterhouses and the monasteries of the Windesheim Congregation were living in small, quiet, unassuming circles of support. As Huizinga noted: "Emotional and spiritual life was cultivated like a greenhouse plant; there was much narrow puritanism, much moral exercise, a stifling of laughter and of basic human drives, and much pietistic simplemindedness" (265). These unofficial folk were gathering and being heard, but they were not known for their mirth.

Thomas à Kempis came from this narrow life. His *Imitatio Dei* is a group of simple sayings around a single point. Its monotonous rhythm "makes it resemble the ocean on a soft rainy evening or the autumnal sigh of the wind." It is miraculous in its even and melancholy power to bring peace, calm, and a quiet resigned expectation and solace. There is something there for the tired of all ages, but the exuberance and laughter of carnival is far, far away.

Still, exceptional privileges of license and lawlessness were allowed in the marketplace, on feast days, and in festive recreational literature. For example, the feast of fools was defended in a circular letter by the Paris School of Theology as late as 1444. It called foolishness our "second nature," and acknowledged our need to allow this nature or force to spend itself at least once a year.

About 1450, the printing press was invented and became the main technology for the coming new age. Print began to change what was known as well as what could be known. Truth-in-a-book became external, clear, certain, visible, repeatable, unchanging, constant, and indisputable. As Ong (1986) has noted, even "if a book states an untruth, ten thousand printed refutations will do nothing to the printed text: the untruth is there forever ... Texts are essentially contumacious" (27).

The birth of the new age during the sixteenth century in Europe was certainly contumacious. Obstinate rebellion was everywhere, and Francois Rabelais (1495-1553) made his way through the shifting powers as a restless survivor. He was first a Franciscan and then a Benedictine monk with a vast interest in Greek and the humanities. He then became a secular priest and studied and taught medicine at the University of Montpellier.

The exaggerated and pungent stories of Rabelais, which he wrote from about 1533 to nearly his death, brought the folk tradition of carnival into print. It challenged the objectivity, control, and permanence that print technology had brought to the new consciousness. He dignified what was supposed to be only for the amusement and entertainment of the powerless, the disenfranchised, and the illiterate.

Rabelais' view of laughter drew its authority from three classical sources that the Fathers of the Church had either not noticed or did not wish to notice. All three sources agreed that laughter has a positive, regenerating, and creative meaning.

Hippocrates' medical treatise asserted that laughter and a cheerful mood on the part of the patient and physician were important for healing. Aristotle observed that children should not be considered to be human beings until they laugh, something that he thought took place about the fortieth day after birth. The third ancient source was Lucian. One of his characters, Menippus, even laughed in the kingdom of the dead!

Rabelais' stories were divided into four books. All were condemned by the Sorbonne soon after printing. In 1545, the first three books were printed in one volume with *"avec privilege du roi,"* but was condemned anyway.

Rabelais was in good company. Erasmus' *The Praise of Folly* was condemned by the Sorbonne in 1543. Erasmus thought his opponents were "racking a butterfly on a wheel" (1979, xiii), but he took their attacks seriously and attempted to remain foolishly wise *(morosophos)* in his revisions.

The Puritans became more visible as a group after the Reformation of the sixteenth century. "High seriousness became synonymous with a deep religiosity. Laughter on the other hand meant frivolity, looseness, an attitude of devil-may-care. It meant everything but the solemnity associated with a Puritan religion" (Sanders 1995, 197),

In England, the government joined the church to make laughter illegal. A 1547 statute outlawed an offensive joke about the Eucharist. In 1559, royal injunctions prohibited jokes against the clergy in general. A 1606 statue made joking references about God on stage forbidden.

The views of Rabelais during the centuries that followed are interesting. They show how attitudes and definitions of laughter changed. For example, during the seventeenth century the feudal system dissolved and absolute monarchy formed. Rationalism and classicism joined to create a new official culture. The ways in which the Middle Ages had allowed our "second nature" to be acknowledged were lost. The official view of laughter became more narrowly defined and cut off from the hearty and realistic laughter of the peasants.

This was the age of Moliere (1622-1673). He developed his comedies from the traditions of the old French farce and the Italian *commedia dell'arte,* but he produced his plays for the court aristocracy of Louis XIV. Moliere's characters were taken from the nobility, and his villains, especially his ridiculous characters, are the bourgeoisie. The peasants were not mentioned.

After the first third of the seventeenth century, Rabelais's writings were no longer understood as being part of the people's festive laughter. He appeared unique and needed interpretation to be understood. The historic-allegorical method was developed at that time to provide the needed interpretation. This method prevailed for three centuries, while the tradition of popular, festive laughter that informed Rabelais' work was forgotten. It was reduced to personal invective.

Laughter's definition continued to narrow in the eighteenth century. During this period the universal outlook of laughter was also lost, being submerged in negation and limited to the private. It was during this century that Rabelais was the least understood.

Voltaire thought Rabelais was "extravagant and unintelligible." Bakhtin found that Voltaire could only understand Rabelais's exuberance as "naked and straight satire." Laughter had been reduced to "bare mockery," precisely the "laughter of Voltaire." It no longer had any regenerating or renewing element left in it.

When English-speaking people think about eighteenth century humor, Swift's "A Modest Proposal" from 1729 probably comes to mind first. Its satire was intended to subvert the status quo as much as any carnival clown or festival fool, but it observed decorum and displayed its wit precisely by not eliciting gales of laughter.

Such wit required a literate and educated audience. This laughter of the mind tricked the insiders into noticing that the reductive, mathematical solutions proposed for Ireland's woes were as disgusting as baby cannibalism. Swift, like his readers, had a stake in maintaining the existing order, and so he used his wit to prod and poke the way to reform.

In the nineteenth century, what Bakhtin called the realism of "eavesdropping and peeping" developed. Laughter was used to express only irony and sarcasm. The grotesque exaggeration of Rabelais that had delighted the sixteenth century was now seen as purely negative. For example, the enormous amounts of food, drink, and clothes needed to sustain the giant Pantagruel, King of the Dipsodes, became seen only as the king's heavy expenses imposed upon the people rather than an abundance.

By this time efforts were made to turn Rabelais into either a rationalist or an orthodox Christian, but his religion and humanity were wider and more deeper-rooted than any simple, one-sided view could encompass. He had ignored all intolerant seriousness and all dogmatism.

Rabelais's humor was not used to hide his atheist tendencies, as some modern scholars have argued, but to point to the comic aspect of the whole world. He spoke out of a tradition that included the crowning and uncrowning of clowns in the Roman Saturnalia and European carnivals. Such laughter was generated from the people's optimism that existed despite their deep awareness that all of our hopes and disappointments arise from the limited potential in any age. There is always a struggle between great and small, exalted and lowly, fantastic and real, physical and spiritual, rising and falling, flowering and growing old, and life and death.

Bakhtin's history showed how the primal awareness of joy can transcend the transient, because in the long run there is the hope that plenitude will prevail over finitude. Laughter grounded in such realism gives one the freedom to deal with whatever comes and to question all who take life or themselves too seriously.

We turn now to another way to organize our discussion of laughter.

We will move from the story of laughter and freedom to the analysis of laughter's cause. For this discussion we will examine the four models described by John Morreall.

Four models of laughter

John Morreall's study of what causes laughter (1983) presents four models for consideration under the following headings: "Superiority," "Incongruity," "Relief," and Morreall's own model, "The Pleasant Psychological Shift." We will look at each in turn.

1. The Superiority Model

The Superiority Model features Plato's argument that what makes people laughable is their self-ignorance. Aristotle agreed with Plato that laughter is basically a form of derision. Hobbes thought that laughter erupts, when there is "a sudden glory," a victory over another person or some entity. Laughter, then, is self-congratulation. Ludovici called laughter an expression of a person's feeling of "superior adaptation," placing Hobbes's view in a Darwinian frame.

The superiority claim calls attention to the difference in importance between the one laughing and the "lower" person who is laughed at. Even when you laugh at yourself, part of your self is put down while another part is raised up.

Morreall observed that this model cannot serve as a comprehensive theory of laughter, for all laughter cannot be reduced to the declaration of importance. Not all laughter is self-serving.

2. The Incongruity Model

The Incongruity Model shifts the focus from feelings to thinking. Instead of the feeling of triumph, this theory is interested in our cognitive reaction to an unexpected, illogical, or inappropriate event. This theory does not deny that feelings of superiority may be involved in laughter, but it is interested in the more abstract notion of incongruity as laughter's primary cause.

An assumption is made that we live in an orderly world, or at least that we grow to expect certain patterns. As Pascal put it, "Nothing produces laughter more than a surprising disproportion between that which one expects and that which one sees."

Kant's theory of laughter included aspects of relief that will be discussed in the next model, as well as incongruity, but the kind of incongruity he identified was curious. It takes place when an expectation "is suddenly transformed into nothing." This was explained by an example. A rich man was unable to plan a funeral because the more money he paid the mourners to look sad, the more cheerful they looked. The laughter comes, Kant said, from the absolute frustration of our expectations. "Nothing" is left to say.

Schopenhauer disagreed. His version of incongruity focused more on the unexpected than being tricked logically into being mute. If the funeral procession were impossible because of rain, it would not be funny. This is a normal occurrence. What makes Kant's example funny is the non-mourning mourners. They are not normal.

Incongruity causes much laughter, Morreall observed, but there are many cases of nonhumorous laughter that do not involve incongruity or superiority. In addition, there can be incongruity that is deeply sad, as with the death of a child, so incongruity is not the sole cause of laughter.

3. The Relief Model

The Relief Model relies primarily on the psychological concept of venting nervous energy. The feeling of superiority and intellectual incongruity are not necessarily dismissed, but they fade into the background.

One of the earliest articulations of the relief theory was Shaftesbury's essay of 1711, "The Freedom of Wit and Humor." He defined laughter as breaking free from constraint. Schopenhauer, mentioned above, also wrote of laughter as the result of an escape from the oppression of

"Dame Reason," as well as springing from incongruity.

Shaftesbury reasoned that when a person enters a situation with pent-up nervous energy, such as that dammed up by a cultural taboo, a release of energy results in laughter. Of course, the situation itself may cause the build-up of nervous energy, as well as its release, as in a joke.

Herbert Spencer added to this theory by his observation that laughter differs from other releases of pent-up energy, because it is not the early stage of a later act. With anger, for example, you might have angry thoughts, clench your fists, crouch, and finally attack the person you are angry with. Unlike anger, laughter does not lead to anything else.

Freud distinguished three kinds of laughter in his *Jokes and Their Relation to the Unconscious*. It was his view that motivation in human activity followed definite mechanical rules of operation that regulate the flow of energy within the human organism. In all laughter situations, Freud wrote, we summon a certain quantity of psychic energy away from some other psychic purpose where it is no longer needed. This surplus energy is discharged in laughter.

Freud's typology of laughter included "Jokes," where the discharged energy comes from *forbidden* feelings and thoughts. "The Comic" is an expenditure of energy that has been saved in *thought*. "Humor" involves stored *emotional* energy. Freud's packets of stored energy, how they are to be distinguish, and how one measures what is superfluous remain unclear.

Whether one refers to Herbert Spencer's view of laughter in his "On the Physiology of Laughter" from his *Essays on Education* or to Freud's more complicated theory that refers to Spencer by name, the critique is the same. It is difficult to crowd all laughter into a single relief model.

Some laughter erupts before there is time for a build up of energy.

For example, it only takes a glance to laugh at some *New Yorker* cartoons. This is true whether or not the content is related to repressed feelings.

Sometimes laughter can be appropriate, fully conscious, and fail to reduce inappropriate feelings. A hostile practical joke may be mean, but it is a good example. The laughter that results from an enemy sitting on a hidden bladder cushion in a big meeting and making embarrassing noises may not relieve the joker's dislike of the person. It may only result in satisfying but revengeful laughter.

Finally, you would expect the greatest amount of laughter to spring out immediately when the threshold is passed for the release of energy, like opening the valve of a steam pipe. Some jokes, however, become better and create more laughter as one thinks about them. The laughter builds instead of declining over time. This model too fails to include all examples of laughter. We therefore need a more comprehensive model.

4. The Pleasant Psychological Shift Model

The fourth model of laughter is Morreall's own. It is called in his words "The Pleasant Psychological Shift Model." It is designed to provide enough generality to cover the cause of all forms of laughter. The "shift" he refers to must be pleasant, for a "shift" could also be charged with sadness.

Laughter is not the shift itself. Neither is it the pleasant feeling produced by the shift. Laughter is the physical activity caused by and which expresses the feeling produced by the shift. The feeling itself might be called "amusement" or "mirth."

This theory is broad enough to include all of the examples of laughter above as well as the laughter of tickling. (Aristotle noted that you cannot tickle yourself, for some surprise or deception must be involved.) It also includes sensory and perceptual shifts, such as in a game of peekaboo or when one is tossed into the air and caught.

Morreall also included a developmental component in his theory. For example, he said the following:

> The child cannot enjoy humor, or even experience it as humor, until he catches on to the fact that the incongruities he is being presented with are only a playful rearranging of reality and not, say, a confusing bunch of preposterous lies. Before a child can play around with his conceptual system, in short, he has to have a pretty solid grasp of that system, and has to feel comfortable in having it violated. (1983, 44-45)

A child's capacity for humor increases in sophistication as intellectual and emotional development continues. This is true for both humorous laughter and nonhumorous laughter, such as winning the lottery or suddenly experiencing safety after danger. Other examples of nonhumorous laughter are the result of embarrassment or hysteria.

Laughter, however, does not continue to develop automatically. For some adults, as Wordsworth wrote, "The world is too much with us." The ability to laugh sometimes atrophies from a lack of use, or it can be taken away by the power of unrelenting seriousness.

This is why laughter and power are so important to keep in mind for the religious educator. Sincerity without humor is closed, dangerous, and demonic. Fanatical certainty breeds intolerance, aggression, and violence. Religion taught in this manner leads to inquisitions, heresy trials, witch-hunts, religious persecutions, holy wars, book burnings, and martyrdoms. We already know this from history. What we have forgotten is the power of certain kinds of laughter as an antidote to closed, unrelenting seriousness.

The hopeful laughter of mirth in the deep and ancient tradition of wise laughter does not deny seriousness. It purifies and completes it. It keeps one's seriousness open to the future without losing contact with the limitations of past, present, or future.

Serious laughter signals that one is experiencing a playful, meditative, and creative sense of life, rather than the sneer of controlling rigidity and the endless hilarity of madness. What we need is a more specific view of laughter to guide our use of power in religious education.

Laughter and complexity

The field of chaos has antecedents in the nineteenth century, but it took recognizable shape during the early 1970s. This was because about that time fast and powerful computers started becoming more available and affordable. "As of 1991, the number of papers on chaos was doubling about every two years" (Williams 1997, 19).

Many journals have been born, and both technical (specialized mathematics written for other specialists) and non-technical books (beginning especially with James Gleick's *Chaos* in 1987) have been written. Garnett P. Williams' *Chaos Theory Tamed* (1997) is a good compromise between the technical and the non-technical introductions.

"Chaos," in ordinary language, means disorder or confusion. This word is a misnomer for the special meaning for which chaos theory uses it. Chaos only *appears* to be present when a system is plotted by a two-dimensional graph with one variable. The line goes up and down, apparently at random. If one uses three variables, plotted simultaneously in computer space, the system will be seen to wander, never repeating itself, as the emergence of a form appears with boundaries that contain the formerly apparent chaos. Chaos and order are, therefore, related to each other over time.

Examples in nature where self-organization takes place without any outside input are: the flocking of birds, the schooling of fish, the rippling of sand, weather forming hurricanes, water molecules moving into laminar flow, stars forming into the spiral arms of a galaxy, and the development of economic markets (Williams 1997, 233).

Self-organization is the main feature of a kind of behavior called complexity. Complexity "is a dynamic behavior that never reaches equilibrium and in which many independent particle-like units or 'agents' perpetually interact and seek mutual accommodation in any of many possible ways" (234). Complex adaptive systems are called emergent systems. What "emerges" are new, more complex levels of order over time. Such systems seem to be "living systems."

We cannot understand such systems by isolating their components or analyzing each component individually. We have to look at the whole system over time.

When we attempt to place "life" at the center of our teaching, then, we become involved with complexity. Life is where there is the greatest freedom and yet the ability to sustain continuity is found. When the system drifts over the boundary into chaos and gets stuck there, it spins apart. When it drifts into rigidity and gets stuck, it grinds to a halt, breaks, and disintegrates. Our teaching and learning, therefore, needs to be in the service of complexity, rather than reduction and control, especially in religious education, which takes for its "subject" the Creator.

What does complexity feel like? How can we identify it? Living systems that are human have the ability to be conscious of this process and to name it, so the question for us is how can we be in touch with this deep impulse for life? What behavioral manifestation is there that we are "there?"

My proposal is that laughter of a particular kind is the behavioral manifestation that complexity is present. To discuss this further, I would like to propose the metaphor of a river. The water of the river is a place of "sensitive chaos" (Schwenk, 1996). It will also meander. The banks do not so much contain it, as guide it for the time being, always open to change.

If our students get stuck on either bank of the river, they will cease to be turbulent, eternally changing, and alive. If they get stuck in chaos, their laughter expresses madness. It is completely disconnected from seriousness. Nothing is sacred to such laughter.

If we get stuck in rigidity, there is too much seriousness, too much control. All is sacred, so laughter becomes the laughter of scorn for the uninitiated, the frivolous, and the unimportant. Only the content of one's own seriousness counts.

The two limits define each other in relation to each other. One boundary is comedy in opposition to tragedy. The other is boundary is tragedy in opposition to comedy. Going beyond tragedy or comedy and remaining there is where the danger lies. The deep channel of the river integrates tragedy and comedy into a resounding joy that is sometimes thundering and sometimes gurgling with laughter.

We are drawn toward tragic people. They arouse pity and fear. We sometimes call them heroes, but at the same time something about them makes us draw back. This "drawing back" is our impulse toward life. This is because, as Northrop Frye (1957) has described, tragic figures become rigid, and more and more committed to the pursuit of their goals. They will endure pain or even death to carry on in the pursuit of their goal. One can become tragically stuck.

One can also become stuck in comedy. In pure comedy Frye observed that the primary theme is the happy integration of the central character into society. While a tragedy might end with people dying on stage, the comedy ends with people getting married. While tragedy arouses pity and fear, comedy arouses sympathy and ridicule. When one veers beyond comedy, however, and gets stuck, then the happy integration into society becomes fantasy. Belonging becomes an illusion.

Warning laughter

A clue to telling when one is getting stuck may be found in Henri Bergson's classical work, *Laughter* (1980), which was first published in 1900. I call this classical, because the Second Book of Aristotle's *Poetics,* the one about comedy, has been lost. Bergson's work is a major candidate for an alternative, even though he makes little or no mention of Rabelais and draws, perhaps, too many of his examples from Moliere.

Bergson said that what makes us laugh is when a living being acts mechanical. A "mechanical inelasticity," such as when someone trips over a stone, is what causes laughter. A comic character is someone who is no longer "ceaselessly adapting and readapting himself to the society of which he is a member. He slackens in the attention that is due to life" (187). The person is "absent" and takes it easy. In our terms, one becomes stuck and loses his or her complexity. Laughter snaps life's larger perspective back into focus.

"Laughter is, above all, a corrective," Bergson argued. It is the result of a "mechanism set up in us by nature or, what is almost the same thing, by our long acquaintance with social life" (188). Laughter is not kind-hearted. It has an objective and moral tone.

Bergson drew a distinction between a tragedy that centers around individuals such as Hamlet or Othello and a comedy that is generally about a type, such as someone who hates people, as in Moliere's *The Misanthrope,* or the miser in his play, *The Miser.*

For our purposes, the types are figures who go beyond comedy into madness and go beyond tragedy into rigidity. The alarm system of laughter is not only about overweening pride or unrelenting fantasy, but more fundamentally it is about our desperate need to create meaning despite the threat of death or madness. Meaning is what is to be found in the deep channel of the river. There the laughter of complexity lives.

The laughter of meaninglessness is found beyond the boundary of comedy in madness. Nothing means anything anymore. Hilarity becomes a habit. When we pass beyond the boundary of tragedy, compulsive laughter is there too. It is the laughter of scorn and the unforgiving laughter of ceaseless competition.

What has been described as complexity provides a rich enough definition of intrinsic motivation for religious education to be useful. The rediscovery of intrinsic motivation has taken place in general education during relatively recent times. We now turn to that discussion.

The rediscovery of intrinsic motivation and the laughter of complexity

In 1965, Mihaly Csikszentmihalyi finished his doctoral thesis, which focused on a group of male artists who worked intensively with great concentration, enjoying their work immensely, and yet who seemed to lack interest in the resulting product for which they got little affirmation from the culture. There were two common explanations at the time about why this happened.

One explanation of this drive was that the artists were sublimating repressed instinctual cravings. Csikszentmihalyi thought there was too much genuine excitement and involvement with the emerging forms and colors to explain it all in terms of a substitution for something else.

A second explanation was in terms of extrinsic rewards. In the mid-sixties, most psychologists were not interested in intrinsic motivation. The behaviorist revolution started by John B. Watson in 1913 had begun to run its course, but the attraction to objective, observable behavior was still persuasive to many. B.F. Skinner was widely read.

Abraham Maslow was an exception to this trend. He distinguished between process and product orientations in creative behavior. Some people worked hard, he said, because the work itself was rewarding. This motivation, he suggested, might be related to a desire for "self-actualization," namely, a need to discover one's potentialities and limitations through intense activity and experience.

Csikszentmihalyi agreed, but he also wanted to know what self-rewarding behavior felt like. He turned first to the literature on play. Play is clearly intrinsically motivated, he discovered. People play for the playing itself, whatever its evolutionary or adaptive value might be.

Studies by that time had shown that even rats did not work exclusively to get food or to avoid shocks. Sometimes they appeared to be motivated by novelty, curiosity, and the exercise of competence.

Richard deCharms then discovered that if you rewarded people for doing things they had initially chosen spontaneously, their intrinsic motivation to do them decreased. This was summarized in a volume he called *The Hidden Costs of Reward*.

Meanwhile, Csikszentmihalyi had discovered what he thought intrinsic motivation felt like. He called the feeling "flow." Flow was felt in a wide variety of pursuits from mountain climbing to painting, and sometimes even in one's work. In 1975, he published *Beyond Boredom and Anxiety*.

The situation in which flow can be felt involves a middle range of activity between tedium and anxiety-producing chaos. From the perspective of the subjective experience alone, work and play could no longer be considered opposites.

The concept of flow gained greater notice in the decade from 1975-1985. Among others, Mircea Elide became interested in flow that displayed its relevance for religious education. He commissioned an article on the experience of flow for the new *Encyclopedia of Religion* he was working on at that time for Macmillan.

What was converging from all of this curiosity was a psychology that focused on optimal experience, rather than pathology. It was outlined in a collection of articles by several authors from different fields called *Optimal Experience* (1988).

The intrinsic motivation of flow and the psychology of optimum experience has important implications for guiding one's religious life and our teaching as religious educators. When we compare what Mihalyi Csikszentmihalyi has described as creativity in terms of "flow" with what Richard of St. Victor (died in 1173) has described as "contemplation" and Catherine Garvey (1977) described as "play," we find the following:

Contemplation	Flow	Play
1. Contemplation is the free		1. Voluntary
2. More penetrating gaze of a mind	1. Concentration is deep 2. Self-consciousness disappears 3. The sense of time is altered	2. Active engagement
3. Suspended with wonder	4. The experience is "autotelic" (worth having for itself)	3. No extrinsic goal
4. Concerning manifestations of wisdom	5. Feedback is immediate 6. Goals are clear 7. Skills match challenges 8. Control is possible 9. Problems are forgotten	4. Links to creativity, learning languages, social roles
(5. Is pleasurable, ecstatic)	(10. Is pleasurable)	5. Is pleasurable

First, all three descriptions include being pleasurable, even if contemplation and flow do not make pleasure or ecstasy one of their explicit tenets. This implication is suggested by the parentheses in the diagram.

Second, all three experiences are voluntary. You cannot force someone to play, create, or contemplate. This means that the motivation must be intrinsic to find the river's deep current without distortion.

Third, flow fills in rather than conflicts with the descriptions of play and contemplation. It adds detail to Richard's "more penetrating gaze of a mind," his "suspension with wonder," and the involvement with "manifestations of wisdom." Garvey's "active engagement" and the related activities of creativity, language learning, and learning of social roles (which is the rudiments of ethics) are also enriched conceptually by this comparison.

It is suggested that what has been discovered, using these three overlapping experiences, is what the complexity, where living systems dwell, feels like. This experience involves being, becoming, and theological play:

1. Being – the absorbing relationship with God known in contemplation.
2. Becoming – creativity as focused on one's continuing journey toward God.
3. Theological Play – the integrating position that involves 1 and 2.

The kinds of laughter that signal each of the above are:

1. Laughter of delight in communion with God.
2. Laughter of discovery in creativity.
3. Laughter of play with God, the deep self, others, and nature.

The nature of the "shift" that is pleasurable, following Morreall's model, is a:

1. Shift to knowing of the spirit by contemplation, as distinguished from knowing of the mind by reason and the knowing of the body by the senses (Richard of St. Victor).
2. Shift to the new frame in which creativity will discover "the new."
3. Shift to the collaborative "field" of play and away from the competitive "work" of everyday.

This is why it is important for religious educators to become connoisseurs of laughter to show the way to the turbulence of the river in which we live and move and have our being. The implications of this discovery for religious education are many, but we will conclude by returning to our focus on the appropriate use of power in religious education.

Conclusion

The big question in any kind of educational setting is always "discipline." To introduce laughter into such a serious discussion seems, well, laughable. When you think of laughter as a sign of the complexity that guides us towards more authentic life, then laughter does not seem so trivial.

Still, how do you get a group of six-year-olds to do what you want them to do? To paraphrase the gospels, you call to them and they do not listen. You play a pipe and they do not dance. You wail and they do not mourn. You offer them something to eat and to drink, but they do not care (Matt. 11:16-19; Luke 7:31-35).

I have two observations to make. First, you have two choices: extrinsic or intrinsic motivation. Extrinsic motivation has the alternatives of positive or negative reinforcement to shape behavior, or there is neutral non-reinforcement to extinguish misbehavior. This is familiar ground that does not need to be covered here again, except to say that some children will bear a great deal of pain to be free. They want to laugh well.

What we sometimes see as a child being "obstinate," "stubborn," or "a behavior problem" may be a human being who is trying to find that playful channel between being stuck beyond comedy or tragedy to stay alive. We seem to be able to respect a painful sacrifice for freedom by other adults when they are politically oppressed, but the same human quality in a child in an educational setting just makes us bad tempered.

A second observation is to underline what Alfie Kohn has recently reminded us about. The title of his book states his thesis: *Punished by Rewards: The Trouble with Gold Stars, Incentive Plans, A's, Praise, and other Bribes* (1993). He argued, following to a large extent the work of Richard deCharms mentioned above, that the most damaging result of rewards and punishments is that they undermine intrinsic motivation.

Intrinsic motivation in religious education is about nourishing and guiding children to discover the way to find the deep channel of complexity in their relationship with God, the deep self, others, and nature. Developing strategies for such a use of power in religious education is the direction we need to go, but we will not go far without serious laughter to show us the way.

Serious laughter is what arises with delight from the complexity of life. It is the lovely sound of a living system that is free from the endless chaos of madness and the death of closed rigidity. It is a sound Rabelais knew well and learned from the illiterate, who, without power, faced the future with hope and the assumption of God's abundance despite all.

The teaching and learning of religion, then, at least the Christian religion, is an art that needs to be guided by this deep river that flows from, with, and to God. It is the source for a powerful "intrinsic motivation" to guide us by the sound of its laughter.

References

Bakhtin, M. 1984. *Rabelais and His World.* Trans. by Helene Iswolsky. Bloomington: Indiana University Press.

Bergson, H. 1956. *An Essay on Comedy.* Ed. by Wylie Sypher. New York: Doubleday Anchor Book.

_____. 1980. *Laughter.* New York: Doubleday Anchor Book.

Csikszentmihalyi, M. 1975. *Beyond Boredom and Anxiety.* San Francisco: Jossey-Bass.

Csikszentmihalyi, M., and I. S. Csikszentmihalyi, eds. 1988. *Optimal Experience: Psychological Studies of Flow in Consciousness.* Cambridge: University Press.

Erasmus, D. 1979. *The Praise of Folly.* Trans. by Clarence H. Miller. New Haven and London: Yale University Press.

Frye, N. 1957. *Anatomy of Criticism: Four Essays.* Princeton, New Jersey: Princeton University Press.

Garvey, C. 1977. *Play.* Cambridge: Harvard University Press.

Gleick, J. 1987. *Chaos: Making A New Science.* New York: Penguin Books.

Huizinga, J. 1996. *The Autumn of the Middle Ages.* Trans. by Rodney J. Payton and Ulrich Mammitzsch. Chicago: University of Chicago Press.

Kohn, A. 1993. *Punished by Rewards: The Trouble with Gold Stars, Incentive Plans, A's, Praise, and Other Bribes.* Boston: Houghton Mifflin Company.

Lindahl, C. *Earnest Games: Folkloric Patterns in the Canterbury Tales.* Bloomington and Indianapolis: Indiana University Press, n.d.

Morreall, J. 1983. *Taking Laughter Seriously.* Albany: State University of New York.

Ong, W. 1986. "Writing is a technology that restructures thought." In *The Written Word: Literacy In Transition.* Ed. by G. Baumann. Wolfson College Lectures. Oxford: Clarendon Press.

Rahner, H. 1965. *Man at Play.* London: Burnes and Oats.

Sanders, B. 1995. *Sudden Glory: Laughter as Subversive History.* Boston: Beacon Press.

Schwenk, T. 1996. *Sensitive Chaos: The Creation of Flowing Forms in Water and Air.* London: Rudolf Steiner Press.

Williams, G.P. 1997. *Chaos Theory Tamed.* Washington: Joseph Henry Press.

Original source:

Berryman, J.W. 1998. "Laughter, power and motivation in religious education." *Religious Education,* **93 (3): 358-378.**

12

Playful Orthodoxy: Reconnecting Religion and Creativity by Education

The problem addressed here arises when one notices that the two fundamental tendencies of religious education, teaching for the closure of orthodoxy and teaching for the openness of the seeker, move in opposite directions. Since both tendencies are dangerous when they stand alone, religious education is confronted with what seems like a cruel dilemma. If one teaches for orthodoxy by memorization, by an emphasis on authority, by the formation of habits, by the promotion of single-minded duty, and by forming an us-against-them mentality, then the result is a deeply held, clear concept and firm practice. The danger is that this can also result in the formation of a rigid, closed-minded, defensive, and sometimes violent orthodoxy. The opposite extreme is also dangerous. Teaching religion in a way that encourages self-direction, wonder, discovery, perspective-taking, pluralism, and inclusiveness tends toward an "anything goes" approach. No clear community is formed to guide and support the growing child's deep identity. Such rootless religion can result in unacknowledged existential anxiety and the loss of deep identity.

This dilemma is, however, false. What appear to be opposing tendencies are actually parts of a larger whole, the creative process. Grounding religious education in creativity is, however, counter-intuitive. Even the words "playful orthodoxy" have the ring of an oxymoron. This is because the opening and closing tendencies of the creative process have been two separate and different things in many people's minds.

The opening and closing tendencies of the creative process become separated when religion shifts its experience base from the creative process to power. Power-based religion is so pervasive in our time that our language has conformed to this separation as if it were natural or even normative. The problem with power-based religion is that it resists the opening aspect of the creative process and favors only the closing tendency. A secondary use of creativity is sometimes applied to power-based religion, which results in limiting the creative process to protecting the system and finding ways to promote its expansion. This adds to the problem and masks the fact that, when religion becomes power-based, it decays as a way for coping creatively with ageless existential issues as well as confronting new situations about life and death. Instead of being a way to cope with trouble, the process becomes trouble itself.

To address this problem we must re-root the teaching of religion in the creative process. To support this conclusion, a long view of religion will be taken to affirm its creative function. Second, the "where" and "what" of creativity will be discussed. Third, the style and stage aspects of the creative process will be examined. The fourth step will be to discuss how religious language can be re-rooted in the creative process. The fifth step examines what kind of teacher is needed to accomplish this. Finally, the question of what method should be used to teach playful orthodoxy will be addressed.

Religion and creativity

The established world religions have long perplexed and frustrated people with their conflicting and exclusive truth claims. Today this conflict threatens the survival of our species and, perhaps, the continuation of life in any form. To gain perspective on the purpose of religion, we shall, therefore, go back to prehistory, long before any of the present world religions existed. This is not done to discover a "golden age" but to propose that religion's fundamental function is to cope creatively with trouble and to celebrate amazing instances of survival.

Jerome Bruner tells us that "trouble" is what prompts stories.[91] The pain and frustration of the trouble forces us to remember a problematic situation with deep feelings and to play with it to see if we can find a better outcome for the story next time. I would add that, when any of our fundamental needs – physiological needs, safety, belonging, self-esteem, or self-actualization[92] are frustrated, we experience trouble.

In addition to telling stories of trouble, we also tell stories of joy when things work out well and in ways that we could not have imagined before they took place. We tell about moments of what might be called "miracle." They go beyond what is normally expected. There are other functions of religious language, such as providing creation stories, parables, and other kinds of meaning, but coping with trouble and celebrating life appear to be the primary functions.

Rituals conserve ways for enacting fundamental stories. They provide a safe place in which the creative process can flourish to create more optimum personal narratives and to celebrate moments of flourishing. The religious practices that arose during prehistory were apparently a way to cope through tradition and creativity with timeless, existential limits and time-sensitive new situations of danger or celebration. This activity probably began with ritualized actions, using symbols, which then developed into rituals with words.

Sometime around 50,000 years ago two great changes took place in our ancestors. A genetic shift provided for the production of speech. Spoken language over time interacted with changes in the brain to produce what Terrance Deacon has called "the symbolic species."[93] A second major change, as early as 13,000 years ago, was the production of food, a farming and herding lifestyle that competed with and surpassed hunting and gathering. People lived in bands of about a dozen people until about 40,000 years ago, and most continued to do so as recently as 11,000 years ago. The shift from hunting and gathering to farming and herding enabled groups of hundreds of people to settle in villages and form tribes. Some tribes then evolved into chiefdoms involving thousands of people, and then into states with populations of over 50,000.[94]

People living in bands used cave paintings, ornaments for the body, and burial practices to cope with trouble and to celebrate life's high moments. The artists appear to have understood their medium; for example, they painted animals on the bulges of walls to make them more realistic. Paul L. Harris notes that this indicates the beginning of "the work of the imagination."[95] Three things indicate this. The artifacts and props "were collectively produced and understood; they served to conjure up an imagined world distinct from the physical context in which they were manufactured or displayed," and in each case the physical context was acknowledged and re-worked so the artifacts could serve their function.[96] In short, the imagination had been born in a way that was deeply associated with religion. The symbols used had been imagined and aided the imaginations of others. Symbols provided a link between the spirit world and the everyday world, conveying energy to the people who saw or touched them.

The imagination is also associated with play. Since modern mammals play, there is no reason to think that ancient humans did not, even as language was only first developing. Play is pleasurable and, therefore, self-reinforcing. It is not the product of play that motivates one to play but the playing itself. It absorbs the player and is entirely voluntary. When combat is reframed as play, the combatants do not actually kill and eat their prey, so play provides a way to practice, to enjoy one's skill, to discover new moves, to try out new weapons, and to live to tell about it. Play is also associated with learning languages and social roles, creativity, and problem-solving.[97]

What-if, or wondering play, gives rise to creating new ways of doing things. As-if, or role play, helps form continuity by ritual and storytelling to induct children into adult roles. These two kinds of play suggest that they are grounded in the exploring (wondering play) and conserving (role play) aspects of the creative process. Religion's early function, then, was to cope creatively with existential trouble and to celebrate the miraculous by play, ritual, art, and storytelling. This was, perhaps, the beginning of the particular kind of discourse we now call "religious," which at its beginning was rooted in the creative process rather than in social power. That is the assertion made here.

The production and storing of food enabled farmers and herders to include specialists in their societies, such as priests and rulers, who did not need to spend their time hunting, finding, or producing food. Among the inventions in these societies was writing, which arose in Mesopotamia somewhat before 3000 B.C.[98] Jared Diamond also notes:

> Bands and tribes already had supernatural beliefs, just as do modern established religions. But the supernatural beliefs of bands and tribes did not serve to justify central authority, justify transfer of wealth, or maintain peace between unrelated individuals. When supernatural beliefs gained those functions and became institutionalized, they were thereby transformed into what we now term religion.[99]

When people began to live under a chief, religion became involved with social power. The drift of religion from individuals creatively coping with trouble and celebrating the survival miracles of people in intimate relationships with each other and the spirit world toward a centralized power shifted its foundation.

Creative coping by means of religious language helped save our distant ancestors as a species. The Neanderthal people, for example, probably did not have much of an ability to use the creative process and died out despite their powerful frames and survival abilities. We, therefore, need to understand better the connection between religion and the creative process to be more clear about how religion can perform the constructive function that it had thousands of years ago, which saved our species, rather than risk destroying it today in religious conflicts.

The public place and private process of creativity

Mihaly Csikszentmihalyi has spent over three decades studying creativity. He discovered that the experience of "flow," which is related to "deep play," is what makes creativity pleasurable and, therefore, self-reinforcing.[100] The tendency to create new ideas and ways of solving problems, however, is not the only clue to our survival. We are programmed with "two contradictory sets of instructions."[101] Human survival is the result of the tendency to conserve as well as to create. Our instinct for self-preservation, self-aggrandizement, and conservation of energy exists alongside our tendency to explore, enjoy novelty, and take risks.

Csikszentmihalyi asked "where" creativity is located to better understand it. He proposed a systems model to define creativity within a network of relationships involving a domain and a field, as well as the creative individual. Creativity takes place when any act, idea, or product changes an existing domain or creates a new one.[102] A domain consists of a set of language rules, vocabulary, and procedures. Mathematics is one example. Religion is another. The second component of creativity is the field, the group of people who act as gatekeepers to the domain. The third component is the individual.

In my book *Godly Play*,[103] individual creativity was described as a movement with an opening (exploring) and a closing (conserving) phase. The opening begins when an established meaning is broken by a crisis, irritated by dissonance, or dissolved by wonder. This initial step in the creative process is followed by the second step, which expends energy to scan for a more adequate kind of coherence to overcome the chaos resulting from the disruption. This might last for hours, days, or years, and it might be conscious or unconscious. The third step is insight. A new, more adequate pattern is formed and forces its way into consciousness via an image, a fragment of a song, a piece of poetry, a dream, or some other means.

After the insight, closure begins: until this point the process has been largely nonverbal and outside the confines of thought. The fourth step in the process takes the insight "received" by consciousness and develops it. The insight is clarified, filled out, and evaluated by the rules of the particular domain in which it was discovered until there is closure. Closure is the fifth step and is necessary to end the endless striving of some people to be satisfied with the development of their ideas.

The whole loop of the creative process is available to all of us, but particular individuals prefer different parts of it. People tend to enter the process at different points, depending on the subject matter, but by and large such preferences are consistent enough to be a general indicator of personality type. Some people love the free-flowing spirit of scanning so much that they do not want to interrupt it with an insight, which takes an effort of focused energy quite different from that used in scanning. Sometimes this energy shift is noticed before the insight is evident such that one can be aware of "having" an idea even before knowing what it is. Other people are so delighted by having insights that they can endure long periods of what they might otherwise experience as pain and loneliness during the chaos of scanning. Once the insight is experienced, however, they are so pleased that they sometimes lose interest and do not develop it.

Conserving people step in after the insight. They cannot stand the loss of meaning during a crisis or the threat of dissonance, and they certainly do not want to participate in the potential "chaos" of wonder. They hate scanning and do not find the insight worth it. They do not even like to be around the "creative" people who enjoy such things. They are not practical.

In step four some people trim new ideas to fit what is accepted by the field. This makes them feel more useful and keeps things in order and under control. At step five, however, the greatest control is maintained with the least risk by limiting one's involvement in creativity to the purely executive step of accepting or denying developed ideas that are proposed. Steps four and five are most attractive to people using religion based on power.

It is important to note, as we conclude this section, that the creative loop can be used to accomplish destructive as well as constructive results. Sometimes an outcome is unknowable, so one goes forward with the process, betting that the outcome will be constructive. Destructive outcomes are, therefore, sometimes accidents. It is also true that one must often tear down something in order to build up a new idea or structure; destruction is sometimes a byproduct of creativity. At other times, however, creativity is explicitly placed in the service of destruction. If religion's domain was developed to help human beings creatively cope with trouble and celebrate survival, then such destruction with intent in the name of "religion" is not religion. It is destructive activity, pure and simple.

Creativity, then, includes both exploring and conserving tendencies. People, however, tend to prefer only parts of the process. This has caused religion to become uprooted from its ground in the whole process of creativity. Religion has been reduced either to opening tendencies or to closing tendencies, leaving the impression that religious education must be based on one or the other rather than both.

There is more to creativity, however, than opening and closing tendencies. Two more important features of creativity will be examined next.

Creativity's styles and stages
The styles and stages of creativity give further definition to its process. This discussion will be guided primarily by Howard Gardner's theory

of "multiple intelligences" and James Fowler's theory of "faith development".[104]

Gardner's *Frames of Mind: The Theory of Multiple Intelligences* was first published in 1983. Ten years later he applied his theory to creativity in *Creating Minds*,[105] which described what we will call "styles" of creativity. Although *Creating Minds* was published three years before Csikszentmihalyi's *Creativity*, Gardner adapted Csikszentmihalyi's idea of using a systems model, which they had already discussed, to help define creativity. Gardner's contribution to this discussion introduced the variety of ways in which people create and the connection between the creativity of the child and that of the teacher.

Einstein was Gardner's exemplar for logical-mathematical intelligence. Picasso illustrated spatial knowing. Stravinsky represented the musical frame. T.S. Eliot showed how a particular sensitivity to words can shape one's creative interests. Martha Graham exemplified kinesthetic creating. Gandhi showed interpersonal creativity at work. And Freud was his model for a person especially in tune to the intrapersonal.

In *Intelligence Reframed: Multiple Intelligences for the 21st Century*, Gardner reported that he had identified an additional frame of knowing.[106] It is found in the kind of person who is especially attracted to patterns in nature. He also discussed why existential, spiritual, or moral sensitivities are important aspects of character but do not qualify as "frames of knowing." One might, therefore, display an existential, spiritual, or moral interest related to the emphasis of any specific frame of knowing.

Gardner also cautioned that his theory of multiple intelligences was not a recipe for education. To run children through all the ways of knowing for a particular lesson is a waste of time and energy for both teachers and the children. An awareness of the multiple ways of knowing is better used to help understand and remedy learning and communication difficulties when they arise so that children can constructively learn to manage them by being aware of their special talents.[107]

In religious education one needs to keep stages as well as styles of creativity in mind in order to insure good communication. We turn now to a discussion about the constraints and opportunities highlighted by stage-development theory.

My involvement with this point of view began as the editor of *Life Maps: Conversations on the Journey of Faith*,[108] which helped pave the way for Fowler's *Stages of Faith*. In Europe, Swiss scholar Fritz Oser championed what he called "religious development."[109] Fowler's faith development and Oser's religious development have been compared and critiqued, and alternative perspectives have been suggested,[110] but the focus here is on two very practical considerations for religious education informed by such theory.

First, the value of verbal and nonverbal communication shifts in importance during development from childhood to adulthood. Children rely primarily on the nonverbal communication system while adults rely on verbal skills. In late adulthood some adults shift back again to rely primarily on the nonverbal system. Religious interests follow this pattern.

Second, we need to teach for the discovery of new ideas and for creating new stages of development. This has implications for both how religion is understood and how it is practiced.

By nonverbal communication I mean facial expressions, vocalizations, gestures, calls, grunts, social grooming, pointing, and other such communication, something that we share with other mammals. This communication does not develop in stages. As confidence grows in one's linguistic behavior, this nonverbal system becomes obscured, although it continues to provide clues to the meaning of words. The lack of awareness of the nonverbal system develops in part because there is such a complete discontinuity between linguistic and nonlinguistic behavior.

The two systems evolved in separate but parallel ways and are produced by different regions of the brain.[111] We can, therefore, describe nonverbal communication with words, as I am doing now, but it makes no sense at all to ask what word expresses a hearty laugh or anguished sob. There is no point-to-point translation. Still, the two systems are bound together: much of what we say relies on nonverbal communication to nuance our verbal meaning. For example, someone might say "Good morning" in such a way that it ruins your day.

Our species is ushered into the realm of verbal communication around the age of two years. The importance given to non-spoken communication declines until a stage of development that Fowler calls the "conjunctive stage" develops in middle or late adulthood. It is then that unspoken communication begins to be more positively valued once again. When adults begin to rely again on subtle cues in relationships rather than on words to make meaning, then the experience of God as presence becomes important again. This signals a second naivete in which a child-like (not childish) sensitivity to play, ritual, and story reemerge as significant ways of knowing.

The second practical implication for religious education from stage theory comes from the fact that the creative process may contribute to the development of new stages. This happens when one is drawn to the next "higher" stage because problems can be solved "one stage up" in a more comprehensive and satisfying way. Hearing about stages "above" one's own creates a dissonance with normal patterns of thinking that sets the creative process in motion to initiate the next "higher" stage.

The opposite occurs, however, when the communication gap between people is more than one stage. Instead of being drawn to the "higher" stage, one is repulsed and frustrated because the "higher" form of discourse is completely unintelligible to the person at the "lower" stage. Care needs to be taken to watch for the two-stage gap, one that can damage present communication and can stifle the development of more complex and flexible religious thinking because it halts the creation of new stages.

The development of new stages in the quest for more adequate ways of making meaning is complex and not always beneficial. The ability to think at "higher" stages gives one the ability to think in broader, more abstract, and flexible ways, but something is also lost with each "higher" step that one moves. The communication of presence and emotional uniqueness is lost, step by step, as pre-narrative and then narrative forms of speaking are devalued and avoided by conceptual thinking and concepts *about* such thinking. Thinking about one's thinking can only take one so far.

For example, a Fowler stage is identified by seven kinds of structures. One of these is the perspective-taking aspect of our thinking. As the creative process moves a person "upward" from stage to stage, the ability to interpret a situation with greater perspective increases. One moves from understanding a situation from only his or her point of view to taking into consideration another person's standpoint. Continued development allows one to assume a hypothetical third-person way of looking at the interaction between the self and another person. Then the ability to take the perspective of a different group, as it observes you, develops. For some people the ability to take the perspectives of conflicting subgroups within a group that is interpreting your actions and thoughts can also be developed.

The above illustration shows the potential, which stage development implies, for greater understanding of religion at "higher" stages, but it also shows how the possibility for greater misunderstanding between stages can develop. To restrict religious thinking to the "lower" stages of development robs humanity of one of its most important tools for creatively coping with trouble, so the encouragement of stage growth is as important as teaching content. It should be accompanied, however, with the awareness, patience, and skill that it takes to be aware of and to sort out cross-stage static in religious discourse as well as to promote a creative involvement with religious content within each stage.

This concludes the discussion of creativity – the public place, personal process, and style and stage considerations. We turn now to the fourth step in our presentation. Just how can we re-ground religious communication in the creative process?

Re-grounding religious communication in the creative process

This section will follow the outline of the four characteristics of the creative process mentioned above. A suggestion about re-grounding religious communication will be offered for each characteristic – the systems and individual aspects of creativity as well as its style and stage implications.

First, let us discuss the gatekeepers in the systems dimension of creativity. They need to respect and to be more open to the theological inquiry of children. Always telling children how to think and feel stifles their creativity. Children need to learn how to think for themselves within their tradition so that they can develop their own authentic and creative ways to cope with existential trouble.

Always telling children how to think and feel creates a second problem. It sets up a power struggle between the validity of the child's experience and the adult's. This not only associates religion with a power struggle, but it also sets up a double bind for the child. The child must either give up his or her felt experience and comply with the adult's interpretation or risk challenging the adult and affirming his or her experience as valid. The child needs both the adult's support as a person in general but especially the acknowledgement that their own felt experience is real. The double bind forced on them by the power struggle requires them to give up one or the other when what they need is both.

Recognizing young children as theologians also has a benefit for adults. It acknowledges the children's closeness to God and their lack of interest in power-based religion. If it is true that our spirituality is located in our nonverbal communication system and ought to be grounded in the creative process, then children, who are not yet completely coopted by adult religious language or religion as power, have especially important contributions to make to the larger theological conversation.

Second, the whole creative process, steps 1-5, needs to be emphasized when playing the religious-language game with children. As noted above, people are usually drawn to particular parts of the total process. To help re-root the use of religious language in the creative process, children need to be encouraged to use the whole process when thinking theologically.

For example, a scanning child, who appears to be merely wandering around the open classroom, needs to be supported to discover an insight. An insight child needs to be encouraged to develop his or her idea. A development child needs to be discouraged from copying other children's work and encouraged to discover his or her own unique insights. The executive child, who only wants to say which developed insight is accepted or not, needs to be challenged to set out on the whole risky voyage of discovery.

The pleasure of using the whole process is greater than engaging in only truncated parts of it. Children, however, do not know how self-reinforcing this is unless they are guided and supported to make such a discovery. Since play is voluntary, this cannot be forced. Children need to be invited, guided, and intrigued to take part.

Third, when we turn to creativity styles, we enter one of the most enjoyable and overlooked areas for reconnecting the use of religious language to the creative process. Children in general often go unsupported in their natural tuning to a unique frame of knowing. This is especially true in the area of religion because the link between a child's preferred frame of knowing and religion is not always immediately apparent.

Adults also need to be aware of their own frame of knowing so that they do not project it onto children as if it were the only possible means for religious expression. As noted above, there are as many ways of creatively coping with trouble as there are ways of knowing, so adult guides need to be alert to the richness of these possibilities.

Children, like adults, need to play to their strengths. Not only is that where the most natural talent lies but also the most security. The creative process does not work at its optimal level unless it can do so in safety, so style support is important for both creative potential and the security in which it can bloom. Words are usually the dominant mode of communication in religious education. They are to be memorized or interpreted in a prescribed way. Both strategies – memorization and prescribed interpretations – bypass the child's creative process. Matters are even worse if a child prefers the language frame of creation, as T.S. Eliot did. The child's unique gift of verbal creativity is often suppressed as an error or at least troublesome behavior in the typical religious education setting.

Children naturally in tune with the other seven ways of knowing are also suppressed when language is the main means of teaching. The antidote to this is for the teacher to be sensitive to children's awakening styles so they can be encouraged. This affirms each child's preferred way of knowing and includes it in what counts as "real" for creatively coping with trouble and celebration in religious knowing.

Fourth, re-rooting religion in the stages of development has two dimensions. The first is to acknowledge how creativity takes place within one's primary stage of knowing. This results in better learning of content and gives a solid base for sorting out cross-stage static when working with others. The second is how to encourage the growth of stages themselves.

One of the difficulties and delights of working with children in a circle of mixed ages is that there might be three or even four stages represented, assuming childhood is from 2-12 years of age. Even in each of the three major periods in this age – early, middle, and late childhood – lovely differences are evident. Each child is moving through the stages at his or her unique rate, despite statistical guidelines. Sometimes children even mask their natural stages by memorizing a higher vocabulary and syntax to please adults. When such children encounter something new, however, they "drop" in stage and re-engage their language with the creative process at their natural level.

The use of play, ritual, and story for teaching and using religion to celebrate life and cope creatively with trouble works as well today as it did in prehistoric times. Play is located in our nonverbal communication system, so it does not divide into linguistic stages. Ritual is a combination of the nonverbal and the verbal, so children can find in it what they need. Story is the natural spoken medium for children, as well as for adults. The combination of all three, therefore, is the most appropriate way for teaching religion so that it can be re-rooted in the creative process.

Well-designed teaching involving play, ritual, and narrative is open to all the stages of language meaning. This is achieved when the core of the metaphor out of which each sacred story, parable, or ritual action is discovered and becomes the heart of each lesson and teaching object. Children, using such materials, do not need to keep the language in mind as they reflect on it. They can move the story, parable, or rite about with their hands as it lies before them on the floor. This strategy also means that the storyteller does not have to worry about matching the lesson's language with each child's stage since the teaching is open to all stages. The children reveal *their* stage orientation when they respond, so the teacher does not have to guess. All stages can be valued equally and yet treated appropriately in such a situation. When stage differences become apparent to the children, as they wonder together about the lesson, the mentor can also show them how to work out the differences with patience and respect. Coping with cross-stage static is valued and modeled in this way.

The open, Montessori-like setting is important in such teaching for many reasons, but it is especially ideal for stimulating stage development. Children will naturally hear "upper" stages in a multi-graded classroom and be drawn to them in the safety of the teacher's support for all stages.

These four kinds of interventions – the public arena, the personal process, respect for style, and the two aspects of stage analysis – are needed for teaching religion in a way that can help reconnect the use of religious language with the creative process. There are many more such interventions that can be made, but these four illustrate that such grounding is possible.

The teacher was often mentioned in the above discussion. This raises the question of what kind of person is best qualified to teach religion to children if the goal is to re-root religion in the creative process.

Who should teach religious communication?

Two general qualifications for the teacher of religious language can be covered quickly. First, the teacher needs to be fluent in the language of the tradition being taught. Second, the teacher-guide and mentor needs to be comfortable with the discovery method and teaching in an open classroom, where children can make choices from among constructive alternatives. This is rather straightforward. What is more complicated is the teacher's stage development and role. It is this third qualification that will concern us now.

Erik Erikson called those who take a genuine interest in the coming generation "generative." When generativity does not develop in adults, there is instead "an obsessive need for pseudo-intimacy or a compulsive kind of preoccupation with self-imagery – both with a pervading sense of stagnation."[112] The teacher of religion needs to be truly generative if he or she is going to help ground religious communication in the creativity of the child.

An ability to be comfortable in the rituals of such teaching is also necessary. In *Toys and Reasons: Stages in the Ritualization of Experience,* Erikson defined ritual as "a *creative formalization,* which helps to avoid both impulsive excess and *compulsive* self-restriction."[113] The grounding of religious language in the creative process needs such "an agreed-upon interplay." Ritual, as a clear pattern of classroom management, is what holds the child and adult together in the same language-learning game. It is within the safety of this interplay that the stage and experience gaps between childhood and adulthood can be bridged when teaching religion to children while learning from them.

For such interplay to be successful, Erikson tells us, the adult needs to be comfortable with being "a numinous model in the next generation's eyes" as well as a "judge of evil and the transmitter of ideal values." When the adult is not comfortable and playful in this role, then the ritual becomes ritualism, and the mentoring authority of the adult degenerates into what Erikson called "Authoritism," the nonverbal communication of the teacher as self-important and judgmental. Children need instead the safety of ritual interplay with a generative, adult guide and a safe, constructive community of children in which to be creative.

Erikson was appreciative of the power of play to help negotiate all the key psycho-social crises across the life span, but it was especially important during the "Initiative versus Guilt" crisis, which Erikson called the "Play Age." Play becomes especially important again, it seems to me, when an adult turns toward the coming generation because this "turning toward" is largely nonverbal.

Since children are not yet as co-opted by language as adults, one cannot distract them from adult nonverbal communication. They naturally pick up any conflict between the spoken and the unspoken message. This means that the teacher must be authentic about and enjoy his or her "turning toward" children to give religious language its appropriate nuances.

We have been following Erikson to this point. We will now shift to Fowler's stage analysis. As one makes his or her way through the stages of faith development, there are exciting and useful changes, such as the shift from primarily valuing and using narrative to the use of ideas to create meaning. What happens later during the conjunctive stage, following my interpretation, is that thinking about one's thinking in increasingly complex and abstract ways finally becomes the dead end of an infinite regress. Fowler talks about the "postcritical rejoining of irreducible symbol as power and ideational meaning,"[114] which takes place during this stage, but I would like to add to that an emphasis on the reassertion of the nonverbal communication system.

After experiencing several stages of cognitive development, one cannot go back to the naivete-without-options of childhood when one relied primarily on the nonverbal. The adult, therefore, must choose in particular situations to allow nonverbal communication to reassert itself if one is to continue to grow toward epistemological maturity.

An example of nonverbal communication reasserting itself is when one chooses not to analyze Holy Communion while participating in it, even though the ability to do so is available and respected when used in other contexts. Instead, one allows the nonverbal communication system to dominate the experience and the quality of relationships that make the experience truly communion with God, others, the deep self, and nature.

In addition, having passed through several stages, one begins to realize that each step toward more abstract and flexible thinking also subtracts an emphasis on the intimacy that the "lower" stages share.

Moving through several stages and experiencing the gain/loss each time helps one become more stage neutral, neither too attached to "higher" stages nor too repulsed by the "lower" ones. This frees one to see truly where children are in order to support where they might go as they develop their use of religious language.

In theory the way to bridge the gap between children and adults is for the adult to match the stage of the child or to speak one stage beyond the child's customary way of speaking. Unfortunately, this can feel to the child like being "talked down to" and is typically and understandably resented. An extreme example is the patronizing, singsong voice some adults use when addressing children. When adults are truly generative and conjunctive, however, they do not "talk down" to children. The child, therefore, knows that he or she has a true play partner and that the game is one of mutual growth with God, the adult, and the community of children. With a teacher like this, religious language can be re-rooted in creativity. Unfortunately, most adults do not easily become generative and conjunctive. This is usually a property of an adult's later years. The compromise is to teach teachers how to teach in a way that incorporates into their teaching *role* as many of these characteristics as possible.

In addition to an awareness of stage constraints and possibilities, the teacher also needs to have a special appreciation for the uniqueness of religious language. Ian T.Ramsey (professor of the philosophy of Christian religion at Oxford in 1951 and the bishop of Durham in 1966) identified this uniqueness. He argued that there is an "empirical placement of theological phrases," so religious language cannot be reduced to some sort of emotional venting. It involves an "odd discernment" and requires a commitment to the linguistic domain to be made before it can be used well and understood. A teacher, therefore, needs to develop, in Ramsey's terms, "a nose for odd language."[115] The "oddness" is more than religious language's difference from scientific language and other linguistic domains. It also includes, it seems to me, a religious language that supports and then redirects one back into the nonverbal communication system where our spirituality is located.[116] An awareness of this also needs to be incorporated into the teaching role.

We have described the role of the teacher needed for rooting religion in the creative process. Let us now consider what the goal of one's teaching ought to be if that is take place.

Teaching playful orthodoxy

We human beings do not learn "language in general." We learn particular languages, such as Arabic or Chinese, and even within a particular language, such as English, we learn specialty languages – such as medicine, law, or religion – and each specialty language in turn has its own sub-functions. To understand mathematics, for example, we begin with a particular base system, such as base ten, before learning other base systems or speaking about mathematics in general. Its sub-functions are "putting together," addition and multiplication, and "taking apart," subtraction and division, comparable with Christianity's sub-functions of parable, sacred story, liturgy, and knowing silence. Europeans, to take another example, learn Western music and its many formal sub-functions, such as a symphony, to distinguish music from noise. Once rooted in Western music, they are then able to recognize and appreciate other kinds of music, and are at the same time open to learn from new forms that they might discover.

Religious communication works similarly. We need to learn a particular religious language system well, such as Christianity, if we hope to understand another religion, such as Islam, or to make meaningful comments about religion in general. What follows is a description of a way to teach "how to speak Christian" that is wholly rooted in the creative process so that it includes both the rooting of orthodoxy and the openness needed to grow and to meet new challenges.

Children are invited into a circle with a mentoring storyteller. The surrounding room is carefully laid out with the materials of sacred stories, parables, and liturgical action. An additional function of the Christian language system, silence, is also taught, but the means for this kind of communication comes from the children themselves. While other teaching materials are silent and can still communicate in their silence, the human beings in the room are the only ones who can "make silence" and communicate back-and-forth in multiple ways through their relationships. This makes these four kinds of communication a substantial part of the complete Christian language system, and the part-whole relationship becomes clear to children at the level of intuition from age two years onward. The complexity of the Christian system is not simplified, but if presented appropriately in this way, the whole system is taught when any part of it is taught.

The spirit of the teaching is playful, but it is also tough and clear about the rules. No game, even language games, can be played without rules. Clear boundaries provide safety and the means for being together in the same game. A clear ritual, then, defines the time spent. It is as carefully developed and prepared as the space in which the play takes place. The deep structure of the Holy Eucharist provides the rules for profoundly playing this orthodox yet open Christian language game.

Children are invited to enter the teaching/learning time and space only after they are "ready." They need to learn *how* to be ready because this language does not work unless people can make the "odd discernment" necessary for it to work. They bring their existential troubles with them to be juxtaposed with the power of religious language and God's presence in the community of children. The lesson is then presented, and in the wondering and expressive art that follows the children can creatively cope with these troubles while the language is being learned. This shows that the Christian way of communication is important and that the pleasure of learning it comes from how its use satisfies the need for deep existential meaning, the result of using it well. A feast and prayers are shared, and respectful goodbyes are said, one by one, with a sense of blessing and constructive closure.

The adult guides show, rather than merely talk directly about, how to use religious language to make meaning. It takes preparation, wonder, and play. It is assumed that children naturally know God. What children lack is the language and a community in which to be at play with God as creators themselves in God's image. Learning the art of "how to speak Christian" in this way supplies the language needed to interact with their natural spirituality to move toward maturity.

The curriculum is an integrated spiral for children between the ages of two to twelve. If adolescents have grown up in such classes, many additional options for teaching are available because the language is already creatively rooted.

Adolescents who have not been raised this way can benefit by starting at the beginning with this approach, as can adults.

The basic lessons are repeated year after year. This repetition provides a way for children to practice one of the unique properties of this language system. The new can be found in the old. The content of Christian language is never exhausted, but it takes practice and creativity to find its hidden meanings and God's presence there. This is another aspect of the oddness of religious language when compared to other linguistic domains.

On the other hand, the spiral of the curriculum adds complexity and additional lessons in later years. For example, the lessons about "The Creation" and "The Faces of Christ" (the story of Jesus) are told as single lessons, and then children are invited to formulate an incarnational theology by placing the tiles from the two lessons together, as they see fit, into an integrated whole. Later, around age ten or eleven years, "The Creation," "The Faces," and the lesson about Paul are joined with part of the lesson about baptism to create an experience of the Holy Trinity. This recapitulates the development from narrative to concept in the history of theology and parallels the stages of faith development that children are moving through at this time in their lives.

It is not possible to describe the whole method here, but resources are readily available to do so. The method is called Godly Play and was explicitly begun around 1972, although some of the theoretical aspects date back to 1960. See, for example, *Godly Play, Teaching Godly Play,* and *The Complete Guide to Godly Play.*[117] The history of this method's relationship to Montessori education is traced in volume one of *The Complete Guide.* One important website to consult is also available at godlyplay.org.

Conclusion

Our ability as religious educators to ground religion in the creative process is critical for the survival of our species. When religion is grounded in power, its danger to life has been made obvious by centuries of violence. Furthermore, the only kind of religion able to counter the threat of "power-based religion" is one that is rooted in creativity. Out-creating "the destructionists" is our only hope.

Original source:

Berryman, J.W. 2005. "Playful orthodoxy: Reconnecting religion and creativity by education." ***Sewanee Theological Review,*** **48 (4): 437-454.**

Part 5

Ethical considerations when working with children

Preface to Part 5

Some readers may not be familiar with Berryman's writing in relation to ethical considerations when working with children, both in research settings and in religious education. Yet it is a theme about which he has written for more than thirty years, often in relation to his early work as a chaplain at the Institute of Religion in the Texas Medical Center in Houston where he worked with children with cancer, and later as Director and Senior Fellow of the Center for the Theology of Childhood, where his worked focused on religious education. In many instances, the ethical dimension was addressed by Berryman through a careful weaving of it into the prose of the various texts of chapters and journal articles he authored. However, there are several papers written by Berryman which have as their focus the ethical dimensions of working with children. The contributions in Part 5 center on these particular writings.

The first contribution was written while Berryman was Senior Teaching Fellow at the Institute of Religion, Houston, Texas. In it, he explicitly outlines an ethical process for involving sick children in research with a concentration on the developmental or structural aspects of that process, specifically in relation to three key questions those children may ask: "What are you going to do to me?", "What must I do [in the research]?", and "What if it doesn't work?" He draws on the theories of Piaget, Kohlberg and Fowler in an attempt to address these questions, suggesting the importance of a careful listening in order to match the discussion of the research with the level of causality understanding of the child.

Showing children the art of worshipping, and how we should relate to them during worship is the focus of the second contribution. In it, Berryman suggests ways in which to put an ethic of respect into action during worship services. Many of the themes developed in other writings are drawn upon here as Berryman outlines the notion of an ethic of respect, such as the function of religious language in creating meaning at the edge of knowing and experiencing, and the double bind which asks children to dismiss the value of their own experiences in favour of the adult's interpretation of those same experiences.

The final contribution addresses the problem of power imbalance in the classroom when theologizing with children. A theological conversation with children ought to entail a coming together of adults and children to talk about God with as much equality and truth as possible, since the notion of a conversation implies equality in the conversation partners. However, the problem Berryman acknowledges is that when adults and children engage in a theological conversation, the participants are not equal in power. The double bind for children again presents itself: if they acquiesce to the adult's language, they will have to give up the language with which they have been attempting to make meaning, or, if they do not acquiesce to the adult's preferred language they risk alienating the adult. Berryman suggests the Godly Play approach as a means by which adults and children can cope with their respective double binds in constructive ways. It is an approach which helps to reduce the power differential between children and adults so that as much freedom as possible for the children to express themselves may be provided without being unethical about giving them with the best tools to think theologically.

13

Discussing the Ethics of Research on Children

We adults talk a lot about children. Our discussions usually stereotype what children think and feel, because they are not present to challenge our false assumptions, directly with words or indirectly by their actions. Our adult conversation about children in this workshop is not untypical. We have present physicians, scientists, ethicists, lawyers, educators, and theologians, but we need some children to speak for themselves.

We adults all speak partial truths about children becoming subjects of research. The ethicists and lawyers tend to assume that they ought to decide what children can and should think and feel. They speak of "voiceless children," "the not comprehending child," "the unperceiving child," and "the child incapable of making his or her own choices." It is true that children do not think and feel as adults do, but the conclusion that they should not be included in the ethical discussion is a cruel distortion of what I consider to be the main purpose of having an ethical discussion with another human being, especially with a child. The main point is to be with children on the threshold of unknown territory and to let them know that you will stay with them through their sickness and the proposed research. The right involved is the right not to be abandoned by another of one's species, and the correlated duty is the duty to be a translator across the developmental distance between the adult and the child, rather than to acquiesce to it.

John Holt represents the position of a perceptive educator and child advocate. He urges on us another partial truth. Saying that we cannot know anyone in his or her depths, regardless of age or stage of development is only partially true, because the answer to overgeneraliziation is not overparticularization. The cure for both distortions is to be so fluent in your general knowledge of children that you can freely depart from it in the presence of an individual child when it is dictated (and it always is). Cramming people into developmental molds only means that the person doing the stuffing is rigidly projecting his or her uninformed, general knowledge. However, using knowledge of developmental trends as a reference point can help prevent one from projecting unexamined assumptions about an individual child.

The physicians and scientists speak partial truths in terms of what can be counted, weighed, measured, and reduced to numbers about cancer. The implication is that the child is a cancer container and that cancer is their real point of interest. Although narrowing one's focus into an area of specialization leads to advances in research, the truth is partial because the child and the cancer cannot be separated. The war on cancer is also a war for healthy, developing, happy children. The scientists and physicians at M.D. Anderson have this as their goal, and this conference is a struggle to keep the children in focus, but the fact remains that the truth they speak is only partial.

The partial truth I want to put forward is that the primary purpose of having an ethical discussion with children or adults is to unlock their loneliness. To talk about what another person ought to do with them is to come close to that place of unspeakable dreads and hopes, for centuries recognized by children in fairy tales that start at the edge of a dark and dangerous forest. How will they find their way and who will be their guide?

The ethical conversation ought to be an end in itself, an antidote to deep loneliness. It is not a debate or combat. It is a sign of the love and caring that only members of the same species can give each other.

This is true whether we seek to enable the child to consent to research and make an informed decision about it or to obtain the child's assent to a course of action that parents, friends, relatives, or doctors have already decided on. How much the child should be the decision-maker depends on how each family and child make decisions and how well the adults hear and speak the child's language.

I wish to say a few words about why we adults tend to not recognize our duty to be with children in their loneliness and to become good translators. I would then like to outline how I see the entire ethical process so we can concentrate on the structuralist aspect of that process. We can then focus on the structural differences between the thinking of adults and that of children and try to find a way to neutralize the developmental distance between us with special reference to three questions that the child has but does not always express: "What are you going to do to me?" "Why must I do it [the research]?" "What if it doesn't work?" I intend to suggest ways in which the adult and the child can be together despite their developmental structural differences. If these ways can carry such a burden, then we can "live happily ever after" with the child, despite the dangers in the dark forest of research and threatened health.

In earlier times children were so invisible that the concept of "childhood" did not exist. There were infants and there were adults. The real distinction was made when infants were no longer dependent on their mothers or nurses for their physical needs.[118]

Despite a tremendous gain in adults' ability to conceive of and to know children, we still seem to operate generally by two myopic myths. We continue to think that children will understand if we talk to them as if they are adults, and we think that they are always happy, or at least they ought to be so. Our myopia is probably rooted in not wanting to see the world of the child because there are parts we would not like to remember and because of the obligations to be a trustworthy guide it would place on us. There is also the fact anyone knows who has lived in a foreign country. It takes a great deal of patience, energy, and good will, as well as skill, to be a good translator.

Carole Klein has written with sensitivity, respect, and informed insight of the emotional world of the child. In *How It Feels to Be a Child*,[119] she carefully removes the mask with the painted smile on it to examine the child's fears, loneliness, guilt, anger, dreams, shame, sexual feelings, and emotions mixed up with parents and parenting persons. We will now turn to the child's thinking as we discuss the ethical domain, but the feelings are of equal importance.

The ethical domain: an eclectic view

When one thinks of moral reasoning and ethics, there is a tendency to think only in terms of decision making or the structures of moral reasoning. There is a wider domain for our ethical discussion with the child that includes perception of the facts, reasoning about them, the faith context in which one decides and acts, and evaluation of one's action. This is a closed process that begins again with either the same or a new perception of the world of facts, depending on the results of the evaluation. It takes several research traditions to trace the structures and content of the process through this fact, reasoning, acting, and evaluation system.

The first part of the process deals with the "facts." What we see as facts involves our needs. Need levels have been studied by Maslow.[120] We tend to see what we need to see. The structures by which we think about the world of facts have been studied by Piaget.[121] His work adds an appreciation for the mental structures in the developing concept of causality by which the facts are tied together.

In the judgment phase of the ethics process, one must rank one's values to decide what to do. Rokeach has studied this process,[122] which provides the content for the judgment along with the facts. This content is woven together with thought structures used in moral reasoning. These structures have been isolated into six developmental stages by Kohlberg.[123] He has suggested that the higher the development, the more likely one is to do what one thinks one ought to do. At the highest stage, however, one encounters the cosmic perspective and asks, "Why be moral?" Kohlberg's analysis spills over into questions of faith and religion in his discussion of despair.

The content of the third phase of the ethics process is the developing ego strengths that have been traced by Erikson[124] through eight stages of psychosocial crises. The faith climate has been studied structurally by Fowler,[125] who has isolated six "faithing" structures that include the work of Piaget in logic and Kohlberg in moral reasoning. If one does not have a clear sense of one's faith world, a "trustable" environment, then the paralysis of anxiety very likely sets in. One senses a danger, but cannot identify it. One does not know whether to stand and fight or flee. Decision and action are paralyzed. The structures of faith and the content of one's ego strength are both interwoven with the judgment and acting aspects of this ethics process. They also look forward to the evaluation that follows.

The evaluation part of the ethics process expands on the "operant conditioning" analysis of B.F. Skinner, going beyond his hesitation to explore beneath the skin for meaning to include motivation as well as reinforcement issues. As we monitor our reinforcement, we continually adjust in ways that are not always clear to us, but there are occasions when we do struggle to make something new. The "something new" might be in terms of content, such as new ideas or visions of the world, or in terms of new structures by which to assimilate the world and be in equilibrium with its structures.

There are times when we are not satisfied with the status quo, even when it is positively reinforcing. At other times the environment reinforces us negatively and yet there is the inner motivation to overcome that pain to find something new. This is true in individual cases, although not significant statistically.

The one kind of evaluation calls for something new in terms of content. In the tension of the painful old and the anticipated new, random thoughts begin to break to the surface of consciousness, often in art or in dreams. This is the primary process kind of thinking discussed by Freud and expanded on by Maslow[126] and later by Arieti.[127] These random ideas are an amorphous cognition that is consciously and analytically worked through by the secondary process, which tests it against the present view of reality. The synthesis of the old and new realities creates the new world of "facts" in which ethical situations are seen.

The second kind of evaluation deals not with the content of new ideas, but with the structures for thinking about reality. A structural disequilibrium gives rise to the motivation to reestablish balance. The structures of the mind change to better match the structures in the outside world whether in nature, such as causality, or in society, as with moral reasoning, or in the ultimate environment, with faith.

This account of evaluation as a kind of creativity completes the circuit of the ethical process. The feelings have been carried by what we have called the "content" aspect of the circuit and the relations between these feelings have been carried in the form of what we have called "structures." Our goal now is to see how these structures can block or aid communication between the adult and the child as together they deal with the emotionally charged ethical questions surrounding proposed research in which the child is the subject.

Interstage communication: a key

The structures we have been discussing fall into stages. Our discussion with the child about how the research works involves the stages of thinking about causality that Piaget isolated. To discuss the question of whether the child ought to become a subject for research involves us in the use of the stages isolated by Kohlberg for doing moral reasoning. To discuss what there is to ultimately rely on and trust, we need to use the structures isolated by Fowler by which we do our "faithing." All three of these persons hold the following assumptions about the way these stages work:

1. Stages are action systems.
2. Transformation of structures from stage to stage cannot be explained by associationist learning (contiguity, repetition, reinforcement, etc.), but only by the development of organizational wholes or systems of internal relations.
3. The development of cognitive structures is the result of the interaction between the structure of the organism and the structure of the environment, rather than the direct result of maturation or of learning in the sense of shaping the organism's responses to accord with environmental structures.
4. The direction of the development of the structure is toward greater equilibrium in the organism-environmental interaction so that the individual neither is dominated by the perceived object or situation nor dominates it, but allows for balanced interaction.
5. The stage development process is hierarchical and invariant. One does not get to stage 4 before going through stages 1, 2, and 3. One does not lose the ability to use the earlier stages.
6. Although the content can vary as to thoughts and feelings that accompany thoughts, the structures are uniform. Both Piaget and Kohlberg have had their stage theories verified across cultural lines.

The key to talking between these structures is to understand what kind of communication can take place between different stages. Rest, Turiel, and Kohlberg studied this question to discover the appropriate way to intervene to promote moral development. Their study was reviewed by Rest in 1973 and again commented on in 1976.[128,129,130] Two things are relevant to our interests: stage comprehension and stage preference.

Stage comprehension was first determined by asking the subjects about moral dilemmas and scoring the structures in their discussions of what was fair in each situation. The subjects were then given samples of six different stages of response and asked to rephrase them in their own words. The recasting of these stages in their own words was then compared to the subjects' spontaneous stages. It was discovered that the restatements of the stage that was one above a subject's spontaneous stage tended to be cast in the logic of the spontaneous stage. This tendency grew more pronounced the farther from one's spontaneous stage the statements moved.

Stage preference was studed in addition to stage comprehension. Among three alternatives for preference (-1, +1, +2), the stage least preferred was one stage below one's spontaneous stage. The second most often rejected was two stages above one's customary stage of thinking. The most preferred of the three alternatives was one stage above one's most used stage.

Since we are looking for optimum communication, we should aim first for a match with the child's spontaneous stage. If we are in doubt, we might aim a bit high as a second choice, because there would still be good comprehension one stage above the spontaneous stage and the child's preference is the greatest for this stage. If we try to communicate at a stage below, it will be rejected as too naive, and if we try to communicate two stages above, it will probably be garbled in the child's translation into his or her spontaneous stage.

Missing the mark can have tragic results. In the first place, the children will not really be informed about the facts of the research in a way they understand. This not only infringes on their right to be informed, but also prevents them from knowing how to help in the research and healing process. Second, the children will be out of touch with the adults around them. Third, they will not only feel the distance between them and adults, but will begin to wonder if their own perception of reality is wrong because adults say it is. They will begin to mistrust their own perceptions in this process that Laing has called "the policies of experience,"[131] when self-estrangement is the last thing they need.

With this discussion of interstage communication in mind, we can turn to the three specific areas in which we might expect to discuss the proposed research with the child. These will correspond roughly to the first three parts discussed in the ethics process.

What are you going to do to me?

The first question concerns the natural reality in the research. It is a question about science, but we must refer to Piaget's research into the child's concept of causality to know better how to answer the question in his or her terms. Piaget's fourth book, *The Child's Conception of Physical Causality,* written with the help of 17 collaborators, is our source.

The researchers used several approaches. They asked the children to tell them how things such as clouds and water moved. Another approach was half verbal and half experiential. They enumerated movements and parts of machines and asked why and how the movements were performed. A purely experiential approach used simple experiments, such as dropping a pebble in a glass of water. The children were asked how and why the pebble went down. Children were also asked to draw pictures of bicycles to show how the parts worked together.

Seventeen kinds of causality were isolated; these fell into rough stages from birth to 2 years, 2 to 7, 7 to 12, and over 12. Table 1 shows the types seen at the stage from 2 to 7 and 7 to 12 years.

The listing of the types of causality distinguished by Piaget and his colleagues suggests the carefulness with which adults need to listen to children to learn how they see the world of nature. This same careful listening is needed to match one's discussion of the research with the level of causality understanding of the child.

Table I. Types of causality as distinguished by Piaget

Age 2 to 7 – precausality

1.	Motivational	Things and events are sent by God or people
2.	Finalistic	The last step defines the reason
3.	Phenomenistic	Simultaneous events are causally linked
4.	Participatory	Similar things are related causally
5.	Magical	Acts, gestures, or words cause events or protect from events
6.	Moral	A theory or event exists because it is necessary
7.	Artificialistic	Someone turns on events
8.	Animistic	Internal forces, alive and conscious, shape things
9.	Dynamic	Physical internal forces cause movement

Age 7 to 12 – true causality

1.	Reaction to surrounding medium	The surrounding medium supplies continued force impetus
2.	Mechanical	Outside forces cause movement
3.	Generation	One event or thing is the mother of another
4.	Substantial identification	No more birth and growth of things, but some idea of mass needed to have one thing generate another
5.	Condensation and rarefaction	Matter differs by degree of packing
6.	Atomistic	Ultimate matter is conceived
7.	Spatial	Use of perspective is employed in cause and effect
8.	Logical deduction	Density and specific gravity are becoming concepts on causality

Although we will concentrate, in the three questions children have in mind about research, on the ages from 2 to 7 and 7 to 12, it may be helpful to mention what comes before and after the two stages of causal conception identified above. From birth to 2 years, the child's view of the world is self-centric and is locked in a sensorimotor record for the most part, rather than in language. When children turn the instrument of physical action onto themselves for discovery, as previously they used it on the world about them, they discover an inner consciousness, a self. This self then becomes the index for understanding everything else in the world. Everything has a living, conscious center of causation within it, as the self does. The child becomes a naive theologian and sees spirits in everything.

Three general kinds of development carry the child forward from birth through 7 years. The first evolution is desubjectification. The tendency to see the world entirely in personal terms gradually fades. Second, the ability to trace a series in time develops. The feeling of "before and after" develops, along with differentiation of time and space, until the child can fill in the intermediary steps between cause and effect. A third line of evolution is the progressing ability to form and break down classes and see equivalences in different shapes. The child develops the ability to rearrange mentally what he or she could rearrange physically. The first and third strands of development have general application, whereas the second one, causal links, is unique to the development of the child's concept of causation. These evolutions finally stabilize into a new set of relationships to form the stage of causality conception outlined in Piaget's phrase "true causality."

During the period from 7 to 12 years, the gains along these three lines of development continue and consolidate. Children move from a world they interpret as naive theologians to a world they interpret as naive empiricists. They slowly develop desubjectification, the sense of before and after, and the ability to handle classes and equivalences, until their fascination with facts begins to fade and they move, about age 12, into the world as discovered by the new naive logician. Their confidence moves from what they can hold in their hands or perceive through their other senses to what they can develop by logical necessity. They move, in Piaget's terms, from transduction to induction and finally to deduction.

How, then, shall we answer the naive theologians or the naive empiricists when they ask what will happen to them in the research proposed? We need more than words alone. Children throughout these two periods need something to work with to really understand what is going to happen. A rag doll works very nicely.

The way one holds a doll tells a child a lot. You can show the child what is going to happen without going into details. The doll can be left with the child to accompany him or her in the research and the nurse can carry out her duties with the doll first so the child will know what is going to happen. Questions can be posed to the doll that the child might not be willing to discuss directly.

The naive theologians will understand what they are talking about if everything is personalized. The fluids "want" to come and make the child better. Even chemotherapy or surgery can be personalized this way. There are many animistic or theological nuances throughout the hospital that we adults have lost the ability to see. The naive theologians may be the most difficult to translate for because we adults often learned painfully that we were stupid and silly when we thought like that. It is hard to get over approaching the world as filled with "thou's" and the intimation of a larger "Thou." That kind of thinking is weeded out by parents and stamped out in school, but with it goes a whole kind of knowledge that is difficult to apprehend in any other way.

The naive empiricists still connect the why with the how, so they have moral questions at the outer limits of their causal conceptions. They want to know how it is really going to work, but they don't want you to overanswer. The doll will be as useful for them as for the naive theologians, but they will talk to and be with the doll in a slightly different way. Playing out the research procedure will be very helpful for both the naive theologians and the naive empiricists, but the latter will need more help getting everything together because they will be interested in more details in their play.

The doll is, finally, a multistage medium through which much of the translating can take place without having to have a perfect match of structures. Not only do children need to have concrete objects to move around to do their "thinking," but showing eases some of the burden on the logic structures for communicating. Moreover, the doll is an intermediary between the two parties to the conversation. It introduces a primitive "objectivity" to the meeting that would not be present if the adult used the child to show what was going to happen. This reduces some of the emotional charge to the conversation.

The doll is not a perfect example of what I mean by a "multistage medium" for communication. The parables used in the next two sections are, because the adult and the child participate in the same medium with the same words, although their understanding of the meaning in the medium can be very different. More conscious translating by the adult is required for the use of the doll than is required in the parables, when presented correctly. With this in mind, we can turn to the next aspect of the ethical discussion with the child.

Why must I do it?

The previous question raised issues infused with moral considerations for the child from 2 to 7 to 12 years of age. We move now from a discussion of the facts in the moral situation (good ethics require good facts) to moral reasoning about the situation, from questions of natural reality to social reality questions. As we have implied already, in the young child these two questions are not very differentiated, but for purposes of analysis we have separated them here.

The developmental structuralist approach to this question probably began with Socrates as recorded by Plato, but the work of Kohlberg in recent years has been the most helpful.

Kohlberg builds on Piaget's research tradition and findings, despite the fact that he sometimes refers to his findings as "warmed-over Dewey." Piaget's stages of logical structures are considered necessary but not sufficient for stage changes in moral reasoning. This is because the logic stage may have been developed through interaction with the natural world, but not yet faced with structures in the social world that cause the imbalance motivating accommodation and stage development.

Moral reasoning is divided roughly into three large periods: preconventional, conventional, and postconventional thinking. Most Americans fall into the range of stages 3 and 4 by the time they are adults. They employ conventional moral reasoning. The children we are considering, those from 2 to 7 and 7 to 12 years of age, typically engage in preconventional moral thinking. A summary of Kohlberg's stages is important so we can better grasp some of the problems involved in interstage communication (Table 2).

The relevance of these stages is apparent at once. Talking with children about how it is fair for them to be research subjects in terms of universal principles or a social contract would he heard in garbled bits and pieces as premoral or preconventional reasoning. The strain of trying to understand that sort of talk would soon turn off the attempt to listen and children would begin to give adult-pleasing answers to bring the discomfort to an end. Loneliness would remain locked.

Table 2. Stages in moral reasoning (Kohlberg)

	Premoral reasoning (2-7 years)
Stage 0	No moral reasoning present.
	Preconventional moral reasoning (7-12 years)
Stage 1	Punishment and reward in physical terms.
Stage 2	Trade-off as yardstick of fairness.
	Conventional moral reasoning (12+ years)
Stage 3	Good behavior as measured against peer and social groups.
Stage 4	Legal measures of justice and fairness.
	Postconventional reasoning (12+ years)
Stage 5	Laws can be changed to meet needs (social utilitarianism).
Stage 6	Social reference extends to all humankind.
Stage 7	Cosmic perspective – overt philosophy and religion.

A discussion employing conventional reasoning would be better heard. The duty of the children in terms of sacred or political law, however, would probably still be heard in terms of adults laying down the law with implications of physical reward and punishment. Stage 3 type reasoning involving feelings of the family or classmates or some other special group might be heard for what the adult was saying. For example, it might make sense to become a research subject to help another person if that person were in a relevant group and known by the child.

The moral imperative to try to match the child's structural stage remains so that the discussion can become an end in itself, the end being to be with the child in a profound way. The difficulty of making that perfect match is obvious. The adult cannot employ his or her own moral reasoning. Translation of structures changes one's moral position, although the outcomes, the "Yes" or "No," might remain the same. This puts the adult under a strain that might block out the message. Perhaps using a multistage medium to share the discussion can help. This is not to say that one should not try for a perfect match in structures, but only that this multistage medium might hedge one's bet a bit and also be a better way to be with the child than reliance on language alone.

One multistage medium I have been experimenting with has been the parables of Jesus of Nazareth. They seem able to provide fruitful interaction with any stage of reasoning. This ambiguity makes them an ideal mode of communication for two persons at different stages of reasoning. Each can remain true to his or her way of expressing the moral question and yet be in deep communion with the other person. This means that the nonverbal communication will not flood the child with mixed signals.

The Parable of the Good Samaritan is a good example. It should be presented with an economy of words and with concrete materials for its multistage nature to really work. I use golden boxes as settings for the parables and have one that shows how a parable is a story inside a story like a box can be inside a box. All the props are laid out on an underlay, which in this case is burlap to represent the desert. Other props include a strip of felt for the road, a city at either end, and black felt rocks on the side of the road. The figures include the person who was hurt and left beside the road, as well as the two persons who "passed by on the other side" and the Samaritan who stopped to help. They are two-dimensional and laminated to slide over the underlay and felt as the story is told.

After the presentation of the parable, the child and the adult can wonder together who was really a "neighbor" or friend to the person who was hurt. The child can pick from among the figures who he or she would like to be. The discussion can be extended by paintings of the parable, and the parable box can be left with the child so he can work it through again alone.

Even if children grasp the facts of the situation, work through their ethical position with a parable, and want to help themselves or another person by being research subjects, the ethical discussion is not complete. They also need discussion of certain faith questions with facts and moral reasoning, to establish both the trust to go forward and something to rely on if things do not happen as planned. That question is discussed next.

What if it does not work out?
This question moves us beyond both natural and social reality to ultimate reality. It is more than a question about the child's death if the research does not succeed. It is a question of what the child or anyone can rely on when, despite one's understanding of science and one's best moral judgment, things do not work out. It has to do with how one's whole world hangs together.

The structures of faith development have been studied by James Fowler[132]. The structuralist and visceral approaches seem complementary. Both are necessary to adequately grasp the faith phenomenon. We will limit our discussion here, however, to the contribution of the structuralists to discussing ethical questions with children in their fullest form.

Building on the research and method of Piaget and Kohlberg, Fowler identified six stages of faith development. Each stage is averaged by scoring persons on seven variables within each stage. The variables used to determine one's faith stage average are: the structures of logic, world coherence, role-taking, authority, bounds of social awareness, form of moral judgment, and the role of symbols. The structures of faith development extend beyond the interaction with the natural world examined by Piaget and interaction with the social world examined by Kohlberg to the interaction with the most comprehensive limits to one's life. Faith stages include logic and moral reasoning stages. Logic is necessary but not sufficient for a faith stage change (Table 3).

As a medium for multistage communication about ultimate reality, I would like to suggest the Parable of the Good Shepherd. Part of my work at the Institute of Religion has been to examine many media to see if they have this capacity. Certainly sacraments do. Probably sacred history and sacred ethics do if they are presented carefully and appropriately. Prayer and liturgy probably do, too, when presented appropriately. This is something that religions have known by intuition for centuries, but must continually be rediscovered.

I am indebted to Professoressa Sofia Cavalletti of Rome for having rediscovered much of how to use these multistage media with children in our time. Her entry point was made by applying the Montessori Method to the teaching of religion to young children. Of all her insights, the use of the Parable of the Good Shepherd seems to be the most profound. This can also be presented using simple strips of cloth and figures.

Table 3. Stages in faith development (Fowler)

Stage 1	Episodic and alogical world view.
Stage 2	Mythical-literal world view: authority relates to trust: limited social awareness (around age 6).
Stage 3	Ideas shape world view: tradition is recognised: symbolism is multidimensional (around age 12).
Stage 4	Ultimate matters are either/or questions.
Stage 5	Rarely achieved. Dialectical logic is typical; universal moral principles (around age 30).
Stage 6	Very rarely achieved. Transcendent loyalty, ontological awareness (around age 40).

Although the details of the presentation may differ, when children are asked to paint back the parables, the same sorts of paintings appear at different stages. Children from about 2 to 7 years paint the sheepfold with the sheep inside as the dominant feature. Beginning at about age 7, the Good Shepherd begins to dominate. By about age 12, the children become interested in the difference in "leadership" between the Good Shepherd and the Ordinary Shepherd. Regardless of what aspect of the parable the children focus on, they seldom confuse the Good Shepherd with their parents. He is something bigger and more comprehensive in his constant caring.

Like fairy tales, the parables of Jesus communicate on many different levels. One brings to them what one knows and the structures by which one knows. They are something to walk with through the journey of human faith. They do not contain the growth of someone beginning his or her journey and they retain many levels of meaning on which a person late in the journey can reflect. Often an unspoken need can guide a person to one parable or another. It certainly does for the children who cannot explain why they want to do a certain parable over and over again. Of all the parables, the one most important for children in a hospital seems to be that of the Good Shepherd.

There is a difference between parables and fairy tales that is also important for the child in the hospital discussing with an adult the prospects of research in which he or she will be the subject. Fairy tales are about the realities of growing up, but these children are faced with having their growing up cut short. Many of the parables are about an invisible kingdom within and among us that continues to grow despite all, even failing physical health. Parables such as the one about heaven or the mustard seed say this in ways that one is hard pressed to exhaust or improve on.

In any case, the use of such a multistage medium as the Parable of the Good Shepherd helps us communicate with the child across the developmental distance. Being in the parable with the child unlocks his or her loneliness and allows the adult to be a companion in the child's dangerous journey.

"Living happily ever after"

In striving to clarify what the developmental structuralists have to say about our ethical conversations with children, I have had a twofold hope. On the one hand, I wanted to widen the concept of the ethical discussion to include the whole ethical domain, the facts, the reasoning, and the "faithing." If we were going to deal with more than one ethical conversation, we would have gone further into the part evaluation and creativity play. My second hope was to provide some insight into how adults can become better translators in their conversations with children about matters of ultimate importance, such as whether or not a child ought to become a subject of research. Both hopes, the why and the how of the process, were formulated to help unlock the loneliness of the child faced with such a situation.

Bettelheim has noted that, when fairy tales end with the formula "and they lived happily ever after," the child does not fix on the promise of eternal life to take the sting out of dying and illness.[133] They end that way to assure the child that a satisfying bond between human beings can form despite being lost or suffering trials in dark forests or in the land of the giants. The promise is there of emotional security and permanence, despite their flooding emotions. The parables go even farther. They say, in their many ways and on many levels, that everything is really a Thou, as the naive theologians of 2 to 7 years sense, and that the Thou loves them in a way that keeps on growing, despite everything.

Original source:

Berryman, J.W. 1978. "Talking ethics with the child." Pp. 85-101 in *Research In Children: Medical Imperatives, Ethical Quandaries and Legal Constraints*, **edited by J. van Eys. Baltimore: University Park Press.**

14

Children in Worship – An Ethic of Respect

So painful were the stories being told that I couldn't believe my ears. We were in a "children in worship" meeting, and the leader had asked us to tell about our childhood experiences. There were the usual stories about misunderstandings, but it was the pain and anger expressed that surprised me most.

My experience was different. I am an Anglican now, but I grew up a Presbyterian. When the elements for holy communion were passed along the pews I reached out one time to take the wine. It was in beautiful rosewood carriers, and the little cups captured various shades of red in their liquid prisms. My father's hand grasped mine and drew it back. I was excluded, but I was also sitting with my family and my father said in a warm whisper, "You can have that when you're older. First you need to study and understand what we're doing."

My Dad had valued the sacramental act and me by talking to me in a personal way. His voice carried neither threat nor anger. He slipped me one of his mints, and I settled back to look at the stained-glass windows and symbols carved in the wood until the end of the service.

I was lucky. One of the stories shared at the workshop was told with wringing, twisting hands and a voice full of pain edged with anger.

A young woman described how as a child she had peeked around the end of the pew to watch people go forward, sometimes in tears, to be "saved." She wanted to go forward and felt she was supposed to, but she feared God was going to break through the roof in anger at any minute. He (and she meant "He") would get her before she could get to the preacher who would "save her."

One day she finally took the enormous risk. She ran terrified and crying to the preacher far down the aisle at the front of the church. He lifted her up and praised God. He shouted about her "tears of joy" at being saved.

The pain and misunderstanding associated with worship are not intended; they happen by default. This article seeks to offer perspective and suggest the issues involved in showing children the art of worshiping, so that what worship intends will be communicated.

In the Book of Common Prayer of the Episcopal Church the baptismal covenant includes the phrase: "Will you strive for justice and peace among all people, and respect the dignity of every human being?" The answer given is one of intelligent will that accepts our human failings and flaws but hopes for the strength of accomplishment. The people say: "I will, with God's help." Respect is the theme of this article. The exercise of the will is a matter of ethics.

The "is" and "ought" of respect

There is no natural and easy respect for children built into our adult relationships with them. We have not always recognized the dignity of children as individuals who experience life in an authentic and valuable way. That is the only clear result that emerges from the history of parent-child relations.

Lloyd DeMause, a pioneer in the historical study of childhood proposed what he called a "psychogenic theory of history."[134] For most of this history adults seemed to be unable to see children as beings distinct and different from themselves. Sometimes they projected unacceptable feelings about themselves onto the child. Or they perceived the child as someone to take care of them. The child was thus a combination of a devil and an adult.

DeMause identified six successive historical modes for the

relationship between parent and child. The relationship shifted over the centuries from infanticide to abandonment to ambivalence to intrusion to socialization and finally to the contemporary mode, which is helping. At times it seems as if DeMause is writing a history of child abuse, but the progressively more humane pattern of child rearing that he found is encouraging – that is, until we discover that this is not the pattern found by other historians.

Philippe Aries found that the concept of "childhood" didn't exist during the middle ages.[135] His research was based primarily on paintings, but he also consulted dress, games and pastimes, manuals, school life and disciplinary practices. By the sixteenth century children were seen as sources of amusement and relaxation.

In the seventeenth century adults began to enjoy "coddling" children and realized that they were different from adults. They were seen as being innocent and weak. The era's moralists were particularly interested in their training and the correction of their behavior.

Children continued to be trained and corrected in the eighteenth century. Besides being viewed as fragile creatures in need of protection and reform, they were thought to need special measures to encourage their health. By midcentury the modern view of childhood had emerged. The child's presence and existence became a concern, with the result that the child took a central place in the family.

John Sommerville discovered a "rise and fall of childhood" rather than the continual rise of empathy found by DeMause.[136] He noted that in the nineteenth century a tragic and odd occurrence took place.

The greatest exploitation and the greatest glorification of children took place at the same time. Poems by Blake, Wordsworth and others reflected a yearning for childhood. Stories included the outrage of Dickens, the irony of Mark Twain, the sweetness of Barrie's *Peter Pan* and the logical puzzles of Lewis Carroll. This interest in childhood for itself contrasted sharply with the social fact of weary, underpaid children forming the backbone of industry from the mills to the mines at the expense of their education and health.

Philip Greven's studies about child-rearing patterns and theology among the Protestants in this country during its early centuries are also interesting.[137] He found that the evangelical, moderate and genteel theological groups had parallels in child-rearing.

The evangelicals wanted to suppress the child's will by breaking it. The moderates wanted to induce self-control by bending the child's will. The genteel tended to raise self-assertive children by encouraging the will.

Rigorously repressive and authoritarian parental control was not always a knee-jerk reaction of unlearned adults. This philosophy was reflected in the domestic rule of The Reverend Jonathan Edwards, the most influential evangelical theologian in the eighteenth century. Another example is Susanna Wesley, the mother of John Wesley. She bore "Methodism" itself by her carefully controlled pattern of daily life that governed the life of Methodism's founder from the day of his birth.

Examples of the moderates are different. They were caught between the poles of duty and desire and sought a middle way. They learned how to compromise but still believed in the need for self-denial. While the evangelicals were self-suppressed, they were self-controlled. The Adams family of Braintree, Massachusetts, is the best example.

The genteel families valued fond affection over conscientious discipline to shape the relationships between the generations. Still the necessity for correct and proper behavior within the family contexts was not neglected. Fear as inconceivable, duty as taken for granted, and reverence and unbounded love distinguished these families from most of their contemporaries.

The family of Governor Thomas Hutchinson, the most eminent and admired as well as the most, ardently hated defender of British authority in colonial Massachusetts, is an example. A second example is the Allen family in Pennsylvania, which produced James Allen, son of a very wealthy and prominent man in the colony. William Byrd's family in Virginia is a third example.

The pervasive preoccupation of evangelicals with sin, corruption, grace and new birth was not shared with as much feeling by the moderates, among whom were many Presbyterians and Congregationalists. Concern with the state of one's inner being was almost absent from the genteel. They were drawn to the ritual, ceremony and stable institution of the Church of England.

Linda A. Pollock studied parent-child relations from 1500-1900, limiting her sources to England and America. She has provided the best literature review and analysis of the sources. She concluded that "instead of trying to explain the supposed changes in the parent-child relationship, historians would do well to ponder just why parental care is a variable so curiously resistant to change."[138]

The only differences in the historical record she examined were those of style. What she did find in the period under study was parental acceptance of responsibility for the protection and the socialization of children and recognition of their dependency.

The study of history is important. Even the brief survey above raises many issues for adults about how we naturally relate to children in worship and elsewhere. Respect for children clearly is not natural to all parents in our time or before. History will not make decisions for us, but if we ignore its teachings it will rule us, ethical or not. As the natural relationship between children and adults is not clear, we should attend to what we "ought" to do, which constitutes a move from history to ethics.

Jesus and respect for children

To discover how we ought to relate to children in worship, we can look at the center of our tradition, the Christ. There was a generating, seedlike quality to Jesus' view of children.[139] It stood in contrast to the rest of the ancient western world. In Sparta, Athens and Rome children were either personal property of the family or father or raw material to be educated to serve the state. They were not valued for themselves. Even in Jerusalem children were valued as bearers of Torah and not as unique beings.

In Galilee Jesus blessed children as beings valuable in themselves. He perceived their parabolic quality, setting a child in the disciples' midst to show that one must become like a little child to enter the kingdom.

Children were the insiders and the disciples were the outsiders. Children are in the kingdom naively and naturally as they play theologically at the edge of their being and knowing. Their rapid growth means that they must live primarily at the edge of being and knowing. Play is the primary way they acquire knowledge.

Children are not always gates into the kingdom or parables of kingdom entry; sometimes they mirror our unbelief. Jesus said his generation was "like children sitting in the market place and calling to their playmates, 'We piped to you, and you did not dance; we wailed, and you did not mourn'" (Matt 11:16-17).

John the Baptist had come fasting and austere. Jesus had come in a more relaxed, social way. But some could hear neither approach. Not everyone has ears to hear, adults or children.

Jesus' basic teaching about children is that they are parabolic signs of our own lives if we want to enter the kingdom. They are clues for us to learn from if we want to know how worship works as communication. The approach to the holy brings us to the edge of our being and knowing, but we have lost our sense of play at that boundary situation. From children we can regain it.

To approach the mystery of God, we need to be able to wonder. Children wonder naturally. Adults need to decide consciously to wonder, which almost precludes the experience until we become childlike. We learn how to become childlike from children, as Jesus showed us in his parable.

Putting the ethics of respect into action

The play of worship is not like a play in which we recite our lines or assume the role of mute spectators. Some think the congregation is the audience, the participants the clergy and God the prompter. Kierkegaard's parable suggested that the people are the players, the clergy the prompters, and God the audience.

The first way to put the ethic of respect into action is to ensure that children not be given a conflicting message about how to worship. Sometimes we are so intent on teaching or controlling their behavior that we cannot worship, so we tell them to do what we are unable to do.

When we feel one way and promote or encourage another, children will learn from our actions, not our words. They will also perceive that worship is to be done in an unauthentic way; in other words, it involves a lie. No one intends to convey that message, but such a hidden curriculum of that kind is sometimes taught by default.

The second way to put the ethic of respect into action is to avoid the temptation to play God. We do not know what children know when they worship. Although we can sometimes look indirectly into the world they inhabit through the two narrow windows of art responses and play responses, we have no direct access. Much of what I have personally seen in these types of responses does not easily fit into the traditional scheme of cognitive development.[140]

Young children have emotional lives of their own and struggle with the same kind of existential issues adults do. They merely do it differently and are often unable to speak of it in a way we can understand.

Some years ago Carole Klein wrote a book called *How It Feels to Be a Child*.[141] The book indicates that the adult assumption that children are always happy is not true. The "myth of the always happy child" is a complicated adult dismissal of children's feelings. We often fail to consider that normal young children experience fear, loneliness, guilt, anger, dreams, shame and sexual feelings but do not have the language to express these powerful shifting waves of emotion that sometimes threaten to overwhelm them. Worship and religious language in general can be very helpful in coping with these global feelings.

Instead of engaging in the blasphemous assumption that we know what children think and feel, we need to listen and watch carefully. Telling them how they think and feel is not only to play God but to trap them in a terrible double bind.

When we tell children how they think or feel, we are proposing that either they give up the experience as they have felt it or the trusted adult's interpretation of that experience. The double bind asks them to turn against the value of their own experience or that of the adult relationship and the safety of knowing that adults know the way things really are. There is no way out of the double bind except by our being more sensitive and respectful of children and their world.

The third way to put the ethic of respect into action is to beware of the danger of idolatry, worshiping the act of worship itself. Worship is the way we communicate with God in Jesus Christ.

Worship and its tools to create communication, religious language, can become as much objects of worship as a golden calf and just as dangerously comic.

The religious language we use to communicate with God and each other in worship is powerful and specific in function. The language of science, law, art or any other language domain we choose is also very powerful when used appropriately. All do their work well, but religious language exceeds other communication domains in helping human beings cope with their existential limits.

The language of religion

A primary function of religious language is to create meaning at the edge of knowing and experience.[142] Playing in language at the horizon's edge requires a special set of tools that disclose the mystery of God's presence, hidden and revealed.

Our need for meaning at the edge of our being and knowing draws us into religious discourse naturally. The existential issue of meaning joins with death, aloneness and the threat of freedom to "box us in" at the limit of who we are and what we can know.[143]

Religious language consists of parables, sacred stories and the action and symbols of liturgy. It relies on striking metaphors that reveal but hide the relationship with the creator so that its implications for coping with our human possibility and limit is indirectly revealed to us in a way that stimulates our creativity.

The functions of parable, sacred story and liturgical symbol and action are part of the religious language system in the way that adding, subtracting and infinity are part of the language of mathematics.[144] The two languages make meaning but about different parts of life and death.

Some would say that children do not have existential and ultimate concerns such as death, the need for meaning, aloneness and the threat of freedom.[145] Another view maintains that children should not be exposed to religious language because it will be misunderstood, causing them to become confused.[146] While this can happen, it need not if children are respected. We should be working continually on ways to present sacred stories, parables and liturgical symbols and action appropriately to children and with respect.[147]

True, children cannot identify or explain metaphors, but they use them naturally when playing with language to generate sentences and language itself.[148] If they learn how to use the metaphors of religious language, they can use them creatively in learning how to cope with existential issues.

Howard Gardner has argued in *Frames of Mind that* there are "multiple intelligences" that develop in different ways on their own timetables.[149] All individuals have a certain susceptibility to the encoding of particular symbol systems as individuals. He has identified intelligences that are linguistic, musical, logical-mathematical, spatial, kinesthetic and the intelligence of the self. I would add to this list the deep code of religious language that is empirically grounded in the experience of the limit to being and knowing.

Teaching the art of worship

We have already outlined three principles that help to protect teaching the art of worship from unintended messages: (1) avoiding conflicting messages; (2) avoiding blasphemy and the potential double bind it entails; and (3) avoiding the idolatry of worshiping worship (and religious language) itself rather than using it to worship God.

The principles tell us what we need to guard against. What we need to do is become master teachers: persons who perform their art as masters and who teach by example. We will resemble teachers of any art, such as painting.

There are art historians, art critics and chemists who make paints, artisans who make easels and stretch canvas, sellers of paintings, people who buy paintings, workers who hang paintings in halls and homes, philosophers of the aesthetic and numerous others who are attracted to painting, but only the painter paints. To learn how to paint one needs to go to the painter and to paint.

To teach children about worship one needs to worship well and authentically. This is our primary responsibility, not trying to change them or telling them how to think and feel when they worship.

The *imago dei* is not a form stamped in clay. It is the awakening of the creative process in other created creatures. This process feeds back into the creator's activity to overcome entropy by creation and destruction by construction.

We express our *imago dei* when we show respect and sensitivity for the child in worship. The child completes the circle with God and shows us the way to wonder and play so that we too can continue to grow in worship and the appropriate use of religious language.

Erik Erikson has suggested that to move beyond the generativity versus stagnation period of development human beings need to be needed. He says that "maturity needs guidance as well as encouragement from what has been produced and must be taken care of."[150] It is a way to enter that "post-narcissistic love of the human ego – not of the self – as an experience which conveys some world order and spiritual sense, no matter how dearly paid for." Such love helps us balance our ego integrity versus despair when we encounter our mortality.

In the next generation when people gather to talk about children in worship, perhaps, they will tell very different stories from those I heard this year. Perhaps more adults will tell about feelings, such as giving thanks and lifting up their hearts when they were children. Perhaps they will do this because we practiced the ethic of respect.

Original source:

Berryman, J.W. 1989. "Children in worship: An ethic of respect." *Liturgy: Ethics and Justice,* **7 (4): 53-59.**

15

Theologizing with Children – A Parable Approach

A theological conversation is when people talk together about God. There is a strong sense of coming together, informality, and equality in the term "conversation" that goes back to the Latin word *cum* that in Italian became *con,* and is translated into English as "with". Conversely, in English the term "con" can also indicate a relationship that is deceitful or an intriguing falsehood. Theologizing with children, then, ought to be a coming together of adults and children to talk about God with as much equality and truth as possible.

The problem of power in theologizing with children

The major problem when children and adults engage in a theological conversation is that it is *not* a conversation. This is because the participants are not equal in power. The adult, merely by being an adult, dominates the discussion's questions and answers by his or her physical size, perspective taking ability, experience, emotional authority, cognitive development, physical control, and in other ways – many of which work at an unconscious level.

Both children and adults experience this power difference as a double bind. For the adult it involves teaching. What the adult says about God *teaches* both by its form and content, even when the adult *does not mean to teach* and values children's freedom to express themselves in their own terms. At the same time the adult has an *ethical duty to teach* the art of how to use the best language possible in the best possible way for such discussions.

The double bind for children is that if children acquiesce to the adult's language, whatever it may be, they will have to give up not only the language that they are attempting to make meaning with, but also the immediacy of God that has been experienced. On the other hand, if children do not acquiesce to the adult's preferred language they risk alienating the adult. Either way the result is painful.

The approach suggested here enables adults and children to cope with their respective double binds in constructive ways and also recognizes that language is inadequate for both children and adults to express fully their experiences of God (Berryman, 2001). It will focus on the use of the Parable of the Leaven (Matthew 13:33; Luke 13:20-21) to stimulate theologizing with children and draws on a study of 216 children, 5-12 years of age. Each group averaged 16.9 children and met weekly during the school year for 30 minutes. A total of 89 parable sessions were involved in the whole study, which resulted in about 44 hours and 30 minutes of audio recordings, which were transcribed and studied.

The method is called Godly Play, which is described more fully in *Godly Play* (Berryman, 1991) and *Teaching Godly Play* (Berryman, 1995) as well as in an eight volume series, *The Complete Guide To Godly Play,* completed in 2008 (Berryman, 2002-2008) and translated into German, Finnish, Spanish, and Swahili. The goal of Godly Play is to nourish the spiritual practice of children and adults for the spiritual maturity of both (Berryman, 2004) and the theory of religious education upon which the method is based encourages "playful orthodoxy," which deepens children's roots in a particular religious tradition and at the same time stimulates them to be open to new experiences, new people, and new ways of thinking (Berryman, 2005), so that ultimately in multi-religious settings depth can communicate with depth.

Strategies for coping with the power differential

Five ways to cope with the power differential will now be discussed. The Godly Play approach uses many more such strategies, but this discussion will be enough to establish that this is possible.

One of the neutralizing strategies places the adult in a circle of a dozen or more children. This gives the children's side of the conversation more weight in numbers so that a community of children can be created. The adult remains a powerful but minority partner and works to support the community of children rather than to dominate it. This reduces the adult's dominance without giving up the ethical responsibility to teach the best language possible for theological discourse and the art of how to use it.

A second problem is the developmental differences between adults and children. Physical artifacts are used to tell the story. Since the "pieces" of the parable's language are placed in the centre of the circle of children they add to the equality in the circle and in addition they help all the children, regardless of cognitive developmental stage, to be able to contribute to the community's reflection on the parable because they can "think" with their hands by moving the pieces around to try out different ideas. This also enables them to know this language with their bodies while their minds are still developing.

A third way this approach copes with the power difference is by carefully organizing the environment in which the conversation is held. When a single part of the Christian language system is placed in the middle of the circle it needs linking to the larger system to provide the contextual meaning. The environment, therefore, needs to have the whole system of Christian language set up on low shelves around the walls to surround children in the circle so they will not have to be dependent on adults to provide this context verbally for their theologizing. This also means that the children become aware, at least at the intuitive level, of the variety of genres within the Christian language system because they are *physically* distinguished in the room. They also begin to intuit through their senses how the Christian language system as a whole is different from others such as the language of science that they are being taught in school and the pervasive but mixed language-of-everyday.

Fourth, theologizing with children is conceived of as a spiritual practice for the *mutual* benefit of both the children and adults involved. The benefit for adults is that being in touch with children benefits their spiritual maturity, as Jesus observed. The benefit for the children is that when adults understand better about "becoming like a child" they are better able to mentor children, which in turn helps the children to be more fully themselves, which in turn again helps make them better mentors to adults. Thinking of theologizing with children as a spiritual practice that uses classical Christian language, such as the parables, contrasts this approach with philosophizing because it involves a different language system.

A final observation about how this approach can help cope with power differences is the use of wonder. Children are shown how to approach the Christian language system with wonder to make meaning. The adult guides this, but the children soon enthusiastically join in, because wonder is so deeply associated with play, which is natural to children, and because wonder opens their creative process, which gives them pleasure. The use of wonder is thus self-motivating.

A wondering question differs from a Socratic question. Socratic questions lead the student to the conclusion the teacher has in mind. A wondering question is one that the adult cannot answer for the child. An example is, "I wonder what this (something in the parable) could really be." Wondering questions thus help free children's theologizing from adult control and the tendency of adults to tell them how to think and feel.

There are many more ways that this approach helps neutralize the power difference between children and adults, but these five ways provide enough general background to allow us to look more closely at how a parable can help theologizing with children.

How a parable can stimulate theologizing with children

Five steps will now be outlined to show how the Parable of the Leaven can stimulate theological discourse with children. More information about this presentation may be found in Volume 3 of *The Complete Guide To Godly Play* (Berryman, 2002, 109-114) and the whole approach to parables, including the lessons that synthesize all the parables in the New Testament, may be found in Volume 3 as well (Berryman, 2002, 77-152). The formal application of this approach to children and parables began to be published in 1979 (Berryman, 1979).

The first step to stimulate theological discourse with a parable is to show the children the gold box, which contains it. The box is placed in the centre of the community of children, as the common property of all. This action, the gold box itself, and the use of the word "parable" converge with the anticipation and respect felt by the adult mentor to show that something special is about to happen. The box identifies the genre and prepares the children for exploring what comes next in an appropriate way.

The second step invites the children to wonder about the cloth that is taken from the parable box and on which the pieces of the parable will be laid. Each underlay is a different shape and color. This one is a curved triangle about three feet by three feet and is a warm tan colour. Recent parable scholars, such as John Dominic Crossan (Crossan, 1973, 1976, 1980) have suggested that parables are a genre that stimulates the creative process, but this is not an entirely a modern view since C.H. Dodd said in 1935 that a parable functions by catching the hearer's attention by "its vividness or strangeness, and leaving the mind in sufficient doubt about its precise application to tease it into active thought" (Dodd, 1961, 5). Wondering about the underlay begins the "teasing".

The underlay also invites the children to work together with the mentor to build the parable's metaphor. As the cloth is smoothed out slowly and carefully, it is invested with the storyteller's love and respect so that when the wondering question is asked about what it could really be the children are involved in a personal way.

Children younger than five years are mostly interested in the mechanics of taking the parable box off the shelf, carrying it with two hands for respect, laying out the artifacts to tell the parable, putting everything back in the box, and putting the box back on the shelf. By the age of five, however, the wondering is more articulate. A group of five-year-olds in the study thought that the underlay looked like:

"A pot..."
"A mountain..."
"A triangle with God coming out of it..."
"A lion...'"
"The gold sun..."
"Something that God was showing..."
"God making something..."
"The earth..."
"A sign of God..."
"A mountain with golden paint on it..."
"A golden retriever..."
"A pot and a flower..."
"A triangle God made for us to climb up..."
"A beehive..."
"A big foot..."
"Honey..."

The words "God" and perhaps "mountain" or "earth," suggest that the children are trying to stretch their language to convey a sense of the ultimate that they intuit in the parable. Other references, such as "golden retriever" or "a big foot," are examples of children at play, tossing up as many divergent ideas as they might toss colored balls into the air.

Children 9/10 years of age responded to the same underlay by saying:

> "You know, there are those parables that have such sharp, straight lines. Then there is that one that's close to round, but this has got steps on it, big steps, and it looks a little round because it's so old like this. Yes."
>
> "A nose..."
>
> "A beehive or something..."
>
> "This could be about sweet things cause they're..." She could not sustain her thought, but children often think this underlay is the color of caramel or honey.
>
> "It looks like a pyramid and those are all those different blocks." They were studying Egypt in history.
>
> "Well, when you said, before we even opened the box, if we didn't try, maybe it will be open, but it's just closed right now. Well, that reminds me of the time where the classroom door was closed and everybody was sitting out there for about fifteen minutes. Finally, someone tried the doorknob and it opened."
>
> "It's like you have to find your own way in," another child added. "The desert, a house in the desert..."
>
> "A termite..."
>
> "A sand dune..."
>
> "Sand..."
>
> "Listening to a parable, if you really listen hard, it's like finding a path through life."
>
> "It's so old."
>
> "A cloth and a triangle..."
>
> "The hands motioned that the underlay could be these two things at the same time".
>
> "Beehive..."
>
> "Ice cream cone, an arrowhead..."
>
> "I think that the doors are big trees, to the only people still left, and the last have been cut down and they're logs floating on this

very dirty river. And that's a big floating rock pile – kind of like rock..."

"Father Berryman, you know how you kind of said that you have to try something to see if it, the door, is open or whatever? And like the parable box is always closed, but you can still open it so it's like opening a new way to go somewhere or do something or listen – which *they're* not doing right now!" This referred to children who were not fully participating in the circle.

"It looks like a butterfly."

"Caramel ice cream..."

"You know how you said you can find your way in, everybody... finds a different way in, and everybody's making up all those ideas, and that's their way in, and so people do get the same way in, but most people have a different way."

These children are, of course, more verbal than the five year olds. Their thinking is more complex and their vocabulary is growing. What is most important, however, is what they have in common with the younger group, which is their creativity has been stimulated.

There are four characteristics of play that indicate when personal meaning is being created. The theologizing is enjoyable. It is done for itself rather than for some product outside the play. It is spontaneous and voluntary, which shapes the dynamics of how a group such as this is supported by the mentor. Finally, it involves deep engagement. Garvey observed that these characteristics relate play to creativity, problem solving, language learning, developing social roles, and a number of other cognitive and social phenomena (Garvey, 1977, 4).

The third step is the telling of the parable. It begins in a stylized way, like the "once upon a time" of many stories, and moves carefully through the brief narration of the parable. When children play deeply with the parable laughter begins to erupt as they make discoveries. The quality of laughter in theological discourse is another important sign that the children are creating personal meaning (Berryman, 1998).

The reflection on the parable becomes more complex as more

pieces are placed on the underlay. An example is when the small, gold triangle is taken out of its curious, ornamented box and is "hidden" in the mixture. When children ask directly what it is so one can say something like, "It is what makes the mixture swell up and get big." This neither interprets the leaven for the children nor goes outside the metaphor to explain it. To discuss such experiences as baking bread or buying leaven in a store or using other kinds of language, such as history or science, distracts the children from making personal, existential meaning with the parable. It also distorts the parable since there is no mention in it of baking bread, the history of leaven as a metaphor, or the science of how leaven works. It is about a kind of mixing and swelling that cannot be stopped or undone once started – among many other things.

More about the term "leaven" might be introduced to children, however, in late childhood, because, as B.B. Scott has said, "Traditional interpretations have ignored the negative aspects not only of leaven but also of 'woman,' 'hid,' and 'until all was leaven'" (Scott, 1990, 328). Some older children might now be able to enjoy the interplay between the positive reference to the "kingdom of heaven" and the negative sense of "leaven," which has a long history although it disappeared in English about 1800.

The fourth step invites the children to wonder together about the interplay between the parts of the parable and its wholeness. The sign that this step is about to begin is when the teacher sits back after telling the parable, pauses, and says, "Now, I wonder what this (pointing to any part of the whole of the parable) could really be". The direction the children's wondering will take cannot be predicted in advance. A group of ten-year-olds wondered about the leaven like this:

> "So maybe the big thing (the underlay) is the leaven."
>
> "Maybe that's a giant leaven (the underlay?) and it gets stuck in the bread and the woman gets stuck in the leaven, and that means the woman gets stuck in the bread. And they cook it in this giant

oven and the whole kingdom of heaven is able to eat it." She goes on to say, "The whole people in the kingdom of heaven eat it all. Except the thing is...there's only some crumbs...like candles on earth, so they all drop 'em down..."

"How big is it gonna get," another child asks.

A third child responds, "Too big."

I summarize, "So the kingdom of heaven is ... too big?"

"Yeah, 'cause if you have all those people's souls up there, they've gotta have a lot of room. More people are growing and have more space."

"Maybe once every year God has someone make a leaven and maybe the leaven somehow has some kind of magical thing in it, like the leaven. Yeah, sort of... like power. Has power in it, something magical, some kind of power..."

"Maybe the leaven is the people and it's like God puts all the people in the bread and it rises and rises and rises."

"The leaven is the people and makes heaven rise and rise."

"It could be something that has like loaves of bread that are really, really big. But they're hollow. And so maybe they're hollow inside, but...keeps growing 'cause the..." The child's reasoning was stretched to the point it could no longer be sustained.

"Maybe before God made earth, maybe before the first day, he made that, just have good earth, but somehow something like maybe liquor got mixed into it and made part of it bad. That's why there's so many criminals and juveniles today."

"The leaven might be a little bit of both. And the good grows bigger and it makes the bad grow bigger."

I summarized, "The bread is creation and the leaven is...?" A child finishes my sentence by saying, "Maybe Jesus' body."

At first I discounted the last child's comment. It sounded borrowed and stereotyped but then the child's face changed. The smile seemed to be one of discovery, so there must have been more than memory and will at work even if the words were familiar. The child had made the borrowed words his own.

The fifth step closes the process of theological reflection. It does this in a way that respects the children's continuing wonder and the property of religious language that there is "always more". Ian T. Ramsey argued that this "always more" quality of religious language is one of the "odd" things about its functioning (Ramsey, 1957, 15). Children need to understand this if they are going to "speak Christian" well. Closure, therefore, needs to wind up without leaving the impression that all has been said that needs to be said. When children carry on conversations among themselves as they leave the environment or when they linger to talk more about the parable with the mentor it shows that the right balance has been reached.

We turn now to a discussion of the empirical references for the kind of language used in this approach. When the children's existential issues begin to emerge we know that the theologizing has been appropriately grounded.

The empirical references for theologizing with children

The existential limits to being and knowing are the empirical references for theologizing. Death, the threat of freedom, aloneness, and meaninglessness "box us in". Theses boundaries both limit and define us. The stimulation of any one of these limit experiences activates the other three and overwhelms us. This is why existential issues need to be addressed indirectly, such as by reflection on a parable. This analysis draws broadly on the work of Irving Yalom's *Existential Psychotherapy* (Yalom, 2003) as well as the whole field of existential therapies, ably surveyed in 2003 by Mick Cooper (Cooper, 2003).

The experience of the existential limits is present at any age. Children and adults may differ in the form of their responses, but when language is involved there is usually a kind of language breakdown at this edge of being and knowing. This is because the referents are not things we can walk *around* like a table and find common agreement about. Instead they are like a room we cannot escape from and they are absolutely personal. Existential issues always *confront* us personally with walls of paradox.

First, being born to die is the ultimate paradox and breeder of anxiety, so we push ourselves to be active. Even though we feel more alive when we are active, we also must rest. The need for rest is the opposing term of the paradox. Resting scares us, however, because repose reminds us of death. This danger causes us to become active again, only to rest again. Existential anxiety comes from this continuing yes-no, off-on oscillation.

A second limiting paradox is freedom. We are relatively free, but our wish to be grounded clashes with the threat of groundlessness experienced in freedom, so we move towards freedom until we experience its lack of form then we move away, seeking safety in human structures. These structures then close in on us and confine us. Groundlessness becomes attractive once more and this oscillation between the opposing poles of freedom and structure form a second existential paradox.

Third, there is always a gap between us and what is not-us. We understand that aloneness is built into our existence, but this fact is also a paradox because we cannot sustain life alone. Aloneness is self-conflicting at the cellular level, psychologically, and socially. We wish for contact, for protection, and to be part of a larger whole, but when we move towards inclusion, we recoil, not wanting to be swallowed up by a larger system and disappear. This in turn drives us back towards inclusion and the paradox lives on.

Fourth, we are creatures who need certainty and yet we are suspicious of it, because we know we created it and we are a fallible and changing source. Despite this, we search for certainty, even absolute certainty, as we try to escape this paradox. Both flight toward certainty and standing to fight against it fail to satisfy, because at either extreme the creative process withers without safety so personal meaning dies.

How does evidence of these limit cases appear in children's

theologizing? There are three criteria: content, degree, and paradox. A content that refers to death, meaning, aloneness, or the threat of freedom suggests the presence of the ultimate boundaries. This is also suggested when the most extreme degree of language is used. Finally, when the structure of language shifts to a paradoxical form it indicates that the edge of being and knowing is being experienced. Not all of these criteria need to be present to show that language is existential, but any of the three suggest that this is possible.

There were no statements from the five-year-old children concerning this parable that directly referenced the four existential limits, used ultimate language or were structured by paradox. Early childhood is a time when children's language is like poetry because of their limited vocabulary and playful experimentation. Their God talk contains many levels and shades of meaning, so existential meaning might be *inferred* in what they say but we are looking for something a bit more explicitly existential. By the age of six this begins to appear.

A girl in the study told a story in response to the parable presentation about when she and her mother were hit by a car. She had been a baby then, she said, and was in her stroller. Her mother had to stay in the hospital. Another child told about a glass shelf that broke and her mother got cut and bled. She was still wide-eyed with the memory. Death had confronted these children because the potential loss of their mother suggested that they might die too, like her, without her nurture and care. These stories did not name the existential limits or use ultimate terms and the structure remained narrative rather than paradoxical, but there are hints of all four boundaries in these stories.

The same group of six-year-olds wondered who the woman in the parable was:

"Jesus' mother..."

"Remember that lady who had a little bit of bread and then he said, 'If you give me that little bit of bread and then you shall have plenty and then it overflowed.'"

"Bloody Mary ..."
"God's wife ..."
"God's sister ..."
"God's baby that grew up ..."
"Maybe she could be baptized, maybe ..."
"Maybe it's one of us."
"The woman, maybe it's one of the girls."
"Maybe it's me."
"Maybe it's you."
"It has to have very long hair."

The presence of Jesus, God, and other ultimate figures is linked in these comments with the children in the circle and they show the interplay between the ultimate and those engaged in the wondering about the woman in the parable. The shift to a focus on "me" and "your" shows the personal nature of this relationship with the ultimate. There are hints of transcendence here beyond the existential limits suggested by this interplay, but by means of these ultimate figures, and before speaking more about that we need to consider the pervasiveness of the creative process in human beings.

The creative process aspect of theologizing with children

The creative process pervades the human condition. It has biological, psychological, social, and spiritual aspects and begins in a very physical way. Howard Gardner's theory of modes (kinds of action) and vectors (the direction of the action) suggests that initially the infant's meaning is limited to a few aspects of bodily functioning such as openness and closeness or emptiness and fullness (Gardner, 1994, 108). These sensations are focused particularly in the region of the mouth but may extend throughout the body.

Usually by the second year the world is no longer perceived directly as a coordination of actions. It becomes mediated by symbols by which the child can now construct a complex world of permanent objects. The three developing systems of making, perceiving, and feeling become integrated in an increasingly fluent way if, indeed, they did not originate as a single system. Two kinds of referencing become available at this time, denotation and connotation. Connotation is especially important in the referencing used by the parables.

An understanding of the broad implications of the creative process has expanded in the last several decades. In *The Arts and Human Development* (Gardner, 1994) Gardner did not expand his analysis of the "making system" much beyond the four steps identified by Graham Wallas (1926), but in *Frames of Mind* (Gardner, 1983) he proposed a broader view of knowing than Piaget's logical-mathematical cognition and then in *Creating Minds* (Gardner, 1993) he expanded our understanding of the creative process by integrating it with the seven ways of knowing, already defined in *Frames of Mind,* and provided 20th century exemplars to show how the creative process manifests itself in different types of human beings. Gardner's work was paralleled by Mihaly Csikszentmihalyi's concept of "flow" (Csikszentmihalyi, 1990) and especially his more comprehensive *Creativity: Flow and the Psychology of Discovery and Invention* (Csikszentmihalyi, 1996). This showed that creativity includes a social aspect and that there is a difference between what is historically new and what is personally new. Csikszentmihalyi's concept of "flow," even suggested how this process feels and why it is intrinsically motivated.

What is most interesting for our purposes here is that there is a similarity between the "flow" of the creative process, the experience of contemplation as described in the twelfth century by Richard of St. Victor (Richard of St. Victor, 1979) and play (Garvey, 1977). This similarity has been discussed more extensively in "Laughter, Power, and Motivation" (Berryman, 1998) and gives a larger context.

This similarity compels one to ask if the presence of the Parable-Maker has been carried across the centuries by the power of parabolic connotation so that when one has "the ears to hear" the parable stimulates the creativity, contemplation, and play of today's interpreter. Postmodern literary critics tend to assume that the author's intention and personal history are irrelevant to the interpretation of texts, but in this case it is the mirroring of the creating-contemplating-playing process *itself* that links the author and the interpreter. This much, at least, must be granted and understood as significant in the use of parables to stimulate theologizing with children.

Some parable scholars have intuited something like this idea. Jeremias for example wrote in his great parable study that "We stand right before Jesus when reading his parables" (Jeremias, 1972, 12) and James Breech has argued that the "voice" heard in the parables is one of an unspoken love, which the parables *show* but do not name. This love is "a mode of being which is grounded in the superabundant power which engenders or fathers-forth all that is counter, original, spare, strange; and if love is a concept that refers to the capacity to engage voluntarily with the freedom of the actual other, then it can be said that Jesus was…the most loving and least sentimental man one could imagine" (Breech, 1983, 222).

The flow of the creative process can be artificially divided into six parts, but it is enough to say here that the process moves at many levels – biological, psychological, social, and spiritual – in a circle, making a feedback loop, from the opening of the process to its closing where it awaits to be opened once more. Each aspect of this process draws a particular type of personality to it, so in theologizing with children the adult mentor needs to support children to move all the way through this process, despite their tendencies to prefer and get stuck in one aspect or another (Berryman, 1991, 93-102).

About half of the process manifests itself in language after the earlier steps work themselves out in the unconscious. This means that one needs to look for behavioural signs to see if the early part of the process is moving. Children will display puzzled faces, frowns of concentration, twisting doubtful strands of the hair, or tapping their feet with frustration during the scanning period. A look of surprise and perhaps the laughter of delight will announce the moment when insight finally comes and begins to break into language.

An example of how the creative process is applied to existential issues will now be presented. The following conversation of children about ten years old took place when they wondered what the mixture could really be that the woman hides the leaven in:

"So it's a huge piece of bread..."

"And you can just take pieces off and when you take that piece off it'll grow back again."

"Maybe Jesus. He's making bread for all the poor people."

"It looks like a little man." (The leaven?)

"I think it's like... God is the bread and it's sort of swelling and swelling and people can eat off it but then it just keeps on growing on and on and..."

"Maybe it's holy."

"Maybe it's the bread that the apostles ate before Jesus died." '

"The person was baking bread for the Last Supper."

"How could we have it today?" (Referring to it being in the parable on the floor in front of us...)

"The bread could be communion bread."

"But more powerful... You don't even have to bake it. What did you see? Like there's everlasting love there...could be everlasting bread...And maybe the everlasting bread makes you remember the everlasting love."

"Maybe the everlasting bread and the everlasting love are brothers, or something."

(I asked, "When you start talking about everlasting things, it's really a different way to talk, isn't it?" I was probably pushing too hard for an awareness of the ultimacy in their language.)

"I know, 'cause nothing ever lasts."

" 'Cause there's not anything we know about that lasts forever."

"God does," another child answers.

"And Jesus."

"Except God," concludes the child who a moment earlier had said that "nothing ever lasts."

Existential content was engaged by the creative process in the statements about lasting and not lasting, "huge bread," "God," "Jesus," "everlasting bread," eating and growing again, "Last Supper," and other less explicit references. The structure of these comments have even verged on explicit paradox. For example there is the paradox of bread that will "grow back again" when consumed. There is the person who made the bread who is the woman and also God. There is the ordinary bread that is also holy. Past, present, and future times are no longer firmly distinguished, in addition the infinite and finite overlap. Perhaps, the most compressed paradox referred to was that bread is "everlasting love."

Within the enclosing boundaries of our existence we look for a way out, but there is none. We turn now to the role of God in God talk and transcendence and depth dimensions in theologizing with children. These dimensions are unique to the language and relationships involved in theologizing with children.

The role of God in God talk

We have now discussed the problem of the power differential in theological conversations with children and have suggested strategies about how to make the most ethical balance between teaching and freedom in that kind of discourse. The Parable of the Leaven was used as an example about how to put these strategies to work and then two concepts useful to guide theologizing with children, the creative process and existential issues, were discussed more thoroughly. We now turn to a final question. Will God come to play in the conversation? Neither children nor adults can control this, but it is possible to be alert to God's role in God talk so that one can be open to and cooperate with God's grace in ways like those noted above.

When the relationship of God to theologizing is considered the work of Gordon D. Kaufman becomes interesting. He has argued for thinking about God as "Serendipitous Creativity" (Kaufman, 1993) rather than as a potter who creates a pot. His phrase for God is helpful, as he said, "because (1) it preserves and indeed emphasizes the ultimacy of the mystery that God is, even while (2) it connects God directly with the coming into being – in time – of the new and the novel" (Kaufman, 2001, 414). I would like to adjust this just slightly to say that God in this sense is action, so God needs to be known by the verb form "creating".

When the classical view of God as Trinity is combined with the idea of God as creating, the complexity of God's relationship to God talk, stimulated by the Parable of the Leaven, becomes more understandable. First, God as the Creator is the creating in the universe, including the creating of a creature who creates. Second, God as Jesus is the creating of the parables. Third, God as Holy Spirit is creating within each child as the parables are interpreted. All this creating, alike yet differentiated, joins the children and the adult mentor who are theologizing in a larger kind of being that cannot be completely limited by one's individual and limited existence. The ability to put this into language is limited by human existential limits, however, so that even with a poet as great as Dante the poet's power fails before this final vision. He concluded his *Paradiso* by saying that his desire and will were spinning "...moved, by the Love which moves the sun and the other stars". What is true for adults is also true for children. Difficulty speaking about God is not merely because of developmental or vocabulary limitations.

The adult mentor cannot know with certainty if the children experience God's presence while they are theologizing. All the adult mentor can know is whether he or she experiences God in this process.

This is important because both to teach and to participate as equally as possible in the conversation the mentor needs to show how to be open to God's grace, since that openness is a matter of showing rather than talking. One might play with words, but playing cannot be controlled by words. Neither contemplation nor creativity can be controlled by what is said either. These are matters of relationship and are part of the nonverbal system, a kind of "social intelligence" that has been surveyed in a popular way by Daniel Goleman (2007) in terms of "empathic accuracy" and "resonance" among other kinds of mirroring brain structures. This means that the evaluation of theologizing with children requires more than a study *of children*. It also includes the *adult mentor's experience of God* while theologizing with children, because this approach's goal is "mutual blessing" (Berryman, 2005).

With these considerations in mind we can now complete the metaphor of the four existential "walls" that "box us in" when theologizing with children. As children and adults go "deeper' into the understanding of the genres of the Christian language system, it is more fully understood that this powerful language of parables, sacred stories, liturgical action, and silent contemplation is not to be learned as an end in itself but is to be learned as an art that is instrumental for knowing God and our place in a larger "state" (realm, kingdom) beyond the paradoxical, existential edges or boundaries of our personal existence. To think anything less would be idolatry in Judeo-Christian terms. The Christian language system is then instrumental to knowing God, as Holy Trinity, and as creating. This is known by the aspect of creating, which is playing with Christian language or, as the method used here is called, Godly Play. As God is known more fully by the instrumental use of Christian language, one discovers that there is also no "ceiling" to the "room" that *does and does not* limit our being and knowing by the paradoxical walls of our individual existence. One can "transcend" these limitations into a larger "state" (realm, kingdom) of creating (God) that encompasses our individual existence. This is done by the contemplative aspect of creating, which carries one beyond language into a direct relationship with God.

Conclusion

What we have seen is that children from 5-12 years can make use of the Parable of the Leaven to stimulate their theological discourse. This approach helped reduce the power difference between children and adults so that as much freedom as possible for the children to express themselves was provided without being unethical about providing them with the best tools to think theologically. This approach also invited God to come and take part in the making of meaning so that the Parable-Maker's creative process could be mirrored by that of the children interpreting the parable. The creative process in the universe (God the Father), the creative process in the making of the parable (The Son) and the creative process of the child interpreting the parable (The Holy Spirit) combined to open the possibility that the interpreters might cope with their existential limits by transcending them with "playful orthodoxy". Christian language in this way becomes instrumental to opening the possibility of God's presence becoming part of the conversation so all involved have the possibility of deepening their use of Christian language and transcending his or her existential limits.

References

Berryman, J.W. 1979. "Being in parables with children." *Religious Education* 75 (3): 271-285.

_____. 1991. *Godly play: A Way of Religious Education.* San Francisco: Harper. Reprinted in soft cover 1995. *Godly play: An Imaginative Approach to Religious Education.* Minneapolis, MI: Augsburg Fortress.

_____. 1995. *Teaching Godly Play: A Sunday Morning Handbook.* Nashville, TN: Abingdon.

_____. 1998. "Laughter, power, and motivation in religious education." *Religious Education* 93 (3): 358-378.

_____. 2001. "The nonverbal nature of spirituality and religious language." In *Spiritual Education: Cultural, Religious, Spiritual Differences.* Brighton, United Kingdom: Sussex Academic Press.

_____. 2002-2006. *The Complete Guide to Godly Play,* Vols. 1-6. Denver, CO: Living the Good News. Volumes 7 and 8 will be ready for publication in 2008.

_____. 2004. "Children and mature spirituality." *Sewanee Theological Review* 48 (1): 17-36.

_____. 2005. "Playful orthodoxy: Reconnecting religion and creativity by education." *Sewanee Theological Review* 48 (4), 437-454.

Breech, J. 1983. *The Silence of Jesus: The Authentic Voice of the Historical Man.* Minneapolis, MI: Fortress Press.

Cooper, M. 2003. *Existential Therapies.* London: Sage Publications.

Crossan, J.D. 1973. *In Parables: The Challenge of the Historical Jesus.* New York: Harper and Row.

_____. 1976. *Raid On The Articulate: Cosmic Eschatology in Jesus and Borges.* New York: Harper and Row.

_____. 1980. *Cliffs of Fall.* New York: Seabury Press.

Csikszentmihalyi, M. 1990. *Flow.* New York: HarperCollins.

_____. 1996. *Creativity: Flow and the Psychology of Discovery and Invention.* New York: HarperCollins.

Dodd, C.H. 1961. (revised ed). *The Parables of the Kingdom.* New York: Charles Scribner's Sons. This book was based on Dodd's Shaffer Lectures given at the Divinity School, Yale University, in the spring of 1935.

Gardner, H. 1994. *The Arts and Human Development.* New York: John Wiley and Sons with a new introduction by the author. 1973. New York: Basic Books.

_____. 1983. *Frames of Mind. The Theory of Multiple Intelligences.* New York: Basic Books.

_____. 1993. *Creating Minds: An Anatomy of Creativity Seen Through the Lives of Freud, Einstein, Picasso, Stravinsky, Eliot, Graham and Gandhi.* New York: Basic Books.

Garvey, C. 1977. *Play.* Cambridge, MA: Harvard University Press.

Goleman, D. 2007. *Social Intelligence: The Revolutionary New Science of Human Relationships.* New York: Bantam Paperback Edition.

Jeremias, J. 1972. *The Parables of Jesus.* Second Revised Edition. New York: Charles Scribner's Sons.

Kaufman, G.D. 1993. *In Face of Mystery: A Constructive Theology.* Cambridge, MA: Harvard University Press.

_____. 2001. "On thinking of God as serendipitous creativity." *Journal of the American Academy of Religion* 69 (2): 409-425.

Ramsey, I.T. 1957. *Religious Language.* London: SCM Press.

Richard of St. Victor. 1979. *Richard of St. Victor.* See especially The twelve patriarchs, The mystical ark, and Book three of The Trinity. Ramsey, NJ: Paulist Press.

Scott, B.B. 1989. *Hear Then the Parable: A Commentary on the*

Parables of Jesus. Minneapolis, MI: Fortress Press.

Wallas, G. 1926. *The Art of Thought*. New York: Harcourt, Brace.

Yalom, I. 1980. *Existential Psychotherapy*. New York: Basic Books.

Original source:

Berryman, J.W. 2009. "Theologizing with children: A parable approach." In *Hovering Over the Face of the Deep: Philosophy, Theology and Children*, edited by G.Y. Iversen, G. Mitchell, and G. Pollard. Munster: Waxman.

Endnotes

1 This paper is a revised version of the keynote address presented to the International Convention of the Religious Education Association, November 25, 1979, in Toronto, Canada. The research on which this paper is based was supported by grants to the author and Institute of Religion by the Lillian Kaiser Lewis Foundation and St. Paul's Presbyterian Church, both of Houston, Texas.

2 Maria Montessori, *The Child in the Church,* (St. Paul, Minn.: Catechetical Guild, 1965), p. 23. This is an up-dated and expanded version of E.M. Standing's 1929 expansion in English of Montessori's 1922 Italian publication called *Children Living in the Church.*

3 Rita Kramer, *Maria Montessori,* (NY: G.P. Putnam, 1976), p. 251.

4 Montessori, The Child in the Church, p. 5.

5 Maria Montessori, *The Montessori Method* (NY: Schocken Books, 1964)

6 Montessori, *The Montessori Method,* p. 207. This remark is related to music education in the environment, but the other quotes in the area of discipline are in the two chapters so designated.

7 Montessori, *The Child in the Church,* p. 6.

8 *William James, Talks to Teachers,* (NY: W. W. Norton & Co., 1958), pp. 23-24. Originally published in 1899.

9 A very helpful summary of Polanyi's work is Richard Gelwick's *The Way of Discovery,* (NY: Oxford Univ. Press, 1977)

10 Robert Rosenthal and Lenore Jacobsen, *Pygmalion in the Classroom,* (NY: Holt, Rinehart & Winston, 1968)

11 She did not address herself to children with "deviations" until *The Secret of Childhood in* 1936 which will be mentioned below.

12 Jerome Bruner, "Freud and the Image of Man," *The American Psychologist* 11 (1956): 463.

13 Maria Montessori, *Spontaneous Activity in Education,* (NY: Schocken Books, 1965). First published in Italian in 1918 and English 1917.

14 Ibid., p. 245.

15 Ibid., p. 243.

16 Montessori, *The Montessori Method,* pp. 82-83.

17 Maria Montessori, *The Secret of Childhood,* (NY: Ballantine Books, 1972). First published in English and French in 1938; Italian 1938.

18 Montessori, *The Montessori Method*, p. 371.

19 Montessori, *Spontaneous Activity*, p. 246.
20 Ibid., p. 247.
21 Montessori, *Spontaneous Activity*, p. 217.
22 Montessori, *The Child in the Church*, p. 15.
23 The age brackets for Montessori stages run parallel to Piaget's, but her interest in the planes of development extend beyond cognitive development. Her book *Pedagogical Anthropology* (NY: Frederick A. Stokes, 1913) first discusses this. Published in Italian in 1910.
24 Maria Montessori, *The Absorbent Mind*, (NY: Dell Pub. Co., 1967)
25 Montessori, *The Montessori Method*, p. 371.
26 This reference is not from *The Absorbent Mind*. It is based on articles by Fantappie's secretary which appeared in Italy in *Vita dell'Infanzia in* 1954 and 1956.
27 Montessori, *The Absorbent Mind*, p. 290.
28 This quote and a discussion of Radice's articles can be found in Kramer, *Maria Montessori*, pp. 257-262.
29 Montessori, *The Child in the* Church, pp. 12-20.
30 Eugenio Zolli, *Before the Dawn* (New York: Sheed and Ward, 1954), p. 164.
31 Sofia Cavalletti, "Catechesi e Metodo Montessori," *Proceedings of the XI Congress Internationale Montessori* (September 1957): 1-4.
32 Jerome W. Berryman, "The Work of Sofia Cavalletti," *The Constructive Triangle* 5 (Winter 1978): 32-45.
33 Sofia Cavalletti and Gianna Gobbi, *Teaching Doctrine and Liturgy*, trans. M. Juliana, O.P. (Staten Island, N.Y.: Alba House, 1964). Published in Italian in 1961.
34 Paul Tillich, *Systematic Theology*, 3 vols. (Chicago: University of Chicago Press, 1951-63), 1:115-116.
35 Rita Kramer, *Maria Montessori* (New York: G. P. Putnam's Sons, 1976), p. 252.
36 Maria Montessori, *The Absorbent Mind* (New York: Dell Publishing Co., 1967). First published in English in India in a rough translation of Montessori's Italian lectures. In 1952 it was published in Italy in Italian after a reworking by Montessori and her colleagues. The cited edition is taken from Claude Claremont's translation of Montessori's Italian edition. It was first published in 1958 by Holt, Rinehart, and Winston.
37 Ibid., p. 52. J. B. Watson discussed.
38 Ibid., pp. 93-95. Arnold Gesell discussed.
39 Ibid., p. 57. Montessori's "vital force" theory discussed in terms of both

individual optimum development and optimum development for life in general.
40 Jerome W. Berryman, "Montessori and Religious Education," *Religious Education* 75 (May-June 1980): 294-307.
41 James W. Fowler and Sam Keen, *Life Maps: Conversations on the Journey of Faith,* ed. Jerome W. Berryman (Waco, Tex.: Word Press, 1978).
42 Michael Polanyi, *Personal Knowledge: Towards a Post-Critical Philosophy* (Chicago: University of Chicago Press, 1958).
43 Thomas Kuhn, *The Structure of Scientific Revolutions* (Chicago: The University of Chicago Press, 1975).
44 Tracy, D. *Blessed Rage for Order* (New York, Seabury Press, 1975).
45 Koestler, A. *The Act of Creation* (New York, Macmillan, 1964).
46 Becker, E. *The Denial of Death* (New York, Macmillan, 1973).
47 Crossan, J.D. *In Parables: The Challenge of the Historical Jesus* (New York, Harper and Row, 1973).
48 Polanyi, M, & Prosch, H. *Meaning* (Chicago, The University of Chicago Press, 1975).
49 Ong, W.J. *Orality and Literacy: The Technologizing of the Word* (London, Methuen, 1982).
50 Cavalletti, S. *The Religious Potential of the Child* (New York, Paulist Press, 1983).
51 Rizzuto, A-M. *The Birth of the Living God* (Chicago, The University of Chicago Press, 1979).
52 Bromberg, W. *From Shaman to Psychotherapist* (Chicago, Henry Regnery Co., 1975).
53 Worgul, G.S Jr. *From Magic to Metaphor* (New York, Paulist Press, 1980).
54 Allport, G.W. *The Individual and His Religion* (New York, Macmillan, 1950), p. 30.
55 Goldman, R. *Religious Thinking from Childhood to Adolescence* (New York, Seabury Press, 1968).
56 Batson, C.D & Ventis W.L. *The Religious Experience* (New York, Oxford University Press, 1982).
57 This process is carefully analyzed by James Loder in a book-length essay. Batson studied with Loder at Princeton Theological Seminary. See Loder, JE, *The Transforming Moment: Understanding Convictions' Experiences* (New York, Harper and Row, 1981). Part of the reason that the child cannot speak about this event is the limitation of the child's stage of "faith development" as defined and studied by James Fowler. It is based on the cognitive developmental tradition

of Piaget and the tradition of Erikson. See Fowler, J.W, *Stages of Faith: The Psychology of Human Development and the Quest for Meaning* (New York, Harper and Row, 1981).

58 Gardner, H. *Art, Mind, and Brain: A Cognitive Approach to Creativity* (New York, Basic Books, 1982).

59 Hardy, A. *The Spiritual Nature of Man: A Study of Contemporary Religious Experience* (Oxford, Oxford University Press, 1979).

60 Robinson, E. *The Original Vision* (Oxford, The Religious Experience Research Unit, Manchester College, 1977).

61 Marcel, G. *The Mystery of Being* (London, Harvill Press, 1950).

62 Buber, M. *Between Man and Man* (Boston, Beacon Press, 1955), p. 139.

63 Tillich, P. *Systematic Theology* (Vol. 1). (Chicago, The University of Chicago Press, 1951).

64 Ibid, pp281-282.

65 Ramsey, I. *Religious Language: An Empirical Placing of Theological Phrases* (New York, The Macmillan Co. 1964).

66 Tracy, D. *Blessed Rage for Order: The New Pluralism in Theology* (New York Seabury Press, 1978).

67 Yalom, I.D. *Existential Psychotherapy* (New York Basic Books, 1980).

68 Berryman, J.W. "Montessori and religious education." *Religious Education* Vol 75 1980, 294-307.

69 Cavalletti, S. *The Religious Potential of the Child* (New York Paulist Press, 1983).

70 If Jesus had wished to compare smallness and largeness or power and weakness by a tree and its seed he could have used the cedars of Lebanon, so the accuracy of translating "shrub" rather than "trees" is important. On the other hand, "trees" communicates better for young children. The "trees "in the material is the same relative size to the person planting the seed as a six foot person is to a mustard shrub in Israel today.

71 Berryman, J.W. "Becoming fundamentally scriptural without being fundamentalistic." *Scriptura: Journal of Biblical Studies* Vol 14 1985, 25-74.

72 Berryman, J.W. "Imagination." *Harper's Dictionary of Religious Education* (San Francisco Harper and Row, 1988)

73 Loder, J.E. *The Transforming Moment* (San Francisco Harper and Row, 1981).

74 Gratitude is expressed to the congregation of Reedwood Friends Church in Portland, Oregon, for the invitation to be their theologian-in-residence during

April 1999, and to give the annual Center for Christian Studies Lectures, which included this topic.
75 See Anderson 1990. This delightful survey of the postmodern world was the stimulus for the title of this essay.
76 Kenneth H. Rubin, ed., *Children's Play,* No. 9, 1980 of New Directions for Child Development. (San Francisco: Jossey-Bass, 1980) pp. vii-viii.
77 Catherine Garvey, *Play.* (Cambridge, Massachusetts: Harvard University Press, 1977).
78 Arthur Koestler, *The Act of Creation.* (New York: The Macmillan Co., 1967).
79 Abraham H. Maslow, *The Farther Reaches of Human Nature.* (New York: Viking Press, 1971).
80 Hugo Rahner, S.J., *Man at Play.* (London: Burns and Oates, 1965).
81 James W. Fowler, "Life/Faith patterns: Structures of trust and loyalty" in *Life Maps: Conversations on the Journey of Faith,* Jerome W. Berryman, ed. (Waco, Texas: Word Press, 1978).
82 Madeline Petrillo and Sirgay Sanger, *Emotional Care of Hospitalized Children.* (Philadelphia: J. B. Lippincott Co., 1980).
83 E.M. Standing, ed., *The Child in the Church.* (St. Paul, Minnesota: Catechetical Guild, 1965).
84 Sofia Cavalletti, *Il Potenziale Religioso Adel Bambino.* (Rome: Citta Nuova Editrice, 1979).
85 Jerome W. Berryman, "Montessori and religious education", *Religious Education* 75 (May-June 1930): 294.
86 Jerome W. Berryman, "The work of Sofia Cavalletti," The *Constructive Triungle,* 5 (Winter 1976): 32.
87 Jerome W. Berryman, "Being in parables with children," *Religious Education* 74 (May-June 1979): 271.
88 Jerome W. Berryman, "A gift of healing stories for a child who is ill," *Liturgy* 24 (July-August 1979): 15.
89 Jerome W. Berryman, "Discussing the ethics of research with children" in *Research on Children,* Ian van Eys, ed. (Baltimore: University Park Press, 1975).
90 Deep gratitude is expressed to the Dean, Clergy, Staff, and Congregation of John's Cathedral, Denver, Colorado, where this paper was developed during Ad-it, 1997, when I was their Theologian in Residence.
91 Bruner, J. *The Culture of Education* (Cambridge, Mass.: Harvard University Press, 1996), 142-43.

92 Maslow, A.H. *Motivation and Personality,* 2nd ed. (New York: Harper and Row, 1954), 35-38.
93 Deacon, T.W. *The Symbolic Species: The Co-evolution of Language and the Brain* (New York: Norton, 1997).
94 Diamond, J. *Guns, Germs, and Steel: The Fates of Human Societies* (New York: Norton, 1998), 265-93.
95 Harris, P.L. *The Work* of *the Imagination* (Oxford, U.K., and Malden, Mass.: Blackwell, 2000).
96 Harris, *The Work of the Imagination,* xi.
97 Garvey, C. *Play* (Cambridge, Mass.: Harvard University Press, 1977), passim.
98 *Diamond, Guns, Germs, and Steel,* 218.
99 *Diamond, Guns, Germs, and Steel,* 277-78.
100 Csikszentmihalyi, M. *Beyond Boredom and Anxiety: The Experience of play in Work and Games* (San Francisco: Jossey-Bass, 1975), 74-75.
101 Csikszentmihalyi, M. *Creativity: Flow and The psychology of Discovery and Invention* (New York: HarperCollins, 1996), 11.
102 Csikszentmihalyi, *Creativity,* 28.
103 Berryman, J.W. *Godly Play:* A *Way of Religious Education* (San Francisco: Harper, 1991).
104 See Howard Gardner, *Frames of Mind: The Theory of Multiple Intelligences* (New York: Basic Books, 1983); and James W. Fowler, *Stages of Faith: The Psychology of Human Development and the Quest for Meaning* (San Francisco: Harper, 1981).
105 Gardner, H. *Creating Minds: An Anatomy of Creativity* (New York: Basic Books, 1993).
106 Gardner, H. *Intelligence Reframed: Multiple Intelligences for the 21st Century* (New York: Basic Books, 1999), 47-77.
107 Gardner, *Intelligence Reframed,* 89-92.
108 Fowler J. and S. Keen, *Life Maps: Conversations on the Journey of Faith,* ed. Jerome Berryman (Waco, Tex.: Word Books, 1978).
109 Oser, F.K. and P. Gmunder, *Der Mensch: Stufen Seiner Religiosen Entwicklung; Ein Struckturgenetischer* Ansatz (Zurich: Benziger, 1984). Later published as *Religious Judgment: A Developmental Perspective* (Birmingham, Ala.: Religious Education Press, 1991).
110 Fowler, J.W. and K.E. Nipkow, Friedrich Schweitzer, eds., *Stages of Faith and Religious Development: Implications for Church, Education, and Society* (New York: Crossroad, 1991).

111 Deacon, *The Symbolic Species,* 54, and chapters 8-10.

112 Erikson, E.H. and J.M. Erikson, *The Life Cycle Completed: Extended Version with New Chapters on the Ninth Stage of Development* (New York: Norton, 1998), 67.

113 Erikson, E.H. *Toys and Reasons: Stages in the Ritualization of Experience* (New York: W. W. Norton, 1977), 37.

114 Fowler, *Stages of Faith,* 245.

115 Ramsey, I.T. *Religious Language: An Empirical Placing of Theological Phrases* (London: SCM, 1957), 47.

116 Berryman, J.W. "The nonverbal nature of spirituality and religious education," in *Spiritual Education: Cultural, Religious, and Social Differences,* ed. Jane Erricker, Cathy Ota, and Clive Erricker (Brighton, Eng., and Portland, Ore.: Sussex Academic, 2001).

117 Berryman, J.W. *Godly Play* (see footnote 13), *Teaching Godly Play: The Sunday Morning Handbook* (Nashville: Abingdon, 1995), and *The Complete Guide to Godly* Play: *An Imaginative Method for Presenting Scripture Stories,* 5 vols. (Denver: Living the Good News, 2002-2003).

118 Aries, P. 1962. *Centuries of Childhood* (Robert Baldick, trans.). Vintage Books, New York.

119 Klein. C. 1975. *How It Feels to be a Child.* Harper and Row, New York.

120 Maslow, A.H. 1954. *Motivation and Personality.* Harper and Row, New York.

121 Piaget, J. 1951. *The Child's Conception of Physical Causality.* Routledge & Kegan Paul Ltd., London.

122 Rokeach, M. 1973. *The Nature of Human Values.* The Free Press, New York

123 Kohlberg, L. 1969. "Stage and sequence: the cognitive-developmental approach to socialization." In: *Handbook of Socialization Theory and Research.* pp. 347-480. Rand McNally & Company, Chicago.

124 Kohlberg, L. 1973. "Continuities in childhood and adult moral development revisited." In: *Collected Papers on Moral Development and Moral Education.* Center for Moral Education, Graduate School of Education, Harvard University, Cambridge, Mass.

125 Erikson, E. 1963. *Childhood and Society.* 2nd Ed. W. W. Norton & Company Inc., New York.

126 Maslow, A. 1971. *The Farther Reaches of Human Nature.* Viking Press, New York.

127 Arieti, S. 1976. *Creativity: The Magic Synthesis.* Basic Books, New York.

128 Rest, J., Turiel, E., and Kohlberg, L. 1969. *Level of Moral Development as a*

Determinant of Preferences and Comprehension of Moral Judgment Made By Others. J. Pers. 37:225-252.
129 Rest, J. 1973. *The hierarchical nature of stages of moral judgment.* J. Pers. 41:86-109.
130 Rest, J. 1977. "The research base of the cognitive developmental approach to moral education." In: T. Hennessy (ed.), *Values and Moral Development.* Paulist Press, New York.
131 Laing, R.D. 1976. *Politics of Experience.* Ballantine Books, New York.
132 Berryman, J. (Ed.). 1977. *Life Maps: The Journey of Human Faith.* Wexford Press, Boston.
133 Bettelheim, B. 1976. *The Uses of Enchantment.* Alfred A. Knopf Inc., New York.
134 Lloyd DeMause, *The History of Childhood* (New York: The Psychohistory Press, 1974).
135 Philippe Aries, *Centuries of Childhood* (New York: Vintage Books, 1965). Originally published in France in 1960.
136 John Sommerville, *The Rise and Fall of Childhood* (Beverly Hills, California: Sage Publications, 1982), Volume 140 of the Sage Library of Social Research.
137 Philip Greven, *The Protestant Temperament* (New York: Alfred A. Knopf, 1977).
138 Linda A. Pollock, *Forgotten Children: Parent-Child Relations from 1500-1900* (New York: Cambridge University Press, 1984).
139 Hans-Reudi Weber, *Jesus and the Children* (Geneva: World Council of Churches, 1979).
140 The Children's Center Project was begun formally for research in 1978 at Pines Presbyterian Church and moved to The Institute of Religion in the Texas Medical Center in 1979. It moved to Christ Church Cathedral in 1985.
141 Carole Klein, *How It Feels to Be a Child* (San Francisco: Harper & Row Publishers, 1975).
142 David Tracy, *Blessed Rage for Order* (New York: Sea-bury Press, 1978). Historical background is provided for the theological and philosophical conclusions. One volumenot referred to by Tracy but which remains relevant and lively is Paul M. Van Buren, *The Edges of Language* (New York: Macmillan, 1972).
143 Irvin D. Yalom, *Existential Psychotherapy* (New York Basic Books, 1980).
144 Rudy Rucker, *Infinity and the Mind* (Boston: Birkhauser, 1982). An especially interesting discussion of "infinity" is offered in this book.

145 Daniel C. Batson and W. Larry Ventis, *The Religious Esperinwe* (New York Oxford University Press, 1982). This is one of the most recent and important texts to suggest this. (I disagree with the view.)

146 Ronald Goldman, *Readiness for Religion* (London: Routledge and Kegan Paul, 1965). This is the most important source for this view. (I disagree with it.)

147 This is one task of the Children's Center Project.

148 Howard Gardner, *Art, Mind and Brain* (New York: Basic Books, 1982).

149 Howard Gardner, *Frames of Mind* (New York: Basic Books, 1983).

150 Erik H. Erikson, *Childhood and Society*, 2nd ed. (New York: W.W. Norton, & Co., 1963), pp.266-269.

www.ingramcontent.com/pod-product-compliance
Ingram Content Group UK Ltd.
Pitfield, Milton Keynes, MK11 3LW, UK
UKHW041415180426
11947UKWH00007B/141